微观中国
1-MINUTE CHINA

GUANGXI: GLORIOUS & HARMONIOUS

微观广西

（汉英版）

彭 匈 主编

SINCE 1897
商务印书馆
The Commercial Press
2019 年 • 北京

龙脊梯田　摄影：许沂

丛书策划　聂晓阳　周洪波

主　　编　彭　匈
副 主 编　朱　燕
文字统筹　（按音序排列）
李　慧　廖　珊　潘惠娟　彭　匈　覃　兰
翟香丽　朱　燕

图片统筹　（按音序排列）
陈炜平　谌贻照　邓　霆　罗劲松　唐典胜
谢勇云　许　沂　玉时阶　张小宁

英文翻译　梅　皓〔美〕
英文审订　刘　彤

责任编辑　吕　欣　齐晓宁
装帧设计　云汉设计

Chief Producers Nie Xiaoyang / Zhou Hongbo

Chief Compiler Peng Xiong
Deputy Compiler Zhu Yan
Compilers Li Hui / Liao Shan / Pan Huijuan / Peng Xiong / Qin Lan
Zhai Xiangli / Zhu Yan
Photography Chen Weiping / Chen Yizhao / Deng Ting / Luo Jinsong
Tang Diansheng / Xie Yongyun / Xu Yi / Yu Shijie / Zhang Xiaoning

English Translator Mei Hao（USA）
English Reviewer Liu Tong

Executive Editor Lü Xin / Qi Xiaoning
Art Design YHDesign

我们广西

公元前214年，秦修灵渠，连接长江、珠江两大水系，广西进入中原版图。

岭南始建桂林郡、象郡、南海郡，从此有了“八桂”之说。韩愈诗云：“苍苍森八桂，兹地在湘南。”韩文公运用诗歌的魅力，把“八桂”这一地域概念传遍了祖国的四面八方。从今日版图上看，广西北毗湖南，东邻广东，西接云贵，南临北部湾，面向东南亚。地理优势，一目了然。

显然，在韩愈眼中，广西首先是个神奇而美丽的地方，那里风光迷人，“江作青罗带，山如碧玉簪”；那里民风淳朴，“户多输翠羽，家自种黄甘”。岂止韩愈，杜甫也曾说“五岭皆炎热，宜人独桂林”；白居易亦感慨“岭南无瘴气，柏暑有清风”；李商隐任桂州幕僚时，写下“天意怜幽草，人间重晚晴”。诗人眼中，广西山水，独步天下。故而历朝历代，诗脉不绝。宋人王正功高吟“桂林山水甲天下”，清人袁枚产生幻觉，“分明看见青山顶，船在青山顶上行”；现代诗人贺敬之唱起了陕北信天游：“云中的神啊雾中的仙，神姿仙态桂林的山；情一样的深啊梦一样的美，如情似梦漓江的水。”元帅诗人陈毅把话说到了极致：“不愿做神仙，愿做桂林人！”人同此心，心同此理。多少外国元首政要，于山光水色中，徜徉沉醉，美国前总统尼克松一段感言最具代表性：“我和夫人有机会访问过八十多个国家，一百多个城市，我们毫无保留地说，我们所访问过的城市中，没有一个比得上桂林美丽！”

既说微观，有一个地方不可不去。那是一个叫兴坪的小渔村，它曾接待过两位总统：民国总统孙中山、美国总统克林顿。这地方的奇特，还在于它集聚了山光水色的精华，叶帅都情不自禁盛赞“果然佳胜在兴坪”，这景致印在了1999年版的20元人民币。

兴坪附近，大型实景剧《印象·刘三姐》，每天都在向全世界的游客诠释广西的山水人文精华。

先声夺人的桂林，只是广西进入世人眼帘的第一个窗口。我们往南。

柳州，1200年前，中原来了一位重量级的文化使者，姓柳名宗元字子厚，最终人称“柳柳州”。作为军政一把手的柳州刺史，他革除弊政，移风易俗，发展生产，种果栽花，兴师办学……为官四载，政绩昭彰。柳人怀念，建柳侯祠。内有柳氏衣冠墓，还有一“荔子碑”，韩愈撰文，书柳宗元事，苏东坡书法，世称“三绝”。

今日之柳州，工业重镇，四方瞩目。螺山螺水螺蛳粉，柳钢柳微柳州人。柳州人具有一种工业思维，为常人所望尘莫及。小小一碗螺蛳粉，电商平台竟然做到了几个亿！下一步他们还会弄出什么响动，谁都难以料及。

广西首府是南宁。南宁的城市精神就跟南宁人的性格一样质朴无华，“能帮就帮，敢做善成”。这恰恰是一种胸怀，一种气度。这能让人想起“山不辞垒土以成其高，海不辞涓滴而成其大”。南宁在长大，大家都看得见。中国—东盟博览会一年一度地成功举办，南宁的名气便与日俱增。显然这得了能够辐射东南亚的地理优势。

南宁还有一个优势是别处难以企及的，即地处北回归线附近，典型的亚热带季风区，冬暖夏长，日照适中，雨量充沛，乃北回归线上不可多得的绿洲。龙眼、荔枝、香蕉、菠萝、芒果、木瓜、杨桃、扁桃、菠萝蜜、山竹、榴莲、莲雾、红毛丹、火龙果……南方浆果，林林总总，给世人带来的口福和惊奇，难以言喻。南宁有亚洲最大的药用植物园，进到里面你会思考药用植物与人类的和谐关系，会生发史前神农尝百草之幽思。

南宁人的爱吃会吃能吃，远近闻名。逛南宁夜市，你能吃到天下美味。

邕江上纳左右江之激流，下投珠江奔腾于大海。发展前途，不可限量。

百色、河池的名头，一是与小平同志领导的那场轰轰烈烈的起义联系紧密，二是这里聚居着色彩缤纷的少数民族同胞。广西有壮、汉、瑶、苗、侗、仫佬、毛南、回、京、彝、水、仡佬十二个世居民族。其中壮族人口约1700万，是中国少数民族人口最多的一个民族。

孔子说，“礼失求诸野”。中原早已失传的包括《诗经》桑间濮上的风俗、节庆、音乐、舞蹈，在广西少数民族地区皆循迹可寻。融入“三月三”歌圩，你会想起杜甫的“三月三日天气新，长安水边多丽人”；看见那恢宏的铜鼓阵势，你会想起“窈窕淑女，钟鼓乐之”；听见悠扬婉转的芦笙，你会想到“我有嘉宾，鼓瑟吹笙”。隆林德峨圩场，看见满街叮叮当当的民族服饰，你会忘情地唱起“赶圩归来啊哩哩”。

少数民族聚居地，还有一个贺州。这里堪称各族方言博物馆。究其缘由，这里除了世居多民族同胞之外，自秦戍五岭以来，此地一直是南来北往的交通要冲。宋儒先贤《爱莲说》作者周敦颐出生在贺州桂岭镇，并在这里度过了他的少年时代。贺州宜居，百岁老人之多，可称奇观。黄姚古镇，那里街头巷尾，全是故事。

梧州人有广州情结，广州人同样有梧州情结。梧州这个地方，历史特别悠久。梧州白话，据说是广东粤语的先声；梧州的六堡茶，货真价实是云南普洱茶的前辈。西江唱晚，黄金水道直指粤港澳，古城新气象，后发必争先。

说到历史悠久，不能不提玉林。玉林古为鬱州，有“千州万州，不如鬱州”的美誉。中唐时有元结主政容州，经略台上的真武阁，四足悬空，力扛千钧，梁思成等建筑大师叹为观止，誉为“南天杰构”；今有享誉世界的语言学泰斗王力先生，国外大学若设汉语课，必以先生之著作为蓝本。

崇左的花山岩画，民族瑰宝，申遗成功。大新德天，一帘瀑布，横跨两国。书圣王羲之后人王元仁，曾出任崇善县令，在广西各处留下几个擘窠大字，崇左江滨公园的“寿”字，有“千年寿”三字笔意。

自秦汉以降，中原文化滚滚南来，与广西的骆越文化水乳交融，形成独具一格的文化形态。北人驭马，南人驾舟，海上丝绸之路浑然天成。北海、钦州、防城港，都是古代海上丝绸之路的重要始发港。中国的陶瓷、丝绸、茶叶等物，丝路各国琳琅满目的舶来品，互通有无，交流无阻，“舶交海中，不知其数”。刘禹锡诗“连天浪静长鲸息，映日帆多宝舶来”，可窥见盛况之一斑。

合浦博物馆为何不可错过，因为里面藏有各个时期从海上丝路运来的古罗马琉璃杯、波斯陶壶、古希腊缠花金球、阿拉伯项链手串……

……

新世纪以来，世界向广西投来温馨而热切的目光，广西亦以日新月异的变化回馈世界。

2018年是广西壮族自治区成立60周年，由衷感谢商务印书馆主持出版《微观中国》书系。此宏大书系的出版问世，诚为出版界、文化界一件值得称道的盛事。它向广大读者提供了一个拓展宏观视野，把握微观视角的绝佳平台，使大众从体察各地的风光、民俗、人杰、物产中，增添心中的自豪自信。《微观广西》位列其中，作为向庆典奉献的礼品，得其时也。

需要说明的是，时间仓促，或许蜻蜓点水；资料不全，难免挂一漏万。还请各位各取所需，庶几略有裨益。

是为序。

彭匈

2018年10月

Our Guangxi

In 214, when the Qin built the Ling Canal, connecting the Yangtze and Zhujiang rivers, Guangxi came into the territory of the central government.

Three counties were firstly established south of Five Mountain Ranges, i.e., Guilin, Xiangjun and Nanhai. Poet Han Yu of Tang dynasty wrote about these thick forests south of what is now Hunan; the power of his verse made this area, known as "Bagui", familiar to people in regions far and wide. Looking at the current delimitations, Guangxi lies south of Hunan, west of Guangdong, east of Yunnan and Guizhou and north of the Beibu Gulf facing Southeast Asia. Its geographical advantages are clear.

Evidently, in Han Yu's eyes, Guangxi was first and foremost a place of beauty, one with alluring scenery. He wrote of the bright, twisting rivers and mountains that shone like jade. He wrote of the simple life of the people there, countless families with houses upon the green landscape planting citrus. It wasn't just Han Yu who was enamored with this place – the famous poet Du Fu also wrote of the livability of Guilin compared with the hotness of the nearby regions. Bai Juyi also described the fresh air, dense forests and pleasant environment. After Li Shangyin took office in Guizhou, he wrote about how beautiful the cool grasses were at sunset after the rains. In the eyes of these poets, the scenery of Guangxi was second to none, which is agreed by numerous poets afterward. Wang Zhenggong of Song dynasty said, "The mountains and rivers of Guilin are unexcelled". Yuanmei of Qing dynasty wondered at the illusion that he was sailing atop the mountain peaks. Modern poet He Jingzhi also sang the praises of the region, remarking on the other-worldly atmosphere, with the mists, mountains, rivers, and streams gripping the viewer like a dream. General Chen Yi even said he would rather be a Guilin local than an immortal being. There is a clear consensus here. Many foreign dignitaries and heads of state have visited and become intoxicated with the beauty of the scenery here; former United States president Richard Nixon remarked: "My wife and I have visited over eighty countries and more than a hundred cities, but I can say without reservation, none of them are more beautiful than Guilin!"

When talking about quick views, there's a place that you can't miss: a small fishing village called Xingping. It has received two presidents: Sun Yat-sen and Bill Clinton. This place is lovely and mystical; where scenic beauties come together. General Ye Jianying himself was moved by the sights and exclaimed: "the true attraction is really in Xingping". The scenery of Xingping was also depicted on the 20-Yuan note printed in 1999.

Near to Xingping, the play "Impression – Liu Sanjie" takes place. Every day it shows the beautiful scenes and culture of Guangxi to travelers from around the world.

Guilin, although striking and famous, is only the first place worth mentioning. Let's move southwards.

One thousand and two hundred years ago, an essential cultural emissary came to Liuzhou; his name was Liu Zongyuan. He served as the governor of Liuzhou, and wiped out maladministration and changed the customs. He developed production as well as agriculture, focusing on education during his tenure, and affecting great changes. After he left, the people of Liuzhou built a temple in his honor, with a cenotaph inside. A "lychee stele" was erected, where the writings of Han Yu, administration of Liu Zongyuan and the calligraphy of Su Dongpo are the "three wonders".

Liuzhou today is a center of industry. There are the famed snail noodles, as well as the steel and automotive manufacturers. The people of the city have an industrial mindset, which is rarely seen in ordinary men. A simple snail noodle can collect revenue of hundreds of millions of Yuan via E-commerce platforms. One can only imagine what they'll bring about next.

Nanning is the capital of Guangxi. The city and its people have an unadorned character, an attitude of helping and the guts to try and fulfill. This is both a mindset and style of behavior. This makes one think of how mountains and seas grow from small amounts of soil and water. The city of Nanning is growing up, which everyone can see. The China-ASEAN Exposition, or CAEXPO, is held here every year, which continually adds to the recognition of the city. It is a clear indicator of the city's geographic advantage being next to Southeast Asia.

Nanning has a unique advantage. It's right on the Tropic of Cancer, in a typical subtropical monsoon region. It has warm winters and long summers, as well as ample sunlight and rain. Longan, lychee, bananas, pineapples, mangoes, papayas, star fruit, almonds, jackfruit, mangosteen, durian, wax apples, and rambutans all grow here. A wide variety of fruits are a wonderful sight to see. Nanning also has the largest medicinal plant garden in Asia. When you come here, you'll think about the harmonious relationship between medicinal herbs and human beings, just like the god Shennong who was said to discover the herbal medicine.

The people of Nanning excel at and enjoy eating, a reputation that is known throughout China. When browsing the night market in Nanning, you'll be surrounded by a world of delicious flavors.

The Yong River collects the waters from Left River and Right River and flows into Zhujiang River as it heads to the sea. It represents limitless possibilities for development.

Baise reminds us of comrade Deng Xiaoping, who led the wondrous Baise Uprising. Hechi is home to a large variety of ethnic groups. The Zhuang, Han, Yao, Miao, Dong, Mulao, Maonan, Hui, Jing, Yi, Shui and Gelao, minorities all live here. The population of Zhuang people is approximately 17 million, making it the largest ethnic minority in China.

Confucius said, when etiquette was forgotten, you have to seek it in the far-flung area. The customs described in the Book of Songs that have long since died out in the central plains, regarding festivals, music, dance, and meetings can be found among the ethnic minorities in Guangxi. The Song Festival makes you think of the beauties along the river described by poet Du Fu. When you see the grand copper drums, you may think of a verse in the Book of Songs. When you hear the sounds of the reed flute, you may think of how Cao Cao entertained his guests. At the festival in De'e, Longlin, when you see everyone decked out in ethnic dress, beads clinking, you may feel as if you were within a song.

There's another place where ethnic minorities live in large numbers, Hezhou. It's sometimes referred to as a museum of minority languages. It has been home to a large variety of ethnic groups, and a central hub for communications and transport between north and south. Zhou Dunyi, the author of Ode to the Lotus was born in Guiling County in Hezhou, and spent his youth here. Hezhou is a nice place to live and has many centenarians. The streets and alleys of Huangyao Old Town are full of stories.

Wuzhou has affections for Guangzhou, and Guangzhou has attachments for Wuzhou too. This is a place with a long history. The local dialect here is said to be the origin of Cantonese, and the Liubu or "Six Fort" tea here is genuinely a forerunner of the famous Pu'er tea of Yunnan. The West River connects Guangdong, Hong Kong, and Macao. The ancient city, at the same time, starts a new life.

When talking about history, one can't forget Yulin. Known initially as Yuzhou, it was known as a place of great beauty. In the past, the Zhenwu Pavilion was praised by Liang Sicheng and other famous architects as an exemplar of excellent architecture in the south; at present, the works of Wang Li, a world-famous linguist, are still must-read books to learn Chinese.

Concerning Chongzuo, the Huashan rock paintings were listed as a world heritage, and the Detian waterfall connects China and Vietnam. At the Riverside Park, you can see the handwriting of a descendant of the calligraphy master Wang Xizhi.

From Qin and Han dynasties, cultures of Central Plains and Guangxi have been mingled together, forming a brand new cultural. In the north, people drive horses, whereas in the south, people take boats. Naturally, the Maritime Silk Road was formed. Beihai, Qinzhou, and Fangchenggang were all important starting-off points for the ancient maritime roads. Chinese porcelain, silk, tea, and other items flowed out, and imported goods flowed in, with more ships than could be counted along the waterways. Liu Yuxi of the Tang dynasty remarked upon the scenes in his poems.

Thc Hcpu Muscum is a spot not to bc misscd, as it displays some items that arrived on the maritime road: Roman glass, Persian ceramics, ancient Greek golden containers, Arabian necklaces, and bracelets…

In the new century, Guangxi attracts more attention with its rapid changes. Two thousand eighteen marked the 60th anniversary of the Guangxi Zhuang Autonomous Region. I want to thank the Commercial Press from the bottom of my heart for publishing One-minute Guangxi. The excellent One-minute China series is making waves in the publishing circle as well as the cultural world. It provides readers with a broadened view, showcasing excellent stories and content from an interesting angle, introducing the sights, customs, people, and objects of the areas it covers in a clear and confident fashion. It is a gift for Guangxi to be included in this series.

I have to confess that this book is not comprehensive at all, with multiple items being left out due to the time limit and lack of materials. At the same time I am sure this book can provide the readers with a better understanding of Guangxi, a wonderful place that deserves a visit.

It is my sincere hope, and I am sure you will enjoy the book.

Peng Xiong
October 2018

目录 Contents

霞光普照南宁五象新区　摄影：周军

城市 · 觅语
Cities and Sites

“绿城”南宁

“Green City” Nanning

文：朱燕

南宁素有“绿城”之称，草经冬而不枯，花非春而常放，一年四季都绿树成荫。琅东芒果的翠绿、凤岭木菠萝的墨绿、西乡塘小叶榕的新绿、江南扁桃的青绿、南湖相思树的苍绿，构成了一幅丰美且妖娆的“南宁绿”。品读“南宁绿”，只需席地而坐，将自己想象为这万千绿树丛中的一片树叶即可，那如云似水的诗行便会在你胸前自由滑过。

Nanning is commonly called the “Green City”. The plants don’t wilt during the winter, and flowers bloom year-round; the metropolis enjoys green scenery in all four seasons. The green mango trees of Langdong, the deep green jackfruit trees in Fengling, the fresh green ficus in Xixiangtang, the striking colors of almond trees in Jiangnan, the hues of the Acacia confusa trees at the South Lake, all come together to form a rich and enchanting world of green here. Take a seat somewhere in the city as you experience Nanning and imagine yourself as part of the foliage, and you’ll be full of feelings of poetry and comfort.

绿城南宁　摄影：周军

杂食家

Diverse Eaters

文：彭匈

南宁的饮食男女，肠胃坚强无比，但不能称他们为美食家，叫他们“杂食家”更合适。因为南宁人这张嘴的最大优点就是不挑食。水陆毕陈，兼容并包。更有甚者，猫肉蛇肉，来者不拒；鼠肉鸟肉，更是难得。他们有“一鼠顶三鸡”的说法。东西南北中，只要味道好，南宁人都会张开双臂，无条件欢迎。此外，他们还会开着车，到高峰去吃柠檬鸭，到良庆去吃脆皮扣，到邹圩去吃鯰拐鱼……

The men and women of Nanning have strong stomachs, but you can't describe them as gourmands – rather, the term "diverse eaters" is more appropriate. Their most apparent characteristic is that they're not picky. Here you'll find feasts in which all from the land and sea is included – everything's accepted. Cat and snake meat are good to go; mouse and fowl can't be done without. There's a saying here, "a mouse is better than three chickens". The people here will welcome any food from anywhere without reservation or hesitation as long as it's tasty. They'll drive out to Gaofeng for the lemon duck, or Liangqing for crispy-skin braised pork,or Zouxu for catfish…

杂食家的天堂　摄影：陈炜平

世界上最好的快餐

World's Best Fast Food

文：彭匈

坦白地说，这世上还真没有哪种食物叫我如此牵肠挂肚。我的一句“名言”在朋友圈里流传甚广：“我吃过世界各地的各种快餐，最后得出一个结论：世界上最好的快餐，就是桂林米粉！吃到一碗地道的桂林米粉，其效果完全不亚于一桌酒席！”每次回桂林，开头那餐我多半会谢绝朋友们的盛情，而去找一家好的粉店享足口福。

Frankly speaking, no other food in the world tugs at my heartstrings so. One of my "famous quotes" on social media was spread far and wide: "I've had all kinds of fast food throughout the world, and my conclusion is this: the best fast food in the world are Guilin-style rice noodles! A bowl of these is better than the best of banquets!" Every time I go back to Guilin all of my friends are inviting me out for big affairs, but I turn them down to seek out a restaurant serving these.

最具市井气息的夜宵圣地

Night Eats

文：朱燕

在南宁，这条叫“中山路”的小吃街白日空无一人。晚霞刚落，迈进夜宵的节奏就明快起来，四面八方的大排档、烧烤摊、小吃店摆起了各自的阵势，各种各样吃过没吃过的亚热带水果也陆续登场，空气中顿时弥漫着各种诱人的香味。人们悠闲随意，高声喧哗，痛快畅饮，大快朵颐……中山路陪伴着一代代南宁人出生、成长，而街道两旁已有上百年历史的骑楼建筑也随着年月更迭变得日渐斑驳，愈有韵味。

In Nanning, there is a street, “Zhongshan Road”, which is devoid of people during the day. As the sun sets, however, it starts to bustle with the night-time eating crowd. There are dai pai dong, barbecue stands, snack stalls and the like everywhere. All kind of subtropical fruit are on offer, and as soon as things kick off, the atmosphere is filled with the voices of people and scents of food. People come here to relax, clamor, and partake massively in food and drink. This is a street that has grown up with generations of people in Nanning. The buildings overhanging the road in some places are more than a century old, and have seen iteration after iteration of business there; their histories are full of stories and flavor and become increasingly so over time.

中山路小吃街　摄影：陈炜平

桂林男子一枝花

Guilin Guys

文：彭匈

桂林的文化气脉，一直就没有断过。经过如此这般反复熏陶，即便木头一根，也会生出几分灵气来。只要相处一段时间，你就会发现，桂林男子身上总有那么一点子别的地方男人难以企及的贵族气和书卷气。在桂林男子的骨子里，精细的东西要多些，比如琴棋书画，比如诗文摄影，比如园林盆景，比如家馔小吃……

The character of Guilin is one that has developed over the ages gradually and continuously; it is one that is imbued with spirit and cultivation. If you interact with them just a little, you will discover that the men of Guilin have a character that’s both refined and scholarly. This is something in their bones, something which gives them a tendency towards the more delicate things: instruments, chess, calligraphy and paintings, poetry, photography, gardens and bonsai, excellent food and other consumables…

一条叫东巷，一条叫西巷

East and West Alleys

文：朱燕

在桂林的东西巷慢行，能真切感受到世界的界限分明。繁华喧嚣与朴实幽静在王城根下呈现两个世界，这两个世界显示了一个城市不同的文化色彩和历史底蕴。置身巷子一户人家，那雕花门窗虽已被岁月的烟火熏得失去本色，却仍可让人遥想昔日的景象……是谁曾在西窗下读书？又是谁在庭院发出阵阵叹息？思绪后，人顿时会生出“旧时王谢堂前燕，飞入寻常百姓家”的沧桑之感。

桂林的东西巷　摄影：罗劲松

Walking through the East and West Alleys in Guilin, you can feel the clear demarcation between realms.When you walk around Wangcheng Wall, you will find two different worlds: one is loud and complex, while the other is simple and silent. The contrast is a testament to the different cultural and historical heritage of the city. Looking at a home in the alleyway, with the carved wooden frames of the doors and windows worn away by the trials of the years, one can still imagine the scenes of days long gone by. Who used to read under the west window here? Who had sighed within the courtyard? After thinking for a while, one will think of the poetry of Tang-dynasty poet Liu Yuxi: “Swallows which skimmed by painted eaves in bygone days, are dipping now among the humble home’s doorways. ”

西街的美丽与骄傲

Pride and Beauty of the West Street

文：朱燕

这里，曾接待过 150 多个国家的元首和有关领导；这里，是艺术大师徐悲鸿曾居住过的地方。徐悲鸿在 1935~1937 年间两次到阳朔，以西街为住地，游历山水，独爱阳朔天下无双的遇龙河的秀山丽水，在此创作出《漓江烟雨》等一批价值连城的美术作品。可以说，在西街每一寸青石板上都印刻着天下名人的足迹，就连那些无名的小店，也留下了他们的微笑和身影。这是西街最大的美丽与骄傲。

This is a place that has hosted heads and leaders from over 150 countries. When the famous artist Xu Beihong visited Yangshuo, he lived here and wandered about. He had special love for the mountains and waters of Yulong River. Inspired by them, he produced Misty Rains of the Lijiang River and other top-rated works. It can be said that the slab stones here all contain the traces of the comings and goings of various famous figures; in every nameless small store are the traces of their shadows and smiles. This is the pride and beauty of the West Street.

紫荆花开，诗意柳州　摄影：谌贻照

柳州人的工业思维
Working Mindset

文：彭匈

跟柳州人打交道，三分钟，你能觉出他的直率和痛快；三个小时，你能领教他的豪爽和利索。柳州人有点不善言辞。你同他多讲几句他不感兴趣的话题，他就会请你“讲点别的”，有时还会甩过来一句“答你都困”，就是“懒得同你讲”的意思。柳州人干事的风格，可以概括为一种工业思维——小小一碗螺蛳粉，在电商平台，他们能做到几个亿！

When interacting with the people of Liuzhou, after just three minutes you can feel their straightforward and direct character. After three hours, you may feel that bold and orderly character. These people are not necessarily the most eloquent. If you speak for a while about a topic they find uninteresting, they may encourage you to say something else. They don't mind talking directly about what they want, and if you're boring them, they will let you know. One can say they have a “working mindset” – they can turn traditional snail noodle business into e-commerce with revenue in the hundreds of millions.

奇石情怀
Nice Rocks

文：彭匈

柳州人对于奇石的兴趣，几达不可理喻的地步。石迷石痴，不乏其人，说起石头，悬河滔滔。尽管柳州人的玩赏水平已达到相当的高度，然而我更欣赏的是他们的商业眼光——柳州人竟然把石头鼓捣成了一个不小的产业！逛过柳州奇石市场的人，没有不感慨万千的。

The people of Liuzhou are very into “curious stones”, to the extent that almost puzzles outsiders. There are people all over the city who are “rock enthusiasts”, and enjoy talking about them whenever they are mentioned. These people are good at enjoying themselves and their hobbies, but what I enjoy even more is their eye for business–they've turned these rocks into quite a little industry! The “curious stone” markets of the city are a place full of people and action.

2017 年柳州国际水上狂欢节的壮观场面　摄影：谌贻照

柳州白沙大桥　摄影：李斌

桥梁博物馆

Bridge Museum

文：朱燕

从空中俯视，柳州是被柳江包围着的。被誉为“桥梁博物馆”的柳州，在柳江河上建成、在建、规划建设的跨江大桥已达20几座。它们是：双冲桥、柳江铁桥、柳江大桥、河东大桥、壶东大桥、文惠桥、静兰桥、高速公路洛维大桥、红光桥、友谊大桥、阳和大桥、龙屯立交桥、潭中高架桥、飞鹅立交桥、三门江大桥、文昌桥……每座桥梁都有自己的特色，在柳江上是一道不可多得的风景。

Looking down from above, one will find that Liuzhou is surrounded by the Liu River. The city is known as a “bridge museum”, because there are more than twenty bridges built, being built, or planned to be built upon the river. They are the Shuangchong Bridge, Liujiang Iron Bridge, Liujiang Bridge, Hedong Bridge, Hudong Bridge, Wenhui Bridge, Jinglan Bridge, Expressway Luowei Bridge, Hongguang Bridge, Friendship Bridge, Yanghe Bridge, Longtun Overpass, Tanzhong Elevated Bridge, Fei’e Overpass, Sanmenjiang Bridge, Wenchang Bridge… Each bridge has its own characteristics and provides an indispensable view.

国内唯一全海景跑道

Seaside Run

文：朱燕

防城港是中国“海上丝绸之路”的始发港之一，拥有4万多平方公里海域，是中国沿海最干净的海域之一。“2017中国—东盟国际马拉松大赛”在广西防城港市鸣枪开跑，这是中国第一个全程全海景马拉松，全长42.195公里的沿海跑道由全塑胶铺成。“中国—东盟国际马拉松”作为国家级IP赛，联动东盟、辐射10国，是第一个在中国田径协会以国家及国际组织注册成功的国际马拉松。这场马拉松的举办，让人们开始用另一种目光打量这座城市，感受这座城市，欣赏这座城市，述说这座城市，点赞这座城市。

Fangchenggang is one of the starting harbors on the Maritime Silk Road. It has more than 40,000 square kilometers of territorial sea, one of the cleanest in China. In 2017 it was the site of the China-ASEAN Marathon. As the starting gun's shot rang out, runners took off on a 42.195 kilometer seaside run on an all-polymer course. A state-level competition, it connects ten countries and is the first sea-view full marathon in China, as well as the first marathon registered with both the Chinese Athletic Association and an international organization. This marathon is bringing new notice to this city, causing people to observe, feel, enjoy, describe and like this city.

全海景马拉松赛道防城港北部湾海洋文化公园段　摄影：周军

水都
Water Capital

文：朱燕

每当洪水挟着各种杂物从四面包抄涌来，这边的孩子们又是紧张又是新奇，大声嚷道："水浸街了！水浸街了！"那边人声喧哗，搬运工人大包小包进行抢运。人们在二楼窗口打水洗衣，一只只小艇在街心前行……在许多人心中，洪水与猛兽同义，但在梧州人看来，他们对洪水的定期拜访已养成了一种习以为常的心理，仿佛一年一次感冒似的自然。

Every time the waters come flowing, bringing objects from around, the children here are both nervous and enthused, yelling, "The street is flooding!" Movers rush to transport all manner of packages, large and small. People on the second floor take water from outside their windows to wash clothing, and boats float down the street. For many people, the flooding water is like a beast of prey, however, for those in Wuzhou, regular flooding is a normal thing, just like catching a cold once a year.

通向广东之路
The Road to Guangdong

文：朱燕

梧州人爱吃粤菜，爱说粤语，爱唱粤曲，爱去广东购物和玩，连平日在朋友圈发的帖子也多与广东有关。"通向广东之路"是许多梧州人的心理情结。土生土长的梧州人觉得自己骨子里更像是广东人，因为他们从小接触的大多数东西都与广东有关，在心理上早已习惯倾向广府文化，所以对广东的认同感远超于广西其他地方的人。

The people of Wuzhou like to eat Cantonese food, speak Cantonese, listen to Cantonese opera and go to Guangdong to eat, shop and play. Many of the posts they make on social media have to do with Guangdong Province. This is the attitude of people in Wuzhou, the "Road to Guangdong". The people who are born and grow up here feel that they in their bones are people of Guangdong. They have been in contact mostly with things and events of Guangdong since childhood; their culture is slanted towards that of Guangzhou. For this reason, they have more familiarity with Guangdong than people from elsewhere in Guangxi.

评论

神秘的南国风情

Southern Vibes

文：朱燕

北海的天似乎很低，街道两旁的树也就显得格外高大。那是海榕树，用粗壮虬曲的枝撑开的巨伞，浓密又沉郁。还有假槟榔树，笔直顶上天空，羽毛状的叶子四散成优雅的弧形，显得刚强又柔媚。街上行走的人，喜欢戴着尖顶的斗笠，不管男女。女的在斗笠下挂一块大手帕，遮住面颊。扑面而来的，是一股神秘而迷人的南国风情，让人无端生出许多遐想。

It feels like the sky in Beihai hangs very low; the trees on either side of the streets are strong and tall. These are banyan trees; their thick and twisted branches form huge parasols, drooping and heavy. There are also Alexander palm trees which poke upwards at the sky; their feathery leaves float about along arcing paths, full and elegant. The people walking along the street wear conical bamboo hats, both male and female. The women hang a handkerchief from the hat to protect their face – this is an alluring southern scene, one that gives rise to all kinds of thoughts.

现实中的“鹅城”

“Goose City”

文：朱燕

姜文导演的电影《让子弹飞》，为观众塑造了一座北洋年代的“鹅城”，城里有金钱美酒，有占据鹅城的恶霸，有号令山林的悍匪与行走江湖的骗子。这座充满欲望与争斗的鹅城，令人惧怕又向往。而现实中的“鹅城”位于广西西部。百色，之所以被称为“鹅城”，不是因为那里喂养的鹅多，是因为它的行政区图特别像一只展翅高飞的天鹅。这是一个英雄的地方。这里有好多美丽的传说，都是关于鹅的。

Jiang Wen’s film Let the Bullets Fly created an image of the “Goose City” of the Beiyang period, with the wealth, resplendence, tyrants, bandits, and tricksters of the time. This “Goose City” full of desire and conflict raises eyebrows today. In reality, the real “Goose City” is situated in western Guangxi. Baise, which is also known by this name, isn’t so called because many geese are raised here. Instead, it’s because the administrative district is shaped like a goose spreading its wings. This is a place of heroes. There are many legends here, all of which are about geese.

百色起义纪念馆全景 摄影：周军

“岭南都会”之美

Lingnan Metropolis

文：朱燕

说起“岭南都会”——玉林的美，你可以说是因为玉林境内秀丽的山水、奇异的古迹、繁荣的商贸、锦绣的田园、浓郁的侨乡风情给你留下了美不胜收的印象和回忆……但是，老玉林人或是热爱玉林的人，都会用一种毋庸置疑的语气悄悄告诉你一个玄而又玄的原因——这里走出过一个杨玉环，这里至今还留存有“贵妃井”。

When speaking about the “Lingnan Metropolis” – the beauty of Yulin, you may be talking about the beautiful landscapes within the city, the mysterious remains of times past, the flourishing commerce, the splendid fields, or the prosperous villages full of sights that will impress and leave you with memories. However, the old people of the city, as well as those who have come to love it, will tell you assuredly that there is another reason for the allure – this is the place of origin of the famous beauty Yang Yuhuan, who was selected as a high-ranking concubine (Guifei) during the Tang dynasty. A Guifei Well is still kept here.

令人神往的三姐故里

Story of Sanjie

文：朱燕

壮族歌仙刘三姐的故乡——宜州，是一座有着 2100 多年历史的古城。它位于广西东南面，东邻柳州市 120 公里，西距河池市 76 公里。相传，歌仙刘三姐的家就在宜州下枧河的下枧村，她常与乡亲上山砍柴，下河打鱼，开荒种地，采茶对歌……至今，下枧村旁还有刘三姐对歌遗址；下枧河岸的峭壁上，当年刘三姐打柴用过的“扁担”“汗巾”仍依稀可见。

Famous Zhuang singer Liu Sanjie’s hometown, Yizhou, is a city with more than 2,100 years of history. Situated in south-west Guangxi, it’s located 120 km to the east of Liuzhou, and 76 km west of Hechi. According to the legends, Liu came from Xiajian Village on the Xiajian River in Yizhou; she’d frequently cut firewood upon the mountain with other villagers, fish in the river, and create farmland, singing as she went. There are still traces of her presence in Xiajian Village today: on a cliff along the river here, the carrying pole and cloth she used to carry firewood are faintly visible.

宜州市刘三姐乡流河社区中枧屯特色生态公园村美景　摄影：朱昌敏 马境

天等人，不等天！

Tiandeng

文：朱燕

天等因为指天椒而驰名中外，被誉为“天下第一辣县”。凭着指天椒这股火辣的狠劲，天等人在京城用数十年先后开了400余家桂林米粉店，把北京人和桂林人都震惊了。天等，在壮语里是“矗立的石头”之意。一个以石头命名的城市，其中隐含着多恶劣的生存环境，可想而知。所以，“活着”对天等人而言，是一件不易又幸福的事。正因如此，他们喊出了一句响亮的口号：“天等人，不等天！”

The chilies of Tiandeng are famous both in China and abroad; Tiandeng is known as the “number one county for chilies”. They are quite spicy, and the people from here have established over 400 rice noodle shops in the capital in a few decades, astonishing the locals. “Tiandeng” means “upright stone” in the Zhuang language; it’s easy to see that a place with a harsh environment could be named for a rock. For the people here life isn’t easy. They are said to be especially resistant to harsh environments and weather.

天等县都康乡　摄影：蒙海

爱读书的博白人

Smart Bobai

文：朱燕

外地人对博白人的印象是"聪明"！是的，博白人的聪明首先体现在读书上。历朝历代，博白聪明的读书人层出不穷。如被人称为"读穿书胆"的王力先生，便是博白"聪明仔"的代表。博白人对读书的重视还体现在独特的风俗习惯上。比如每个学期开学时，家里人都会让小孩子吃点芹菜和葱蒜之类，芹菜寓意勤奋，葱寓意聪明，蒜寓意会算。在博白，如果孩子"抓周"选取了文房四宝，长辈会特别高兴。

When outsiders meet the people of Bobai, their impression is "how intelligent!" That's right; evidence of their intelligence is foremost visible in their habit of reading books. In the times of the dynasties, the people of this city were always into the books. The distinguished linguist Wang Li was a native of this city and evidence of this culture. The people of Bobai's respect for books is reflected in their own special customs. At the start of each semester, the people of the city make for their children a meal of celery, spring onions and garlic, as the names for these vegetables "qin", "cong" and "suan" evoke the sounds for the words for "hard-working", "intelligent" and "capable of calculation". During the ceremony for babies in which they grab at objects representing a profession, parents are delighted if their children grab for writing implements.

现代大港的繁荣

Big Harbor

文：朱燕

钦州是天然深水良港，孙中山先生在其雄心大志的《建国方略》中将其规划为"南方第二大港"。100多年前，刘永福、冯子材援越抗法使钦州名震中外。今日的钦州港，三墩公路如巨龙出水，龙门十二泾大蚝鲜美，三娘湾白海豚逐浪，保税港熙熙攘攘，一幅碧海蓝天与大工业同在的和谐景象。

Qinzhou is a natural deep-water harbor of high quality. Sun Yat-sen in his plan for building the new country described it as the second-most important in the south of the country. More than a century ago, Liu Yongfu and Feng Zicai fought against French troops to assist Vietnam and made the city famous. Today at the harbor, the Sandun Highway emerges from the water like a giant dragon. Oysters grow, white dolphins swim in the water, and the bonded port bustles with activity as blue oceans and skies coexist with industry.

钦州港 摄影：陈炜平

细碎的率性组合
On the Edge

文：朱燕

镶嵌在中越边境上的凭祥，是一个最没有“城市气”的城市。从这个角度而言，凭祥也是一个率性的城市——它根本不屑于城市的固有形式。凭祥整个城区不大，街道也屈指可数，更没有流水一样熙攘的行人。它是细碎的，它由市区、弄尧、弄怀……一连串名字筑起了自身的完整和原真。

Pingxiang, situated upon the border with Vietnam, is a city without the air of a city. It has a natural feel, rather than a constructed feel of a planned city. The entire urban area is small, with only a few roads, and no bustling crowds. It's a quaint place that comprises a center and a few radiating roads, a named place that has a complete and natural character.

贺州寻访
Hezhou Visit

文：朱燕

贺州三省通衢，建制两千年。如今街道两旁的店铺和民居，仍有许多为明、清两代及民国初期修建的两层砖木结构楼房。你可由着双脚牵引，自东门街开始，循着十字街、县前街、南门街、三元街、玉马街、上关街、下关街……一路下去，寻访昔日的县署、学堂、花园、城隍庙，以及“桂水喷香”的桂花井。出东门，还可在古人修建的青石码头上遥望魁星楼、文笔塔倒映在江中的影子，凭吊不复存在的“临江晚钓”。卖早粥的铺子开门了，吃点云吞、糍粑、榨粉，然后租辆车北上去富川。

Hezhou, at the intersection of three provinces, is the site of two millennia of construction; even today along the sides of the streets there are brick and wood structures from the Ming and Qing dynasties as well as the following period. One can head out from Dongmen Street, thread through various old thoroughfares to see the former county seat, the academy, the gardens, the temple of the town god, and the Sweet Olive Well. Exiting the east gate, one can look out at the Kuixing Building from the old stone pier, and see the reflection of the Wenbi Building in the waters of the river. One can visit and ponder over the old fishing site on the river. In the morning when the congee stalls open, one can sample some wontons, and thin rice noodles, and then take a cab to Fuchuan.

评论

荷城
Lotus City

文：朱燕

位于广西东南部的贵港市，是一座有着2000多年历史的古郡新城，自古以来遍种荷花，被称为“荷城”。目前，贵港市有800多种荷花、200多种睡莲，已成为长江以南种植荷花品种最多的城市。荷给了贵港绿色的眼睛，修炼了贵港人的审美情趣。很多个无所事事的下午，人们流连在荷塘边，趴在塘坝的草地上，满屏清爽，极目娇艳，娉娉婷婷，暗香浮动……

Guigang City is situated in the southeast of Guangxi, and has more than two thousand years of history – it's a new town in an ancient county. Lotuses have been planted everywhere since old time here, hence its nickname. Currently, more than 800 varieties of the lotuses grow there, with more than 200 kinds of water lilies. This is the place with the most types of the flower south of the Yangtze River. These plants have given Guigang green eyes, and have cultivated the aesthetic interest of the residents. On an afternoon when you haven't much to do, you can go to the side of the lotus ponds and lie down on the grass, taking in a beautiful scene as breezes blow and blossoms float.

美丽荷城——贵港　摄影：黄大将

“发卡弯”间漂移
Guangxi Drift

文：朱燕

开车行驶在河池的盘山公路上，车外景物呈弧形倒退，轮胎的震动是克制的爆动，方向的变换是被征服的欲望，这是你打开桂西北山区的最正确方式以及独特体验。住在周边的人，假日都爱到这里骑行，挑战一种极限，用自行车速降来感受盘山公路的惊险和刺激。

When driving along the mountain roads in Hechi, you see the scenes fly past; your tires rumble as you switch back and forth through the turns. This is the unique experience of driving through the mountain roads. People who live nearby love coming here on holidays for a challenge. They bolt down the mountain roads on a bicycle in pursuit of excitement.

河池市环红水河山地自行车赛的车手行进在盘山路上　摄影：周恩革

“候鸟人”的养生天堂

Migrating for Health

文：朱燕

每年十月左右，巴马周围的几个村庄就会被来自全国各地的“候鸟人”挤爆门槛。他们当中以老年人居多，往往要一直待到第二年四五月才离开。这段时间，巴马最低温度只有七八度，正是无虫无蚊的季节，舒适宜人。巴马的这些“候鸟人”不同于普通的游客，他们大多抱着养生治病的目的而来，在这里待上短则一个月、长则几年，过着和当地人一样买菜做饭的日子，在这著名的“长寿之乡”使劲呼吸清新的空气，安心畅饮清冽的山泉，静静享受这世外桃源的清幽朴实，诚挚地憧憬着将幸福绵延得更长更久一点……

Every year around October, the villages around Bama are flooded with a glut of “migrating health seeker” from around the country. Most of them are elderly and come here to stay until next April or May. It is a comfortable time without insects or mosquitoes since the lowest temperature is only seven or eight degrees. These “health migrant”, different from normal travelers, mostly come here to keep fit or treat ailments. Some stay here for a month, and some for years. They buy vegetables and cook like the locals, enjoying the clean air and pure mountain water of these “longevity village”. Passing their days in this earthly paradise, they earnestly yearn for the continued happiness.

“候鸟人”的养生天堂——巴马　摄影：陈炜平

中越边陲，国门之城

The Border

文：黄耀东 黄兴忠

走进中越边陲的东兴市，一股浓郁的边关风情扑面而来：以欧式建筑为主要风格的街道上，来回穿梭着商人和游客。其中有很多戴着面罩的越南妇女，她们是这个城市独特的风景。东兴的迷人不仅在于它旖旎的风光，还在于历史给这座城市留下了一个又一个印迹：大清国界碑、零点纪念坛、中越人民友谊公园、北仑河中越友谊大桥……这些印迹赋予东兴作为国门之城、边关之城的使命。

At the border city of Dongxing, facing Vietnam, one gets a real feeling of foreign culture. The streets are mainly lined with buildings in European styles which welcome merchants and travelers. One also sees some Vietnamese women wearing face masks, forming a part of the scenery of the city. What attracts one isn't just the graceful scenery, but also the traces of history that have been left here: the Qing Dynasty Border Demarcation Stele, the Zero-point Commemorative Altar, the Sino-Vietnamese Friendship Park, and the Sino-Vietnamese Friendship Bridge upon the Beilun River. These are all signs of the special status of the city.

一家亲

Family

文：禤盈秋

中国—东盟博览会，已成功举办了十多届。同事阿芳，是位美丽的越南姑娘，常赞道："广西山美水美人更美，又热情好客，特别喜欢这里，是个宜居宜游宜商的好地方！"每每听见她的赞美，我总是笑呵呵地说："嫁到我们壮乡来吧，保你幸福开心一辈子。"或许，说者无心，听者有意。后来，她真的嫁到了南宁。

Thc China-ASEAN Expo has alrcady bccn hcld for tcn ycars. My collcaguc Ar-Fong, a beautiful Vietnamese woman; remarked with admiration: "The scenery of Guangxi is gorgeous, people are friendly and inviting; I really like it here. It's a great place to live or travel!" Whenever I hear that, I will laugh, "Then marry one of our Zhuang men, and you'll be blessed for the rest of your life!" I was just joking, but maybe she took it seriously. It turned out that she really got married with someone in Nanning.

一年一度的中国—东盟博览会　摄影：周军

灵渠　摄影：张小宁

历史 · 寻踪

Past and Pursuit

徐悲鸿南宁画马

Horse Painting

文：李慧

徐悲鸿在抗战时期曾先后10次往来广西。白崇禧在《口述自传》中把徐悲鸿列为对广西有重大贡献的15位外省精英之一，其中言："徐悲鸿……到广西来，黄主席很器重他，特别在桂林设'艺术学院'，请他当院长。徐以画马闻名全国，我亲自在南宁看他在五分钟内画一只马，很生动。"

Xu Beihong visited Guangxi ten times during the Anti-Japanese War. In Bai Chongxi's oral autobiography, Xu is listed as one of the 15 great heroes from outside Guangxi. He says, "When Xu Beihong came to Guangxi, Chairman Huang paid him much respect, and established an 'Art Academy' in Guilin and invited him to serve as its head. Xu was famous for his paintings of horses all over the country, and I personally saw him paint a horse in just five minutes in Nanning. It was moving."

齐白石钦州三尝荔枝

Lychees and Qi Baishi

文：李慧

齐白石在1905 ~ 1909年间，来过4次广西，其中3次在钦州。巧的是每次都正逢荔枝季，齐白石大快朵颐。归去后他开始创作《荔枝蜻蜓图》《荔枝蚂蚱》等作品，把岭南佳果的倩影在画作中留存。他还曾在诗中写道："此生再过应无分，纤手教侬剥荔枝（尝有歌女剥荔枝啖余）。"这位多情才子对当年钦州美女亲手喂他吃荔枝的情景念念不忘。

齐白石荔枝画　摄影：谢勇云

In the period between 1905 and 1909, Qi Baishi came to Guangxi four times, three of which he went to Yinzhou. It just happens each time lychees were in season. He ate loads. After he left, he did a few works, including Lychees and Dragonfly and Lychees and Locust, portraying the excellent fruit of the Lingnan area. He also depicted in his poem how a beautiful singing woman fed him with the fruit. This left quite an impression upon him.

苏东坡为合浦龙眼做广告

Su Dongpo Creates Ads

文：李慧

苏东坡在广东惠州吃荔枝，写下了“日啖荔枝三百颗，不辞长作岭南人”的名句；品尝了广西合浦的龙眼之后，又作出了《廉州龙眼质味殊绝可敌荔支》一诗，大赞龙眼“累累似桃李，一一流膏乳。坐疑星陨空，又恐珠还浦”。如今这两首诗已成为这两种岭南佳果的绝妙广告词。

When Su Dongpo ate lychees in Huizhou, he wrote: “eating three hundred lychees in a day makes one want to become a long-term resident of Lingnan”. When he tried the longan in Hepu, he wrote a poem, Lianzhou’s Longan Can Definitely Take on Lychees in which he gave great praise upon the fruit. Today, these two poems are widely used to promote the fruits of the Lingnan area in ads.

李商隐诗中的桂林平乐

Pingle in Poems

文：李慧

李商隐曾宦游广西一年有余，留下不少佳作。初见桂林，他的印象是“城窄山将压，江宽地共浮”，其中意境不让韩愈。他的住处在独秀峰西侧。雨后赏景，他写下了脍炙人口的“天意怜幽草，人间重晚晴”。后到昭州（今广西平乐）任职，他又以诗句真实记录了当地的奇风异俗、原始风貌，如“桂水春犹早，昭州日正西。虎当官道斗，猿上驿楼啼”“户尽悬秦网，家多事越巫”等。

Tang dynasty poet Li Shangyin served as a government official in Guangxi for a year and produced some good works. When he first saw Guilin, he wrote about the small city, the lofty mountains and the wide rivers. His artistic conception was on par with that of Han Yu. He lived to the west of the Solitary Peak. Once when he was admiring the scenery after the rain, he wrote a famous poem, the second line of which reads “after the heavens have finally graced the grasses with rain, the skies clear before night comes”. Later, when he went to Shaozhou (now Pingle), he recorded the local sights and customs with vivid details and fine verses.

评论

荔子碑的时空穿越

Lychee Stele

文：李慧

今天柳州柳侯公园里的柳侯祠内，留有一块记载柳宗元事迹的绝世宝物——荔子碑，它集中国文学史上“唐宋八大家”中的韩愈文、柳宗元事、苏轼书于一体，也称为“三绝碑”。湖南永州柳子庙根据荔子碑拓本复刻了一块，称“柳子碑”；四川眉州三苏祠亦有一块，称为“柳州碑”；湖北黄冈的东坡赤壁碑阁收藏的经典巨制《景苏园帖》石刻中也有荔子碑的化身；光绪六年（1880年）荔子碑还曾东渡日本重刻。

Today at the Liuzhou Temple within Liuhou Park, there is a treasure that records the acts of Liu Zongyuan. It collects the works of Eight Literary Masters of the Tang and Song dynasties: the text of Han Yu, the deeds of Yang Zongyuan, and the script of Su Dongpo. It's also called the "Stele of the Three Greats". At the Liu Zongyuan Temple in Hunan there is a copy of this stele, called the Liu Zongyuan Stele. At the Three Su Temple in Meizhou, Sichuan, there is another, called the Liuzhou Stele. At the Red Cliff Stele Pavilion in Huanggang, Hubei, there is a copy of the stele, too. In the sixth year of the Guangxu period (1880), the stele was even copied in Japan.

书法大家的自恋

Narcissistic Calligrapher

文：李慧

23 岁的米芾曾出任广西临桂县县尉之职。在桂林伏波山还珠洞内，他用原名“米黻”留下一行题刻（米芾之名是他 41 岁后才改的），上书“潘景纯、米黻，熙宁七年五月晦同游”。139 年后，地方官方信孺的幕僚恰好是米芾曾孙，方信孺把米家家传的米芾自画像刻在了旁边。此像据说是米芾自己对着镜子画的，画像上的他长袍大袖、潇洒不羁，一代书法大家“米颠”出尘自恋的形象跃然石上。

At 23 years of age, Mi Fu was dispatched to Gui County to serve as the governor. At the Huanzhu Cave upon Fubo Hill, he carved a line of words: "Pan Jingchun and Mi Fu were here together on the last day of the fifth month of the seventh year of the Xining Era". One hundred thirty-nine years later, an assistant to local official Fang Xinru just so happened to be a great-grandson of Mi Fu. Fang carved in a self-portrait that had been passed down through the Mi family next to the original inscription. It's said that Mi painted the portrait of himself while looking into a mirror, showing a long robe with large sleeves upon an unrestrained character. It is thus the famous calligrapher's likeness came to be upon the wall here.

宜州南楼那盏心灯

South Building

文：李慧

黄庭坚 60 岁时被贬宜州，栖居南楼，在这里度过了人生中最后一年多的时光。据他的日记体笔记《乙酉家乘》记载，在当地，黄庭坚广交了 50 余位朋友，很多都是当地百姓。淳朴热情的宜州人民送给他各种礼物，包括含笑花、粟米、山药、蜂蜜、竹笋、木炭、人参、木瓜、芭蕉、竹床、竹席等，达 59 种之多；赠酒共有 10 次，最多的一次收到 12 壶。这些“礼轻情意重”的馈赠温暖了黄庭坚的心。

Litterateur Huan Tingjian was demoted and sent to Yizhou at sixty. He lived at the South Building, where he spent the last year of his life. According to his diary, he made more than 50 friends there, many of them the local ordinary folks. The simple and kind people of Yizhou gave him all kinds of gifts including magnolias, grain, Chinese yams, honey, bamboo shoot, charcoal, ginseng, papayas, plantains, bamboo beds, bamboo mats, and others. They brought him alcohol ten times in total, one time bringing him twelve pots at once. These simple gifts made a significant impact on Huang and warmed his heart.

秦观的浪漫与哀愁

Romance and Sorrow

文：李慧

秦观年近五十被贬至横州（今广西横县）。没想到七夕词写得最浪漫的他，抓生计也是一把好手。他教会了当地百姓种桑养蚕，发展经济，还撰写了我国现存最早的一部蚕桑专著《蚕书》。51 岁时，秦观遇赦北还，途经藤州（今广西藤县），与友人游光化亭，聚饮大醉，“醉卧古藤阴下，了不知南北”，梦吟佳篇《好事近》，“后索水欲饮，水至，笑视之而卒”。如此含笑而逝，也许是他毕生最后的浪漫。

When Song dynasty poet Qin Guan was approaching fifty, he was demoted and sent to Hengzhou (now Heng County). As a master of love poems, he surprised others when he showed great skills in making a living. He taught the locals how to grow mulberries and raise silkworms, develop the economy, and published the earliest treatise on silkworm cultivation that is still extant in China. When he was 51, his transgressions were forgiven, and he returned north. On the way, he passed through Tengzhou (now Teng County) and visited the Guanghua Pavilion with a friend. They reveled and drank heavily. “Drunk, I lie down in the shade of vine leaves, knowing neither north nor south.” He mumbled the poem Good Things Are Near and asked for water. However, when the water arrived, he just looked at it with a smile, and then died. Dying with a smile upon his face may be the last romantic thing he did in his life.

永福百寿图

One Hundred Words

文：李慧

永福县百寿镇百寿岩，因岩壁上南宋时所刻的“寿”字得名。字高 1.77 米，宽 1.48 米，为阳刻，而每一笔笔画之中又阴刻了共 100 个小“寿”字。字中有字，且字字有出处：有蔡襄、虞世南、王羲之等名家所书，也有金文、石鼓文、西夏台书等各种字体。镌刻工匠也是刀工了得，把各大名家笔触特点一一还原。一个“寿”字，百种写法，从中看汉字流变，跨越千年。

There is a “Baishou Stone” in Baishou Village, Yongfu County, which is so called because there is the character “shou” (“longevity”) carved into it in the Southern Song dynasty. The character is 1.77 meters tall, 1.48 meters wide, and carved in relieve. Between each stroke of the character, there are much smaller versions of it carved in intaglio, one hundred in total. Characters within a character, and each one has its own provenance. There are ones in the calligraphic styles of Cai Xiang, Yu Shinan, Wang Xizhi and other luminaries, and examples of bronze script, stone drum script, Tangut platform script and others. The work of the carver is exceptionally skilled, replicating each brush stroke very accurately. One “shou”, one hundred styles – this is an exhibit of how the history of Chinese characters progressed over a millennium.

“八桂”的由来

Bagui

文：李慧

广西也称“八桂”。这两个字最早见于《山海经》：“桂林八树，在贲禺东。”其名来源一说因秦始皇设立的岭南三郡之桂林郡（郡治布山，在今桂平）盛产玉桂，而“八”者，多也，大也。此后有韩愈诗句“苍苍森八桂，兹地在湘南”；又有杨万里的“来从八桂三湘外，忆折双松十载前”，“八桂”的美名渐渐传扬开来。

Guangxi is also known as “Bagui” (“eight laurels”). These two characters first appeared in the Classic of the Mountains and Rivers: “The forest of eight laurels is to the east of Panyu.” One of the explanations for this is that Guilin County, one of the three counties established by the first emperor of the Qin dynasty, was rich in laurel trees, and that “eight” means “many” or “big”. Tang poet Han Yu later wrote in a poem, “The hazy forest of eight laurels is located south of the Xiangjiang River”. There are mentions of the name from Yang Wanli of Song dynasty and many other poets. The fame of Bagui spread ever since.

评论

颜公读书岩
Poet Yan

文：李慧

与谢灵运并称“江左颜谢”的颜延之，曾任始安郡（郡治在今桂林）太守。当年千里迢迢前往桂林任职的途中，他还特意绕道浔阳去见了比他年长30多岁的忘年交陶渊明，饮酒尽欢。到职后，颜延之写下了有记载的最早描写桂林山水的诗句：“未若独秀者，峨峨郛邑间。”独秀峰南麓有一个山洞，被颜延之开发成了天然的书房，冬暖夏凉，他常常在此读书。后人把这个山洞称作“颜公读书岩”。

颜公读书岩　摄影：邓霆

Yan Yanzhi, a poet during the South and North dynasties, was seen as an equal to Xie Lingyun as a prominent figure in the area. Yan was formerly the procurator of Shi'an. When he set out on the long trek to assume his post in the then capital Guilin, he made a point of taking a detour to see Tao Yuanming, who was thirty years older. They drank and had fun together. After he arrived at the site of his post, he wrote the earliest poem that describes the scenery of Guilin: "I've yet to see a place as amazing as the Duxiu Peak, which towers high between the cities." There is a cave in the Duxiu Peak which was used by Yan Yanzhi as a natural study, warm in the winter and cool in the summer. He frequently came here to read, and later people called it "Mr. Yan's Reading Rock".

范成大的旅游指南
Fan Chengda's Travel Guide

文：李慧

宋代的范成大，曾任静江知府兼广南西路经略安抚使，府治在今桂林。任职两年间，他遍游桂林山水，写成第一部介绍广西的风物志——《桂海虞衡志》。书中分为志岩洞、志金石、志酒、志器、志禽、志兽、志虫鱼、志花、志果、志草木、杂志、志蛮等13篇，内容丰富多彩，生动有趣，让人不忍释卷。

Fan Chengda of the Song dynasty served as the governor or Jingjiang as well as governor and planner of Guangnan Xilu. In the two years he served there he traveled extensively around Guilin and wrote the first guide to the land. The thirteen-chapter book contains descriptions of rocks and caves, metals and stones, liquor, implements, birds, beasts, insects and fish, flowers, fruits, plants, miscellany, and tribes. The contents are extensive and intriguing, painting a vibrant picture that makes one loath to set the volume down.

六旬而八州定

Done in Sixty Days

文：李慧

元结是鲜卑族的后代，原姓拓跋，到北魏孝文帝时才改姓元。50岁时元结调任容州（今广西容县）刺史。元结文韬武略，60天就平定了所辖8个州的内乱。在位期间，他主持修建了经略台。明代在经略台上修建了著名的真武阁。元结曾写过“火山无火，冰泉无冰”的诗句，名闻遐迩的梧州冰泉豆浆就是用他笔下的冰泉水做的。

Yuan Jie was a descendant of the Xianbei people; his surname was originally Tuoba. During the reign of the Xiaowen Emperor of the Northern Wei dynasty, he changed his name to Yuan. When he was 50 years old, he was assigned to Rongzhou (currently Rong County in Guangxi) to serve as a governor. He excelled at both literature and warfare, and within 60 days had pacified rebellions in eight counties there. During his term, he had the Jinglue Platform constructed. During the Ming dynasty, upon it was built the famous Zhenwu Pagoda. Yuan's famous couple "no fire in the fire mountain, no ice in the ice spring" later became quite famous; the Ice Spring Tofu Milk of Wuzhou is named after the spring to which he referred.

南溪山旅游的开发者

Nanxi Pioneer

文：李慧

李渤53岁出任桂州（今广西桂林）刺史。在桂林的两年多时间里，他修整荒弃的灵渠，恢复通航和灌溉，让它焕发生机，造福百姓。兴安百姓修建有“四贤祠”，纪念他和史禄、马援、鱼孟威这4位对灵渠贡献卓著的大贤。桂林南溪山是他开发并亲自取名的，还为之写下深情隽永的诗句。今天的“南溪新霁”是游客最为喜爱的“桂林八景”之一。

Li Bo at the age of fifty-three was assigned to serve as governor of Guizhou (today's Guilin). In the two years he spent in Guilin, he oversaw the restoration of the neglected Lingqu Canal, restoring traffic and irrigation and bringing about a resurgence that won the admiration of the people, who constructed the "Shrine of Four Sages", commemorating Shi Lu, Ma Yuan, Yu Mengwei and him, the four main characters in the history of the canal. Nanxi Hill in Guilin was both developed and named by him, and he wrote long-lasting poems full of emotion about it. Today Nanxi Xinji, or "The Sunny Scene of Nanxi" is one of the eight most famous sights in Guilin.

评论

包拯的偶像

Idol of Bao Zheng

文：李慧

大宋开国贤臣周渭，桂林恭城人。他执法如山、爱民如子的事迹，比包拯整整早了 60 年，包拯将他视为前辈楷模。周渭一生为官清廉，以致去世后因家贫无力下葬，皇上闻之，赐钱十万，方才得以入土为安。恭城建有周渭祠，别名一为“周王庙”，一为“蜜蜂楼”。前者表示民众对他的尊崇，后者是对该建筑特色的生动比喻。

Zhou Wei, a founding minister of the Song dynasty, was a native of Gongcheng, Guilin. He enforced the law strictly and famously loved the people. He was sixty years earlier than Bao Zheng, whom Bao regarded as a model of the previous generation. Zhou served honestly and without corruption, and died too poor to be buried. When the emperor heard of this, he contributed ten thousand, so that he could be put to rest properly. There is Zhou Wei Shrine in Gongcheng, which is also called King Zhou Temple, or Bee Building. The first name refers to the respect the people had for him, and the second to the appearance of the structure.

王阳明的前卫教育

Forefront Education

文：李慧

王阳明曾在田州、思恩、南宁设立书院，延师授业，其中南宁敷文书院经多次重修，至民国初年犹存。自敷文书院后，南宁地区书院逐渐发展起来，至清代达到高峰。现南宁尚存多处王阳明的纪念遗址，如人民公园镇宁炮台内的坐像碑、青秀山上的阳明洞等。他的很多教育理念和现代观念不谋而合，如对儿童采取“愉快教育”“因材施教”等，今天听来尤为亲切。

Ming dynasty philosopher Wang Yangming established academies in Tianzhou, Si’en, and Nanning and invited teachers. The Fuwen Academy in Nanning went through some reconstructions and still functioned up until the Republican Era. After the Fuwen Academy, gradually more and more academies developed in Nanning, reaching a peak during the Qing dynasty. There are still some memorials to Wang Yangming in Nanning, such as the seated statue of him upon the fort in Peoples’ Park, and the Yangming Cave upon Mount Qingxiu. Many of his educational principles agree with those extant in modern days, such as “happy education” for children and adaptive instruction techniques.

评论

徐霞客的“穷游日记”

Xu Xiake's "Budget Travel Diary"

文：李慧

1637年徐霞客从湖南进入广西，足迹遍及全州、兴安、桂林、阳朔、柳州、融安、桂平、玉林、容县、南宁、宜州、南丹等地，一年后才从南丹进入贵州。徐霞客根据这一年的考察经历写的《粤西游日记》，专门记述了他在广西的见闻，其篇幅占了《徐霞客游记》的三分之一，可惜的是，他在南宁一个月时间的旅行记录后来全部遗失了。除了详尽记录广西的奇山秀水、民俗物产等，徐霞客还是系统考察研究广西喀斯特地貌的第一位学者。

In 1637, Xu Xiake entered Guangxi from Hunan, and went all over to Quanzhou, Xing'an, Guilin, Yangshuo, Liuzhou, Rong'an, Guiping, Yulin, Rong County, Nanning, Yizhou, and Nandan, among other places. A year later he finally entered Guizhou from Nandan. Xu wrote an account of this year of travel in Travels to the West of Yue, in which he described what he'd seen in Guangxi. This work constituted one-third of Xu Xiake's Travels. Unfortunately, he later lost all his account of his one month's travel in Nanjing. Xu Xiake gave detailed descriptions of the scenery and custom of Guangxi and is also the first person to research the karst landforms there systematically.

瑶族皇太后

Yao Empress

文：李慧

明朝弘治皇帝朱祐樘的母亲纪太后是出身于广西贺州的瑶族，这有文字记载。明中叶时广西贺县与广东连山县一带的瑶、壮民族起义，明朝多次用兵镇压。贺县桂岭镇一个瑶族土司被杀后，他的小女儿被俘虏到北京，献入皇宫，管理内藏图书。一天明宪宗偶然路过内藏库，被她的容颜谈吐打动，临幸了她，竟使她怀孕了。她侥幸逃脱万贵妃妒杀，偷偷生下一子。这位皇子在安乐堂当了6年的“黑户”，终于有机会和皇帝相认，纪氏也受封为淑妃，但当年她就不幸去世了，年仅23岁。

The mother of Zhu Youtang, the Hongzhi Emperor of the Ming dynasty, was of the Yao people of Hezhou, which is attested in historical records. In the middle of the Ming dynasty, there were some Yao and Zhuang uprisings in He County of Guangxi and Lianshan County of Guangdong. The government dispatched soldiers multiple times to suppress them. In Guiling Village of He County, a Yao chieftain was killed, and his daughter was captured and sent to Beijing, where she was given to the imperial palace, tasked with working in the library. One day the Chenghua Emperor happened to pass by the library and was moved by her appearance and manner of speech. He paid her a visit and impregnated her. She managed to escape being killed by the concubines and secretly had a child. This descendant of the emperor grew up in the Anle Hall in secret for six years and finally had an opportunity to meet and be recognized by the emperor. Ji was made a high-ranking concubine but passed away later that year. She was only 23.

廉吏天下第一

Most Honest Official

文：李慧

于成龙走上仕途的第一站是广西罗城。当时的罗城刚入大清治下两年，盗匪猖獗，民不聊生，他的前两任知县一死一逃。他在这种恶劣的环境下一干就是7年，整顿地方，恢复生产，教化百姓，政绩斐然，朝廷将他举为“卓异”（大概等同于今天的全国标兵）。他为官20余年，3次获此殊荣，但他日常生活的清廉艰苦，也到了不能理喻的地步，康熙称他为“廉吏天下第一”。

Yu Chenglong's first stop on his official career was Luocheng in Guangxi. At the time Luocheng had only been under the administration of the Qing dynasty for two years, bandits ran rampant, and the people were destitute. One of his predecessors had died, and the other had fled. He spent seven years in this harsh environment, bringing about the order to the place, restoring production, and educating the people. He achieved great things, and the court upheld him as an exemplary official of the empire. He served as an official for more than twenty years and was awarded the special honor three times, but he led an unimaginably frugal life. The Kangxi Emperor said he was the most honest official in entire China.

贫穷贵公子，画坛大宗师

Poor Aristocrat, Amazing Painter

文：李慧

石涛是明代分封桂林的靖江王赞仪的十世孙，朱亨嘉的长子，本是地位显赫的王族子孙。清顺治二年桂林城破，他沦为饱尝国破家亡之痛的孤苦少年，在全州湘山寺出家。虽然身世飘零，他却取得了“画坛四大高僧”之一的成就，和八大山人朱耷齐名。石涛有许多流芳千古的名作，更有经典的绘画理论集《画语录》，被公认为“清三百年来第一人”。

Shi Tao was the descendant of Jingjiang Lord of the Ming dynasty and the eldest son of Zhu Hengjia, clearly a prominent personage. In the second year of the Shunzhi Era of the Qing dynasty, the city of Guilin was conquered, and Shi found himself a lonely and helpless child. He went to become a monk at the Xiangshan Temple in Quanzhou. Although his fortunes were down, he became one of the "four great monks of the art circles", on par with Zhu Da. Shi Tao produced the classic book upon paintings Painting Quotations as well as many works that became quite famous. He was commonly recognized as the "best painter in three centuries".

评论

追根溯源《爱莲说》

Home of the Writer

文：李慧

桂林西北 32 公里，漓江支流甘棠河上游，有一个古老的村落，名叫江头村。据江头村周氏族谱所载，他们的先祖乃是北宋大名鼎鼎的周敦颐。周敦颐出生在贺州桂岭，并在这里度过了少年时期。因他写下了千古名篇《爱莲说》，周氏后人将家族祠堂命名为“爱莲家祠”。爱莲家祠建筑工艺精湛，书香浓郁，始建于清光绪年间，历时 6 年乃成。大厅中壁有 6 块木板拼镶而成的巨幅木刻《周氏家训》，读之可晓周氏为何文脉兴盛，代有才人。

Thirty-two kilometers north-west of Guilin, upon the upper reaches of the Gantang River, a tributary of the Lijiang River, there is an old village called Jiangtou (literally means “head of the river”) Village. According to the genealogy of the Zhou clan there, they are the descendants of the Northern Song writer Zhou Dunyi, the author of masterpiece Ode to the Lotus Flower. Zhou was born in Guiling, Hezhou, and spent his young years there. Since he wrote the famous work, the Zhou family later named their ancestral temple “Lotus Flower Temple”. The craftsmanship of the structure is excellent, and the place has literary scent throughout. The construction was started in the Guangxu Era of the Qing dynasty and lasted for six years. Upon the wall of the main hall, there are six wooden panels which are carved with the family’s maxim. Reading them, one can see why the family flourished with talented individuals generation after generation.

北蔡南马

Mr. Ma Junwu

文：李慧

中国近代教育史上素有“北蔡南马”之说。“蔡”指的是蔡元培，“马”指的是广西桂林人马君武。马君武是中国近代获得德国工学博士第一人，国民党元老级人物，曾担任孙中山革命政府秘书长、广西省省长，北洋政府司法总长、教育总长。他是广西大学的创建人和首任校长，还出任过上海中国公学、国立北京工业大学、大夏大学校长。胡适投考上海中国公学时，马君武正好就是他的主考官，后来也对胡适多有提点、庇护。

In recent Chinese education, there is the phrase “Cai in the North, Ma in the South”. “Cai” refers to Cai Yuanpei, and “Ma” refers to Ma Junwu of Guilin. Ma is the first person from China to attain a Ph.D. in engineering from Germany and was a top-level official in the KMT. He served as the secretary-general of Sun Yat-sen’s revolutionary government, the provincial governor of Guangxi, the legal head of the Beiyang Government, and the head of education. He is the founder of Guangxi University and its first president, and also served as the president of Shanghai’s National University, the National Peking University of Technology, and Great China University. When Hu Shi sat exams for Shanghai National University, Ma Junwu happened to be his proctor, and later provided him with support and protection.

红颜薄命说绿珠

Lü Zhu

文：李慧

西晋和王恺斗富的大富豪石崇，当交趾采访使期间曾经路过广西玉林博白县，把当地著名的美女绿珠纳为爱妾，携回河南，建金谷园藏珠。绿珠聪明貌美，能歌善舞，尤善吹笛。每次宴客，石崇必命绿珠出来歌舞侑酒，见者皆失魂落魄，绿珠之美遂名闻于天下。曹雪芹在《红楼梦》中，也通过林黛玉的吟咏，将西施、虞姬、明君（王昭君）、绿珠和红拂（张出尘）并称为“五美”。后骠骑大将军孙秀向石崇强行索取绿珠，石崇推拒，孙秀怀恨，诬告石崇叛乱。石崇被抓前对绿珠说：“我今为尔得罪。”绿珠流着泪说：“愿效死于君前。”遂坠楼而死，石崇全家亦被杀。

Shi Chong was a wealthy man of the Western Jin dynasty, who had been competing with Wang Kai to see who is even wealthier. When Shi Chong was on his way to what is now Lingnan area, they passed through Bobai County in Yulin. He took the locally famous beauty Lü Zhu as his concubine and brought her back to Henan, where he built the “Jingu Garden” for her. She was beautiful and intelligent, excellent at song and dance, and was especially good at playing the flute. Every time he had a banquet, Shi Chong would have her sing, dance and encourage guests to drink, which drove them wild. Her fame spread wider and wider. In Cao Xueqin’s Dream of Red Mansions, through the intonations of Lin Daiyu, he lists Xi Shi, Yu Ji, Wang Zhaojun, Lü Zhu and Zhang Chuchen as the “five beauties”. Later on, General Sun Xiu demanded that he give Lü to him, but Shi refused. Sun was infuriated and falsely accused Shi of treason. As he was about to be arrested, Shi told Lü: “Today I fall for you.” Lü, tears in her eyes, told him: “I’d rather die in front of you.” She jumped out a window, killing herself. Then Shi’s entire family was put to death.

采茶戏《绿珠女传奇》剧照　摄影：陈炜平

南宁的女儿
The Daughter of Nanning

文：李慧

邓颖超纪念馆位于南宁市朝阳路 3 号。在纪念馆马路对面的三角绿地里，矗立着一块刻有“志洁行芳”的纪念石，石头所在位置据考证就是邓颖超的出生处——南宁镇台官邸。邓颖超出生时，父亲邓庭忠重男轻女，差点把她送人，但开明的母亲对她却百般疼爱。她 6 岁随母亲离开南宁到广州、上海谋生，后辗转到了天津。20 世纪 60 年代，邓颖超曾两次回到南宁认访自己的出生地。她说：“我是南宁的女儿，我是喝邕江水长大的。”

The Deng Yingchao Memorial Hall is at No. 3, Chaoyang Road in Nanning. There is a triangular green area across the hall, where there is a memorial stone that has the words “clean will and fine conduct” carved into it. The stone is located at the site where records show Deng was born – the official mansion of Nanning County. When she was born, Deng’s father held boys in higher esteem, and almost gave her away, but her open-minded mother loved her deeply and held on to her. When she was six, she left with her mother for Guangzhou, and then Shanghai to make a living, later ending up in Tianjin. In the 1960s, Deng Yingchao visited Nanning twice and looked upon her birthplace. She said, “I’m a daughter of Nanning, I grew up drinking the water of the Yong River.”

费孝通五上金秀大瑶山
Fei Hsiao-tung and Yao Mountains

文：李慧

费孝通先生曾经说过：“世界研究瑶族在中国，中国研究瑶族在金秀。”1935 年 10 月，刚从燕京大学毕业的费孝通、王同惠夫妇，应广西省政府的邀请，第一次到大瑶山进行瑶族社会考察。调查中两人迷路，费孝通误踏虎阱，腰腿受伤，王同惠出外寻求支援，不幸失足溺水身亡。悲剧发生时正是夫妇俩新婚 108 天。费孝通后来将这次考察的成果整理编成《花篮瑶社会组织》一书，以王同惠的名义印行。此后他又于 1978、1981、1982、1988 年四访金秀瑶山，除了学术考察的原因，恐怕还有毕生难舍的情愫。

Fei Hsiao-tung once said: “When the world researches the Yao people, they look at China. When the Chinese research them, they look at Jinxiu.” In October 1935, Fei Hsiao-tung and his wife Wang Tonghui had just graduated from Yenching University and accepted an invitation from the Guangxi government to perform the first survey of the Yao society in the mountains there. During their expedition they became lost, and Fei fell into a tiger trap, injuring his waist and leg. Wang went out to seek assistance but ended up drowning. This tragedy happened only 108 days after their wedding ceremony. Fei later produced the book The Societal Structure of the Flower-Basket Yao People and published it under his wife’s name. Later, he visited the Yao Mountains in Jinxiu in 1978, 1981, 1982 and 1988 for his academic survey, and for his lingering feelings too.

侠义方寸间

Chivalrous Heart

文：李慧

被誉为“新派武侠小说开山祖师”的梁羽生，生于广西蒙山的一个书香门第。1945年，一批学者避难来到蒙山。太平天国史专家简又文、以敦煌学及诗书画著名的饶宗颐都在梁羽生家里住过。梁羽生向他们学习历史和文学，深受教益。今天蒙山县城东南角有一座梁羽生公园，少年时代的梁羽生常在此处游玩。园中鳌山宝塔塔联“文光映日，到最高处开阔心胸，看乡邦又翻新页；笔势凌云，是真才人自有眼界，望来者更胜前贤”，是梁羽生先生1987年2月回乡探亲时所作。

Liang Yusheng, honored as the “founder of the school of new wuxia novels” was born in a scholarly family in Mount Meng, Guangxi. In 1945, some scholars fled there; famous historian of the Taiping Kingdom Jian Youwen as well as Dunhuang scholar, poet, and painter Jao Tsung-I both stayed at his house. Liang learned history and literature from them, gaining much knowledge. Today there is a Liang Yusheng Park in Mengshan County, at the site where he frequently played as a youth. The Aoshan Tower there has an inscription: “The light of literature shines and broadens one’s ambitions, a page is turned here. The spirit of calligraphy is sky-high; may we hope for more from the successors”. This was penned by Liang when he came back to his hometown in February 1987.

昆仑关战役

Kunlun Fort

文：李慧

昆仑关位于南宁市昆仑镇与宾阳县交界处，距南宁市50公里，地势险要，易守难攻，为兵家必争之地。历史上这里曾发生过多次战役，其中最大、最惨烈的是抗日战争时期的“昆仑关大战”。1939年12月18日，中日双方在这里血战10余天后，由杜聿明率领的国民革命军第一个，也是唯一一个机械化军第5军，歼灭日军第21旅团5000余人，其中班长以上的军士官死亡达85%以上，并击毙敌少将旅团长中村正雄，取得桂南会战的重大胜利。

The Kunlun Fort is situated at the intersection of Kunlun Town and Binyang County in Nanning, about 50 kilometers from Nanning. It’s hard to access and easy to defend, and is an important military location. In the past, many battles have been fought there, among which the largest and most intense is the “Battle of Kunlun Fort” in the war against the Japanese aggressors. On December 18, 1939, the Chinese and Japanese shed blood for ten days. The fifth army, the first and at the time only mechanized corps in China killed more than 5,000 of the Japanese troops and more than 85% of higher ranking officers, including major general Masao Nakamura. It was a great victory in the Battles of Southern Guangxi.

桂平西山舍利子

Relics in the Mountain

文：李慧

桂平西山是中国南部著名佛教圣地，全国十三大佛教圣地之一，也是广西保存最完整的佛教圣地，自唐代起就有高僧驻锡。1989年9月27日，95岁高龄的释宽能法师在桂平西山洗石庵涅槃，火化后留下了3粒舍利子和48粒佛珠舍利。这3粒舍利子是目前世界上有史料记载的第一个比丘尼的舍利子，现供奉在洗石庵内，成为镇庵之宝。

Xishan, or the "West Mountain" in Guiping, is a famous site for Buddhism – the best-preserved site in Guangxi, a well-known place in South China, and one of the thirteen main sites in the entire country. Outstanding monks have lived here since Tang dynasty. On September 27, 1989, 95-year-old Nun Kuanneng achieved nirvana at the Xishi Temple. After she was cremated, three Buddhist relics and forty-eight beads were left behind. These three relics are the first in the world to come from a nun and are stored there today, as treasures.

桂林山水甲天下

Mountains and Rivers

文：李慧

"桂林山水甲天下"可说是桂林最好的广告词，人们一直好奇是谁先写出来的。经过考证，这是南宋时广南西路提点刑狱使王正功，在为进京赶考的学子饯行的"鹿鸣宴"上所作的两首七律中一句。"桂林山水甲天下，玉碧罗青意可参"，朗朗上口，一经提出，广为传颂，从此桂林山水名扬四海。在桂林靖江王城独秀峰读书岩，还可找到 "桂林山水甲天下"的摩崖石刻真迹。

"The scenery of Guilin is truly the best." This line is the best-known sentence used to promote Guilin. People are always curious about who wrote it. Looking into it, we see that it was written by Wang Zhenggong of the Southern Song dynasty, as part of a work he wrote for a party celebrating successes of candidates in local examinations who would go on to the capital. "The scenery in Guilin is truly the best, with the mountains here, and the waters of the Lijiang River." The composition quickly became popular and known widely, spreading the fame of Guilin. The first part of the couplet is even inscribed upon the walls of the famous Reading Rock at the Duxiu Peak in Jingjiang.

刻于桂林独秀峰下岩壁上的王正功诗句"桂林山水甲天下" 摄影：邓霆

靖江王府 摄影：邓霆

阅尽王城知桂林

City of Jingjiang Prince

文：李慧

靖江王城坐落于桂林漓江西岸，是明朝靖江王朱守谦的藩王府，始建于洪武五年（1372 年）。靖江王城外围有国内保存最完好的明代城墙，它比北京故宫早建 34 年，是南京故宫的精华缩影。明朝共有 12 代 14 位靖江王居住于此，历时 280 年。今天的靖江王府，已经和广西师范大学合为一体，作为学校的本部，历史文化与旅游学院的师生在此学习。月牙池畔书香浓，历史积淀与青春朝气相得益彰。

The City of Jingjiang Prince was situated upon the western bank of the Lijiang River in Guilin. This was the site of the palace of Prince Zhu Shouqian. Construction was initiated during the Hongwu era, in the fifth year (1372). It boasts the best-preserved city wall built during the Ming dynasty, 34 years earlier than the Imperial Palace of Beijing – it captures the essence of the imperial palace of Nanjing. During the Ming dynasty, 14 Jingjiang Princes lived here, representing the consecutive rule of twenty-eight decades. Today the Jingjiang Palace is a part of Guangxi Normal University and its central unit where teachers and students of Historical Culture and Tourism Institute study here. Historical heritage and modern glamor combine around the crescent lake.

评论

壮族抗倭女英雄

Zhuang Heroine

文：李慧

广西田阳县田州镇，有一位曾经叱咤风云的壮族女英雄瓦氏夫人。她生活的明代中期，我国东南沿海江浙一带遭受倭寇烧杀劫掠，生灵涂炭。南京兵部尚书张经曾经见识过广西壮族土司组建的地方武装“狼兵”的战斗力，向朝廷举荐用“狼兵”剿灭倭寇。瓦氏夫人响应朝廷征调，以 58 岁高龄率兵千里迢迢自广西跋涉到嘉兴，奋勇杀敌，战功累累，堪称一代抗倭女杰。

Tianzhou Village in Tianyang County is the home of a famous figure, a heroine of the Zhuang people, and a powerful commander. She lived in the middle of the Ming dynasty when Japanese pirates were rocking the coasts of the provinces of Jiangsu and Zhejiang, afflicting great suffering upon the people there. The military minister at Nanjing saw the military might of the “wolf soldiers” under the Zhuang chieftains of Guangxi, and recommended to the court that they should be used to extirpate the pirates. This woman surnamed Wa responded to the order, and at fifty-eight years of age led her troops on the long journey from Guangxi to Zhejiang, where they routed the enemies. She was a true heroine.

王力书百字长联

Wang Li's Couplets

文：李慧

著名语言学家王力教授，与赵元任、吕叔湘等并为“中国语言学三大泰斗”，并和胡适、朱光潜、冯友兰等合列“北大名家名师”。五大洲许多国家的大学汉语专业都把他的《古代汉语》作为基础教材，美国把他的《汉语诗律学》列为研究生必读书，俄罗斯把他的《汉语语法纲要》定为必修教材。今天桂林七星公园月牙山小广寒楼门前廊柱上有 138 字长联，是他 84 岁高龄时为桂林写下的。

Famous linguistic scholar Wang Li, along with Zhao Yuanren and Lü Shuxiang, is known as one of the three greatest linguists of China. He's also known as one of the greats of Peking University just like Hu Shi, Zhu Guangqian and Feng Youlan. In term of Chinese studies, his books are a must – his Classical Chinese is the principal textbook around the world; his Laws of Chinese Poetry is essential for graduate students in the USA, and his An Outline of Chinese Grammar is a must-have text in Russia.Today in front of the Little Guanghan Building at the Crescent Hill in Seven Stars Park, Guilin, there is an inscription of 138 characters upon the pillars in front of the entrance, which was written by him at eighty-four years of age.

语言学家王力的雕像　摄影：陈炜平

桂西北遥远的句町古国

Old Culture

文：李慧

百色市西林县，曾经存在过一个有500多年历史的古国——句町国。它是和夜郎国、古滇国同时期的西南三大藩国之一。20世纪70年代，西林县普驮屯曾经出土过铜棺墓、铜鼓墓，发现了400多件西汉初年的青铜、玉石等材质的随葬品，初步推断为句町古国首领的墓葬，其中以四面铜鼓为葬具的独特葬式为全国首见。普驮屯今天还保留着句町遗俗——欧贵婚俗，即男子入赘当上门女婿，男从女居，很有母系氏族社会的气息。

Xilin County in Baise is the site of Gouding Kingdom, a kingdom that existed for five centuries. It, along with the Yelang and Dian Kingdoms, was one of the three major vassal states in the southwest. In the 1970s at Putuotun in Xilin County there unearthed bronze coffin, bronze drum tombs, and more than four hundred of burial artifacts at the time of early Western Han dynasty made of bronze, jade and other material. The place was assumed to be the grave of the leader of the ancient Gouding Kingdom. The burial using bronze drums was the only one found in China. Today, Putuotun still preserves the old marriage customs that the men marry into and live with the brides' family, clear evidence of a matriarchal society.

元祐党籍碑

Yuanyou Stele

文：李慧

元祐党籍碑，宋代摩崖石刻，世存两块，均在广西。一块存于桂林七星岩龙隐洞，一块存于融水真仙岩老仙洞。碑上人名309，被北宋徽宗一朝蔡京专权列为反对王安石新政的“奸党”一族。却没曾想，借此碑，309人扬名立万，反倒成了佳话。存于融水真仙岩的《元祐党籍碑》所拓为蔡京手书真迹，尤其珍贵。徐霞客慕名而来，在洞中留居13天，写下数千字日记赞叹真仙岩奇景。

The Yuanyou Steles were carved in a cliff during the Song dynasty. There exist only two pieces in the world, both in Guangxi. One exists at the Dragon Cave, Qixing Cliff, and the other at the Laoxian Cave, Zhenxian Cliff, Rongshui. They are the list of 309 people who were considered “reactionary party members” by Cai Jing, the ministry during the Huizong Era of Song dynasty. However, it turns out these people became famous and respected due to these steles. The stele at Zhenxian Cliff has handwritings of Cai Jing himself, and is especially precious. Xu Xiake was attracted by the fame of these sights and spent 13 days there, writing thousands of words of praise in his journal.

评论

遗存有武则天创造的异体汉字的古碑

Evidence of Wu Zetian's Characters

文：李慧

智城古城位于广西上林县，距今已有1300多年的历史，主要由唐城和唐碑组成。这里曾是被武则天封为“万寿公王”的唐代澄州刺史韦厥的隐居地。智城碑被誉为“岭南第一唐碑”，刻于武则天时期，作者韦敬一。碑文盛赞智城山一带风光形胜，具有浓厚的道教文化气息。这座位于壮族聚居区的碑刻反映了唐代中原与岭南地区文化上的紧密联系，碑文中刻入的武则天创造的6个异体汉字更是让人惊叹。

The Zhicheng Old City is located in Shanglin County, Guangxi, and has more than 1,300 years of history. It mainly comprises remnants of a Tang city and Tang steles. This was formerly the site of the residence of feudal governor Wei Jue. Zhicheng stele, known as "No. 1 stele of Tang dynasty in Lingnan area" and was carved in the reign of Wu Zetian. The author Wei Jingyi made high praise of the topology and scenery of Zhicheng mountains, and have a very Taoist tone to them. The stele, located at a place where the Zhuang people live, reflect the close cultural links between the central plains and the Lingnan area during Tang dynasty. Within the text of the stele, there are six alternate forms of characters created by Wu Zetian, which make them quite significant.

全州湘山寺的高丽情缘

Koryo Connection

文：李慧

全州湘山寺，又称“楚南第一禅林”，因全真法师而声名远播。700年前，这里有位铁山长老，曾到高丽国交流。1311年7月，高丽国王派使者回访，赠送了夜明珠、如来佛像、凤翅帽、金字《华严经》、金绣千佛袈裟、金钵盂6件宝物，轰动一时。全州有三江口、钵盂山，韩国也有全州、三江口、钵盂山，两地之间，可谓世代有缘。

The Xiangshan Temple at Quanzhou, known as the "First Chan Temple in Lingnan", enjoys its fame because of Master Quanzhen. Seven hundred years ago there was an elder monk called Tieshan, who had visited the Kingdom of Koryo. In July of 1311, an emissary dispatched by the king of Koryo returned the visit and brought with him a precious pearl, a Buddha statue, a phoenix-wing cap, a copy of the Avatamsaka Sutra in gold characters, a gold-embroidered monk's robe, and a gold bowl, six pieces altogether. The names of "Sanjiangkou" and "Mount Boyu" also exist in present-day Korea, just like in Quanzhou, a reflection of this connection.

评论

古人类的家园

Ancient People

文：李慧

迄今为止广西发现10余处古人类遗址：木榄山人，距今11.1万年左右；柳江人，距今13万至7万年之间；白莲洞人，距今3.7万年左右；麒麟山人，距今3万年左右；甑皮岩人，距今1万至7000年之间……此外还有距今80万年的百色手斧文化遗址和距今4000多年的大石铲文化圈，无不说明史前广西这片热土是古人类栖息繁衍的理想家园。

Up to now, six relic sites of Palaeolithic people have been found in Guangxi: the Mount Mulan Man, about 110,000 years old; the Liuzhou Man, between 130,000 and 70,000 years old; the Bailian Cave Man, about 37,000 years old; the Mount Qilin Man, about 30,000 years old; the Zengpi Rock Man, between 10,000 and 7,000 years old… In addition, there are the remains of the 800,000-year-old Baise Hand-Axe Culture and the 4,000-year-old Large Stone Spade Cultural Group. They all are testaments that the warm climate of Guangxi has been a friendly habitat for humans of all kinds for a long time.

王城里的"状元及第"　摄影：邓霆

广西古代两学霸

Great Students

文：李慧

中国科举史1300年间，连中三元者仅13人。地处偏远的广西，占了2名。所谓三元及第，即乡试举人第一名，会试进士第一名，殿试又点中状元。宜州冯京，广西第一位"三元及第"。临桂陈继昌，则是中国科举史上最后一名连中三元的人物。当时有一联语：高祖当朝一品；玄孙及第三元。高祖指乾隆时重臣陈宏谋，玄孙即为陈继昌。自唐以降，临桂一县出过5名状元、2名探花及291名进士。

In the 1,300 years of the history of imperial examinations in China, there have only been thirteen instances in which someone has achieved three consecutive first-place rankings at the provincial, national, and then palace-level examinations. Two of these people hail from remote Guangxi. Feng Jing from Yizhou was the first one who achieved this feat in the history of Guangxi, and Chen Jichang was the last one in Chinese history. Chen's great-grandfather was also very famous at that time. After the Tang dynasty, Lingui produced five first-degree scholars, two third-degree scholars and 291 successful candidates overall.

擘窠大字
Large Characters

文：李慧

写字、篆刻时，为求字体大小匀整，以横直界线分格，形制硕大，称为“擘窠”。清代王元仁是王羲之的后裔，著名书法家，擅长擘窠书，特别善于巨幅单字。他于道光年间任阳朔、崇善县令，在八桂大地留下几个擘窠大字：阳朔碧莲峰“带”字，高近6米；武鸣起凤山，天下第一“凤”，高4米，宽3米；崇左“寿”字，高2米，宽1米……风格遒劲雄健，极具视觉冲击力。

When writing or carving characters, one constructs a grid to ensure that they are of uniform size. This is especially difficult when they are quite large. Wang Yuanren of the Qing dynasty was a descendant of Wang Xizhi, a famous calligrapher of the Eastern Jin dynasty, and excelled at creating large characters, especially huge ones. During the Daoguang Era, he was posted to Yangshuo and Chongshan Counties. He left a few examples of his works around Guangxi. Upon Yangshuo's Bilian Peak he realized the character dai about six meters tall; on Mount Qifeng he wrote the largest Feng ("phoenix"), four meters tall and 3 meters wide. At Chongzuo he made the character shou ("longevity") two meters tall and one meter wide. The style of the characters is robust and vigorous, full of visual strength.

海上丝绸之路
Maritime Silk Road

文：李慧

两汉时期，合浦港、北海港，皆为海上丝绸之路的重要始发港。唐代刘禹锡描写过其时的繁华景象：“连天浪静长鲸息，映日帆多宝舶来。”今天北海白龙城遗址是当年海上丝绸之路货物集散地，珍珠、玳瑁、丝绸、瓷器、茶叶等，从合浦、北海出发，输送到世界各国；世界各国的货物也纷至沓来。合浦汉墓出土的大量舶来品包括琉璃、玛瑙、水晶、玻璃珠串和古罗马琉璃杯、波斯陶壶、古希腊缠花金球、阿拉伯项链等，见证了当年海上丝绸之路的繁荣昌盛。

During the time of the Han dynasty, Hepu and Beihai Harbors were both important jumping-off points for the maritime silk road. Liu Yuxi of the Tang dynasty described the bustling scenes of these ports, waves undulating, sun shining, and countless boats coming and going. Today the remains of the Bailong ("white dragon") City at Beihai are the site where cargo was packaged and distributed, goods including pearls, turtles, silk, ceramics, tea, and more. These wares headed out to lands all over the globe from Hepu and Beihai. Treasures from afar also came one after another. Unearthing Han tombs at Hepu has yielded a large amount of specimens, such as glass, agate, crystal, beads, and Roman glass, Persian ceramic pots, ancient Greek gold balls, Arab necklaces and the like, evidence of the flourishing trade on the maritime silk road.

中国近代史上唯一一次完胜
Modern Victory

文：李慧

清光绪十一年（1885 年）三月，在中法战争中，年近七旬的老将冯子材带领清军在广西镇南关（今友谊关）大败法国侵略者，取得重大胜利，导致法国茹费理内阁倒台。这场著名的战役就是镇南关大捷，是中国近代反侵略战争史上唯一一次完胜。可惜弱国无外交，最终结果仍然是割地赔款。同时期活跃的抗法力量还有刘永福率领的黑旗军，曾取得纸桥大捷。

In March 1885, as the Sino-French War raged, old general Feng Zicai, almost 70 years old at the time, led his troops to rout the invading French troops at Zhennan Fort (today's Friendship Fort) in Guangxi. It was a great victory and led to the fall of the Ferry Cabinet in France. It's a famous event in the modern military history of China, the only crushing victory the Chinese have had against invaders in contemporary history. Sadly, the country was weak and in the end still forced to cede territory and pay indemnities. Around the same time, the Black-flag Army under the leadership of Liu Yongfu also gained a substantial victory at the Zhiqiao Bridge.

南疆雄关——友谊关　摄影：周军

一门三总督

Three Governors

文：李慧

清朝末年，广西百色市西林县那劳乡岑氏家族涌现了三位活跃在中国近代政治舞台上的重要人物：云贵总督岑毓英、岑毓宝，两广总督岑春煊，时称“一门三总督”，岑氏可谓簪缨世族。今天昆明大观楼上还可以看到工笔楷书刻写的180字“古今第一长联”，落款“西林岑毓英重立”。岑毓英之子岑春煊性好弹劾贪官、庸官，人送绰号“官屠”，与“财屠”张之洞、“人屠”袁世凯并称“清末三屠”。他为官所到之处大力创办新式学堂。山西大学、四川大学等20多所学校前身均为岑春煊所创办。如今整个岑氏古建筑群统称为“宫保府”，为桂西及桂西北壮族地区保存规模最大、延时最长、保存最为完整的土司建筑群。

At the end of the Qing dynasty, the Cen family of Nalao in Guilin produced three sons who became major players on the stage of modern Chinese politics. The governors of Yunnan and Guizhou Cen Yuying and Cen Yubao, and the governor of Guangdong and Guangxi Cen Chunxuan became the “three governors of one family”. Thus, the Cen clan can be seen as one of the noble families. At the Daguan Tower in Kunming today one can still see 180-character “the longest couplet of now and then”, which is signed with Cen Yuying’s name. His son, Cen Chunaxuan excelled at delating corrupt and indolent officials, and became known as the “butcher of officials” – along with the “butcher of wealth” Zhang Zhidong and the “butcher of men” Yuan Shikai; they were the “three butchers of the late Qing”. He worked hard at establishing academies where he took office. Today’s Shanxi University, Sichuan University, and more than 20 other universities in China were established by him. The “Gongbao Mansion” of the Cen clan still stands as one of the largest, oldest and best-preserved Tusi buildings in western and north-western Guangxi.

我在家乡等你

I'll await you at Home

文：李慧

2014年7月22日，第四十五届世界体操锦标赛（南宁）宣传片亮相美国纽约时报广场：“十月，我在家乡等你！”李宁张开双臂，在美国纽约时报广场的大屏幕上向全世界发出邀请，为家乡代言。

On July 22, 2014, the promotional video for the 45th World Athletic Championships in Nanning was shown in Times Square in New York City. “In October, I’ll await you at home!” exclaimed Li Ning as he extended his arms upon the giant screen in the square, inviting the world to come around.

评论

灵渠秀影 摄影：张小宁

北有长城，南有灵渠

Ling Canal

文：李慧

公元前 214 年，位于兴安县境内的灵渠凿成通航。这是世界上最古老的运河。它的流向由东向西，将兴安县东面的海洋河和西面的大溶江相连，仿佛一个大写的英文字母“H”，沟通了长江水系和珠江水系。它还有“世界古代水利建筑明珠”“世界船闸之父”的美誉，是继都江堰之后又一著名水利工程。郭沫若先生曾经赋诗曰：“始皇毕竟是雄才，北筑长城南岭开。”

In the year 214 BC, the Ling Canal was dug and opened to traffic within the borders of Xing'an County. This is the oldest canal in the world, and people think it can equal the Great Wall in North China. It flows from west to east, and connects the Haiyang River of Xing'an's east to the Darong River in the west, forming a large "H" shape, providing a route for traffic between the Yangtze River and Zhujiang River networks. It's regarded as a wonder of waterway engineering in the ancient world, as well as the first example of ship locks. It's another amazing feat after the Dujiang Weir. Guo Moruo once described it in a poem: "The first emperor was truly talented, building the Great Wall in the north and Ling Canal in the south."

融水杆洞乡高培苗寨　摄影：谌贻照

村镇 · 漫行
Villages and Voyages

绣球之乡

Xiuqiu Village

文：朱燕

电影《刘三姐》在中国可谓家喻户晓。片中，壮族砍柴女一边吟唱山歌，一边深情款款地将绣球抛给心上人阿牛哥的场景，让几代人至今难以忘怀。位于广西靖西县的旧州村，就是大名鼎鼎的“绣球之乡”。2300多位村民中，有一半都在家从事绣球制作工作。当地人穿上独具特色的壮族服饰，坐在家门口缝制绣球的场景，成了靖西一道独特的风景。

The film Liu SanJie is well-known in households throughout China. In the film, the female firewood collector sings a folk song as she throws a xiuqiu, a kind of embroidered cloth ball, at Ar-Niu, the object of her affections; this scene is unforgettable to generations of Chinese. Today, Jiuzhou Village in Jingxi County, Guangxi is the "village of xiuqiu". Of the 2,300 residents, half of them work in the production of these cloth balls. Locals wear the special clothing of the Zhuang people, and here the sight of them sitting in their doorways stitching and embroidering these balls is a part of the unique scenery of the village.

壮家绣球女　摄影：张小宁

中国画扇第一镇

Painted Fans

文：朱燕

阳朔福利镇古拙的老街上，最曼妙的一道风景便是画扇。斑驳的青石板路边，几家颇具年代感的铺面里，摆满了大小不一的画扇。这些画扇，小的仅三四寸，大的却有七八尺，形色各异、美不胜收。到过福利古镇玩乐的国内外游客，走时都喜欢带几把画扇作为礼物或自用。这些漂洋过海的“福利画扇”，在异国他乡的客厅，重现了桂林山水的风韵。

On the unadorned old streets of Fuli Town in Yangshuo, the most attractive sight is that of the painted fans. Beside the mottled cobbled pathways, there are stores with a very aged feel full of painted fans, of this kind and that kind, large and small. The small ones are only a few inches across, whereas the largest ones may be a few feet wide. They're diverse and beautiful in design. Tourists from around China and the world always take a few of these painted fans with them when they depart, be they for gifts or personal use. These “Fuli Fans” travel far and wide, recreating the scenery of Guilin wherever they go.

黄姚古镇　摄影：罗劲松

“天涯歌女”落黄姚

“The Wandering Songstress” in Huangyao

文：朱燕

黄姚迎秀街处处都有写生。青色墙面上“欧阳予倩故居”小木牌映入眼帘，就是一处充满故事的景色。这是一间不足 30 平方米的小屋，室内陈设简约恬静，那盏悬于屋顶上的铜油灯、挂在墙上的黑白照片，昏黄的灯光中氤氲出天涯歌女的浅唱低吟。这里不仅见证了著名戏剧艺术家欧阳予倩的诸多经历，也伴随先生度过无数个艺术创作、革命活动的不眠之夜。

There are paintings of natural life everywhere on Yingxiu Street in Huangyao Town. On one of the houses, there is a small wooden plaque that marks it as the former residence of Ouyang Yuqing, a luminary of modern cinema and drama in China. This is a small dwelling no more than 30 square meters in area; the interior decorations are simple and calm, with a copper lamp hung from the ceiling, and a black-and-white picture on the wall, reminding the visitors of the film The Wandering Songstress directed and starred by Ouyang. The site isn't just a testament to the famous playwright's experiences, but also a place that carried him through sleepless nights during his artistic creations and revolutional activities.

良口古镇的鸟市

Liangkou Bird Markets

文：朱燕

三江良口古镇的老街上，最有意思的要数鸟市。来自周围村寨的瑶、苗、侗族人，每天把捉来的画眉鸟拿来卖。那些穿着各式各样服装的男人，一手拿着烟袋锅子，一手提着鸟笼子在街上四处转悠，或是三五成群蹲在街边赏鸟，讨价还价，表情可是非常投入和陶醉。

On the old streets of Liangkou Old Village in Sanjiang, the most interesting thing to see is the bird markets. Yao, Miao and Dong peoples from surrounding villages come each day with wood thrushes they have caught. These men arrive in their traditional clothing, long pipe in one hand and a birdcage in the other, walking about or sitting in groups on the pavement, admiring the birds and talking prices. Everyone is quite into it according to the expressions on their faces.

雁江古镇福盛楼

Fusheng Building

文：朱燕

在雁江古镇众多宅群中，最有看头的是福盛楼。福盛楼是百年商业古镇的象征，位于古镇最繁华的任慈街和隆靖街交汇处。楼共有三层，是雁江古镇上唯一一栋用“红毛泥”（类似今天的水泥）来建造的，其梁柱、门槛等至今仍非常牢固，可见当年楼主人在雁江的显赫地位。

In Yanjiang Old Town, the most interesting structure is the Fusheng (“abundant prosperity”) Building. It’s a symbol of the more than a century of commerce in the old village, situated at the busiest corner, the intersection of Renci Street and Longjing Street. The building has three stories in total and is the only building constructed out of a special type of “red feather clay”, a material which is similar to modern concrete. The beam-columns and thresholds are all still very strong, which are indications of the status of the original owners in Yanjiang at the time of the building’s construction.

人民币上的风景

The scenery on the Paper Money

文：朱燕

兴坪古镇位于阳朔东北部，素有“桂林山水甲天下，阳朔山水在兴坪”之说。孙中山和美国克林顿总统都曾经到访过的小渔村就在兴坪古镇内。20元人民币的背面，用的也是兴坪风光。兴坪古镇除了自然风光迷人，三条老街亦各具特色。当年叶剑英元帅游览漓江，被兴坪风光吸引，写下“果然佳胜在兴坪”的赞诗。

The Xingping Old Town is situated in the northeast of Yangshuo. Guilin is famous for having nice scenery, and Xingpiing is renowned for being exceptionally nice. It was once visited by Sun Yat-Sen, as well as former United States President Bill Clinton. The scenery on the back of the 20-yuan note is a depiction of Xingping as well. In addition to the attractive natural view, it also has three special old streets. When marshal Ye Jianying visited the Lijiang River, he was taken in by Xingping’s beauty and even penned a short verse praising it.

三江侗寨　摄影：陈炜平

广西文化第一村

Cultural Village

文：朱燕

玉林高山村现存有300多幅壁画、100多件古泥塑以及一大批古画、古手稿、古书籍、古牌匾。高山村曾出过4名进士、19位举人、193位秀才，被世人称为“进士村”“广西文化第一村”，可谓名副其实。这里的每一块砖、每一个窗格，无不是高山村百年文化的载体，也是高山村古民居建筑的灵气精魂所在。

玉林高山村　摄影：陈炜平

Gaoshan Village in Yulin has more than 300 murals, more than 100 clay sculptures, and a large number of old paintings, manuscripts, books, and plaques. The village has produced four candidates for the imperial examinations, nineteen successful candidates at the provincial level, and 193 county-level candidates. It's been named "the village of success" and the "most cultured village in Guangxi", two titles which it deserves. Here every brick, every lattice carries the centuries of culture of the village, as well as the true spirit of folk architecture.

玉林高山村　摄影：陈炜平

怀远情结

Huaiyuan Sentiments

文：朱燕

出门在外，怀远人碰上怀远人，话题总少不了怀远如何如何。著名歌手唐佩珠，到哪儿都会自豪地说自己是宜州怀远人，怀远人于是脸上便有了光。唐佩珠的爱人张文明，是一名作曲家，紧紧咬定刘三姐音乐元素，提取草根文化，创作了大量具有地域风情的歌曲，被同行称为“宜州怀远的施光南”。

When elsewhere, people from Huaiyuan County running into each other will always have plenty of topics to discuss on how Huaiyuan is so and so. Famous singer Tang Peizhu and his composer wife Zhang Wenming will always proudly declare that they are from Huaiyuan in Yizhou no matter where they go. Zhang Wenming latched firmly on to the musical elements of Liu Sanjie, extracted the essence of folk culture and created many songs with local features, and thus is called “the tongue of Huaiyuan” by other composers.

四十八弄明珠

Forty-Eight Pearls

文：朱燕

中渡古镇是鹿寨文明的发源地，建于东吴甘露元年（265 年），距今将近 2000 年历史，素有“四十八弄明珠”之称。由于上通桂林，下达柳州，又处在四十八弄隘口，中渡是一条古驿道，明清时曾繁华一时。据记载，大旅行家徐霞客当年就是顺着这里的洛江下抵柳州的。

中渡古镇　摄影：赖建辉

Zhongdu Old Town, the place where Luzhai Culture started, was built in the year 265, almost two millennia ago. It’s commonly known as “the pearl of forty-eight lanes”. It’s a passage to Guilin in the north and Liuzhou in the south. Zhongdu used to be the name of a courier route and was prosperous during the Ming and Qing dynasties. According to records, famous traveler Xu Xiake passed through it on his way to Liuzhou.

中渡镇生态乡村美如画　摄影：陆秀廷

岭南状元村

Scholar Village

文：朱燕

走进不孤村，当你看到村口牌坊两边镌刻着“汝水流清士读农耕绳祖武；南山挺秀德门仁里萃人文”的对联时，定会闻到一股厚重的文化味。在那些农家院落，厅堂里见得最多的持家治学对联都是“劝学篇”：“一等人为家为国；两件事种田读书”“万贯家财不算好；唯有教子读书高”……不孤村被誉为“岭南状元村”，世代诗书飘香，钟灵毓秀，人才辈出。

Walking into Bugu Village, one sees a pair of couplets alongside proclaiming it to be a village of good moral character, upstanding families, scholarly conduct and learning. In this farming village; in the houses and halls, there are inscriptions encouraging study. “A good person can do two things for the country: farm and study.” “An educated family is better than a wealthy one”. The village is known as the “Scholar Village in South China”. It has enjoyed renown throughout generations and produced numerous talented individuals.

秦家大院

Qin Household

文：朱燕

兴安水源头村位于湘江源头，据说是唐朝大将秦叔宝的后裔所居之村，称为“秦家大院”。这里的人们还保留着前辈留下的各种工艺制品及制作手艺。村中老妇爱刺绣。鞋垫、帽子、手帕、围巾、桌布等绣着精致的五颜六色的花纹，就连老人戴的眼镜，都配有绣上花草虫鱼的布口袋。

Shuiyuantou Village, Xing’an County is situated at the source of the Xiang River; it’s said that the people who live here are descendants of the Tang general Qin Shubao, thus it’s also known as the “Qin Household”. The people here have maintained the crafts of their ancestors – the old women in the village like embroidering cloth shoes, hats, kerchiefs, scarves, tablecloths and other items with all kinds of colorful patterns. You’ll find that even the old people’s eyeglasses are all wrapped in cloth bags embroidered with flowers, grasses, insects, and fish.

评论

凤山县百乐坳山路　摄影：周恩革

自古繁华八步镇

Babu Town

文：朱燕

在贺州八步镇内的旧街对岸，隔江耸立着一座石山，叫点灯山。山下有个寨子叫点灯寨。传说点灯寨自宋代起就已经很风光。因为此乃一块风水宝地，吸引了许多外地开采锡矿的人搬来定居，丁财兴旺，街庭若市。一风水先生曾以点灯寨为题作联，但只有上联“点灯高照三家寨”，一位13岁神童以“八步”为题对了下联“担石铺平八步街”。这一联语，描绘了八步当年挑运矿石的民工来往奔忙，以及街上人声鼎沸的繁华景象。

On the other side of the river in Babu (literally means “eight steps”) Town, there is a rock mountain called the “Lamp-lighting Mountain”. Below it is a village known as “Lamp-lighting Village”. It’s said that it was already quite the place to be in the Song dynasty. It’s a “promised land” that attracted many tin miners to settle here, making it into a prosperous place. A Feng Shui master wrote the first half of a couplet: “The lit lamps illuminate this village of three clans…” which was completed by a 13-year old prodigy “The carried stones flatten the streets of Eight Steps”. This is a picture of the busy work of the miners at the time it was written, as well as a vivid picture of the sights and sounds of the streets.

龙潭夕影迷少游

Dragon Pool

文：朱燕

扬美古镇的三界庙前，汇集了一湾深潭。潭边有一巨石酷似龙头，远望去，仿佛一条巨龙在此蜿蜒盘旋，翘首待飞，故名“龙潭”。相传秦少游当年谪居横县时，随好友到扬美赏花，看到龙潭夕影的美景后，便乐不思归。夫人苏小妹思夫心切，托家人送来一首只有14字的七言回文诗，诗曰：“静思伊久阻归期，久阻归期忆别离。忆别离时闻漏转，时闻漏转静思伊。”少游读后，亦赠诗一首：“赏花归去马如飞，去马如飞酒力微。酒力微醒时已暮，醒时已暮赏花归。”才子佳人以回文诗寄托了相思之情，一时成为扬美古镇的美谈。

In front of the Sanjie Temple in Yangmei Old Town, there is a deep pool. There is a realistic giant dragon of stone by the pool, looking far out. It’s almost as if the dragon is slithering around here, ready to spread its wings and fly. Thus, this site is known as the Dragon Pool. According to legend, when Qin Guan, a famous poet was living in exile in Heng County, he visited Yangmei with a friend. Seeing the stunning sunset at the Dragon Pool, he was so moved that he wished not to return. His wife Su Xiaomei, out of intense longing for her husband, sent him a poem in an attempt to bring him back earlier. Qin Guan wrote her back with another poem depicting the scenery there and his experiences. The deep love and the poetic talent showed in these two poems are well remembered by the people in Yangmei.

小说里的地心世界

The Inner World

文：朱燕

人常说，香格里拉是洗净心灵的圣地，而巴马的那氏若村就像凡尔纳小说里的地心世界。那氏若村位于盘阳河源头，村里发现的地下溶洞——水晶宫具有“南国冰川”之美誉。洞内石布成幔，洁白如玉，晶莹剔透，气象万千，既有山舞银蛇、原驰蜡象之壮美，也有雪花飘洒、寒江垂钓之宁静。

People frequently say that Shangri-La is a place that cleanses the soul. Compared with that, Nashiruo Village in Bama looks like the hidden place described by Jules Verne. Situated at the source of the Panyang River, Nashiruo boasts some karst caves. The “crystal palace” underground is a famous site in South China. The stones of various shapes in the caves present a beautiful combination of grandeur and calmness.

月老古榕

Matchmaker Banyan

文：朱燕

平乐榕津古镇的西北端街口处，连理千年古榕群构成榕津一大景观，当世罕见。其中一株古榕根围 8.5 米，高近 20 米，树冠覆盖面积约 1900 平方米，虬枝凌空，拱如明月，覆盖着由盘龙根须构成的天然雕饰拱门，形同鹊桥，又似月老牵线搭桥，故称“月老古榕”。相传，旧时恋情，因姑娘深藏闺中，无法自由相见，遇有说媒定亲，家人便到这古榕前祈愿，每每获得美满姻缘。

The Rongjin Old Town in Pingle has a natural wonder made by a large collection of ancient banyan trees. One of the trees has a perimeter of 8.5 meters at the root and is almost 20 meters tall. The tree’s crown covers an area of approximately 1900 square meters, with branches interlocking everywhere, forming a pattern like a natural arch carved in openwork. It’s called the “banyan of the Man under the Moon”, who was the god of marriage in Chinese mythology. Legend has it that in old times as the girls were not allowed to leave their house, it was hard for them to meet with a mate. Marriages were arranged; thus families would come to this old tree to pray, and those that did it were rewarded with great marriages.

平乐榕津古榕　摄影：程海燊

苍梧晚景

Sunset Scenery

文：陈猛棠

“莫道桑榆晚，为霞尚满天。”苍梧夕景殊胜，常彩霞满天，美如仙境，按徐霞客说法：“大丈夫当朝游碧海而暮苍梧。”据吕仙洞宾题诗：“朝游北海暮苍梧，袖里青蛇胆气粗。三醉岳阳人不识，朗吟飞过洞庭湖。”说明这位神仙大清早从北方海边出发，中途降下云头到岳阳楼喝小酒歇歇脚，最终也还是要赶到苍梧去赏晚景。

“Please do not say it is almost dark, the sky is still filled with red clouds.” The evening scenes in Cangwu are beautiful, with the clouds reddening in the sky like magic. Poet Xu Xiake wrote, “A true man sets out in the morning to view the ocean and stay at Cangwu in the evening.” Lü Dongbin also wrote of these scenes in one of his poems, in which a true man stops by the Yueyang Tower for a drink and a rest on a trip, before heading out to enjoy the evening scenes at Cangwu.

广西楹联第一村

Village of Couplets

文：朱燕

有着“广西楹联第一村”之称的大芦村，最引人注目的就是它悬挂在各家门柱上的300多幅木刻对联。这些对联，世代承传，沿用至今，都是劳氏先人自己撰写的，是他们劳作、居家、仕途、训诫、抒怀的展现。比如“读书好耕田好识好便好；创业难守成难知难不难”“仰天但使心无愧；做事何须世尽知”“好把格言训子弟；须寻活计去饥寒”等，内容清新健康，造诣颇高，涵盖了丰富的人生哲理和朴素的道德观。

广西楹联第一村——大芦村　摄影：陈炜平

Dalu Village is known as the “number one village for couplets in Guangxi”. What is most eye-catching are over three hundred couplets inscribed on wooden boards at the gate of each family’s home. These couplets were handed down by the ancestors who wrote them, and cover topics such as work, residence, official careers, admonitions, and feelings, such as: “Studying is good, fieldwork is good, and knowing good is even more good; innovation is difficult, persevering is difficult, but knowing difficulty is not difficult.” “Do with your conscience, and forget the fame.” “Raise your children well, and work with your hands to avoid hunger and cold.” The contents are simple and healthy, and show a good taste. They’re an encapsulation of the simple life principles and morals of the locals.

韭菜节里韭菜童

Leeks

文：朱燕

在广西与湖南交界处有个被称为“世外桃源”的“诗境的家园”，是三江侗族自治县“十佳生态文化寨”之一的高友村。每年，高友村都会举办韭菜节。寨子大街小巷摆满了翠绿的韭菜，四处弥漫着韭菜的清香，行人中不时走过身着韭菜服的“韭菜童”，而众多游客则在选购刚从山上采来的鲜嫩韭菜。整个寨子如一个热闹的韭菜交易大市场。高友韭菜俗称“大叶韭菜”，其叶长四五十厘米，有的达六七十厘米，叶宽一至二厘米。其味道独特，在百里侗乡声名远播。

On the border between Guangxi and Hunan, there is an “earthly paradise”, one of the “ten famous ecological villages”, Gaoyou Village of the Sanjiang Dong Autonomous County. Every year, the village holds a leek festival. The streets and alleys of the village are filled with leeks, and their fragrance permeates the air all around. Sometimes a “leek child” will pass you in a leek outfit on the street. Many visitors choose to buy the fresh leeks here, and the whole village seems like a bustling leek trade market. The Gaoyou leeks are colloquially called large-leaf leeks. The leaves can be forty to seventy centimeters long, and one to two centimeters wide. Their flavor is distinctive and exceptional. For this reason, they are widely known.

十里梅林，青梅煮酒

Plum Liquor

文：朱燕

“青梅煮酒”的故事有着为人熟知的英雄气息，而在宾阳陈平镇绵延十里的青梅果树林下品青梅酒，更是一幅充满诗情画意的画面。陈平名山，因特殊的石蛋地貌，山民在房前屋后、半山腰上都种着一棵棵的青梅树。每年寒冬时节，满树白梅如雪花般挂枝头，唯美得犹如仙境。至清明，一颗颗青翠鲜绿的梅子挂满枝头，摘一颗咬一口，那酸爽的滋味瞬间让唾液在嘴巴里充盈起来。

The Romance of the Three Kingdoms contains a story about the boiling of green plum liquor that is well known to all. The scene of the extensive groves of green plum trees in Chenping Village in Binyang is one that is full of poetic meaning. The famous mountains of Chenping have a unique rocky landscape; the people of the mountain all plant large numbers of the trees upon the mountain, and every year when the cold winter comes their branches are covered with white blossoms like so many flakes of snow to form a beautiful scene. When the Tomb-Sweeping Festival comes around, the branches are covered in the fruit. Plucking one off and taking a bite, you’ll be rewarded with a delicious mouthful of sour juice that will ignite your senses.

地动河山的千古呼啸

Cries of War

文：朱燕

巴岗古寨，凤山当地壮话称为“巴岗更社”，意为山顶上的营寨。一支考古队曾实地考察，得出巴岗古寨是广西目前保存最为完好、规模最为巨大的宋代军事防御工程的结论。2004 年 6 月，有考古工作者在巴岗古寨掘出一把北方军用砍刀，军刀已断成两截，锈迹斑斑，刀柄之木已被腐蚀无存。月夜下，当一缕月光轻抚那喑哑无声的砍刀，人仿佛能听到地动河山的千古呼啸……

Bagang Old Village is known by a name that means “mountaintop military garrison” in the Zhuang language. A team of archaeologists visited and determined that it’s the best preserved, largest-scale fortification of Song dynasty in Guangxi. In June 2004, an archaeological worker unearthed a Northern Song military knife. It has already split into two pieces and was flecked with rust. The wooden handle had completely rotted away. Under the moonlight, when the light shone quietly over the blade, you can almost hear the cries of war from more than a millennium ago.

蝙蝠送福，飞翔而来

Lucky Sign

文：朱燕

象州运江古埠西南隅，隔江一山酷似蝙蝠，有“天下第一大蝙蝠”之称。在中国民间传统习俗中，蝙蝠因其“蝠”字与“福”谐音，被视为祥瑞之物，运江古埠亦因此被称为“福地”。为了迎“福”，古埠的人们在镇西南隅建筑“迎福双亭”。登迎福双亭，举目眺望，远山近水尽收眼底。浩渺柳江晶莹如玉，百舸千樯江面云集；隔江对岸的“天下第一大蝙蝠”正张开双翅，迎面飞来，大有福气来了挡也挡不住的气势。

At the southwest corner of the old port in Xiangzhou, there is a mountain across the water that looks like a bat, and is known as “the world’s biggest bat”. In Chinese tradition, the word for “bat” sounds the same as “fortune”, and thus it’s viewed as an auspicious sign. The old port is thus viewed as a lucky place. To welcome this good fortune, the people of the old port built two “welcoming pagodas” in the southwest corner of the village. Standing in one of them, looking off into the distance, you’re rewarded with a vast scene of beauty. The water sparkles as if studded with gems as masts and sails drift upon it. The “biggest bat”, across the river, seems to be spreading its wings and ready to fly. It’s as if an unstoppable wave of luck is inbound.

评论

水酒浸泡的壮寨

Light Liquor

文：朱燕

平安壮寨是龙胜龙脊景区一个有名的寨子。寨子 100 多户壮族人家以开垦梯田种水稻为生。这里几乎每家都会自己用米做一种度数很低的酒，酒有点甜，很好喝，当地人称“水酒”。酿酒的方式很原始，一个大木桶，放入发酵的糯米，在一口大锅上用火蒸，酒就会从插在木桶中间的小竹筒里流出来，一滴滴胜似琼浆玉液。

The Ping'an Zhuang Village is a famous site in the Longji Scenic Area in Longsheng. There are more than a hundred Zhuang families who grow rice in terraced fields. Almost every family here also makes a kind of light liquor, which is slightly sweet and very palatable. The locals call it "water liquor". The method of making it is quite simple – a large wooden barrel is filled with fermented glutinous rice and then placed in a big pot on a fire. The liquor comes out from a small bamboo tube in the center of the barrel. It's a truly excellent product.

平安壮寨　摄影：张小宁

钦州大风江口吊养大蚝　摄影：谢勇云

物产·海汇
Flora and Fauna

你好，白色瓜皮小帽

Little White Cap

文：潘惠娟

广西西南部崇左市，喀斯特石灰岩地区，陡峭岩壁上，一群头顶“白色瓜皮小帽”的黑毛猴子团坐一起，悠长的尾巴悠闲挂着。忽然，近旁的树枝剧烈摇动，一只小调皮惊险一跃，落到另一棵树上，自得地啃起叶子。这就是广西特有的白头叶猴。白头叶猴有多数与人类相同的遗传基因及复杂的群体形态，珍贵不亚于大熊猫。北京大学潘文石教授说：“白头叶猴是我们的孩子，它同我们唇齿相依。”

白头叶猴　摄影：张小宁

Chongzuo City in southwest Guangxi is a place of many karst formations. Upon the precipitous slopes, a group of “white-capped rascals” sit together, tails hanging languidly. Suddenly, a branch nearby shakes wildly, and with a cheeky little jump, one makes a leap onto another tree, contently gnawing upon leaves. These are the white-headed langurs[1] of Guangxi. They have a lot in common genetically with humans and live in groups. They are as valuable as the panda. Professor Pan Wenshi of Peking University said, “The white-headed langurs are our children; they’re quite closely related to us.”

1.*Trachypithecus poliocephalus ssp. leucocephalus*

三娘湾中华白海豚　摄影：谢勇云

壮大吧，海洋的精灵

Sea Spirits

文：潘惠娟

钦州三娘湾，优质天然的渔场，是中华白海豚的故乡。在三娘湾看白海豚，要有点运气。日照好的时候，乘快艇出海，关了引擎，耐心静待。白海豚聪明，只徜徉在自己的世界里，跃出海面，再扎进海里，碰上同伴，此起彼伏地跳跃前进，撒欢……

Sanniang Bay in Qinzhou, a naturally excellent fishing spot, is the home of the Chinese white dolphin[1]. You need a bit of luck to see them here. When the sunlight is good, you can ride a speedboat out, turn off the engine, and wait patiently. The dolphins are clever. As they roam about their own world, they may leap out of the water before diving back in. They push forward with their companions, having fun along the way.

从石头里蹦出的珍果

Fruit from the Stone

文：潘惠娟

平南的石硖龙眼，是南方珍果。俗语说，白露吃龙眼，一颗顶只鸡。“石硖”是“石夹”（石缝）的意思。相传在平南大新镇，有座高大的石山，山下有一棵长在石缝里的龙眼树，果质很好，当地人称“长寿果”。石硖龙眼果大肉厚，晶莹剔透，爽脆清甜，糖分高水分少。若将新鲜龙眼晒干或烘干，去壳去核，果干肉厚微褐黄，让人唇齿留香，被称为“桂圆”。

The Shixia longan of Pingnan is a treasure of the south. It's said they're best eaten around the 15th solar term, “white dew”, in early December. “Shixia” means a fissure in the rock, or a cranny. Legend holds that in Daxin Town of Pingnan, there was a tall stone mountain, upon which a longan tree grew from a fissure. The fruit was of excellent quality and called “longevity fruit” by the locals. The Shixia longan has thick flesh that is bright and clear with a crisp, sweet taste. Their sugar-to-water ration is high. If you sun-dry or bake the fruit, after removing the shell, you'll find that the flesh has become slightly brown, and leaves a taste that lingers upon your lips and gums.

1. *Sousa chinensis*

不会凋谢的花

The Flower That Doesn't Wilt

文：潘惠娟

有一种花，长年绵延青翠，夏秋最盛。其花大色艳，红的、白的、黄的、粉的、桃色的，它就是有着“不会凋谢的花”之美誉的朱瑾。朱瑾又叫扶桑，未开的花蕊，会圈成一管小蜜罐，吸上一口，甜甜的，蜜蜜的。朱槿花为广西首府南宁的市花。南宁国际会展中心主建筑穹顶造型便是一朵倒吊着的硕大绽放的朱槿花。

There is a kind of flower that grows most robustly in the summer and autumn and has leaves that remain green year-round. The big blossoms can be red, white, yellow, pink, or peach-colored. This famous flower is the broad-bloomed Chinese hibiscus[1]. Before the flowers bloom, they are small tubes of nectar. This hibiscus is the city flower of the capital of the province, Nanning. The Nanning International Convention and Exhibition Center's curved roof represents a hibiscus flower.

海上的森林，海底的卫士

Forest on the Sea

文：潘惠娟

北部湾的合浦山口，生长着一种神奇的生态群落——红树林。沿着海岸线从潮间带蜿蜒而去，密密匝匝地迎风而立，坚实稳健。它们聪明安静，扎根泥沼，却拥有卓越的净化能力。光照足时，还能看到树下活跃的贝、鱼、虾、蟹。海鸟齐飞，红日白沙，一片美好。潮起潮退，红树林既是海上的森林，又是海底的卫士，默默地驻防着海岸。

At Hepu County beside the Beibu Gulf, there grows a mysterious ecological group – a mangrove forest. Winding from the coast into the intertidal zone, it stands resolutely and greets the wind. The trees are smart and quiet, anchored firmly in the mire, and have an excellent capacity to purify the air and water. When there's sufficient sunlight, one can see the mussels, fish, shrimp and crabs swimming amongst their roots. The seabirds fly, and the red sun shines over the white sand. As the tides come and go, the forest stands there as the ocean's protector, silently watching over the coast.

红树林　摄影：张小宁

1. *Hibiscus rosa-sinesis Linn*

人间第一香

Fabulous Fragrance

文：潘惠娟

广西横县茉莉花和茉莉花茶产量占全国总产量的 80%，世界总产量的 60% 以上。横县整座城就是一朵馥郁馨香的茉莉花。碰上这里的茉莉花节，待上一天，你的身上、头发上、衣服上全是香气，你也变成了茉莉花。花农多爱摘含苞待放的"当日花"，将晚上八九点盛放的茉莉与茶叶吐纳互兑窨制，产出的茉莉花茶口感才鲜灵、醇厚。七八窨后的茉莉花茶，不醉人，人自醉，可列作"人间第一香"。

The jasmine flowers and tea of Hengxian County account for 80% of domestic and 60% of world production. The entire county is a giant, fragrant jasmine blossom. When you stay here for a day during the jasmine season, your body, hair, and clothes will all be infused with the scent of the flower – you will become jasmine. The flower growers pick as the plants are just about to bloom. When the blooms open at eight or nine o'clock in the evening, they mix them with tea leaves to make the fresh and full jasmine tea. The drink is fulfilling but straightforward and has a fabulous fragrance.

貌似鳄鱼，却是蜥蜴

Crocodile Lizard

文：潘惠娟

广西瑶山的鳄蜥，头似蜥蜴，尾长侧扁似鳄鱼，首次发现仅生存在广西大瑶山区，曾和恐龙生活在同一时代。它很老，有 2 亿岁，但身量迷你，行动敏捷。它不爱动，就爱睡；睡着了还不容易被吵醒，不能不怀疑它端着睡姿不过是为了吓唬人。

The Chinese crocodile lizard, Shinisaurus crocodilurus, has a head that looks like a lizard, and a long, flat tail that looks like that of a crocodile. It was first discovered and only lives in the Dayao Mountains of Guangxi, and previously coexisted with dinosaurs. It's an ancient species, more than two hundred million years of age, but it's quite small and moves quickly. It prefers to stay still and enjoys sleeping. When dormant, it's hard to awaken. One might think it's pretending to be asleep for an opportunity to frighten.

瑶山鳄蜥　摄影：张小宁

弄岗穗鹛　摄影：张小宁

广西瑶山白眉棕啄木鸟　摄影：张小宁

万金一蝶

Pricey Butterfly

文：潘惠娟

广西大瑶山深处罕见的金斑喙凤蝶，最新的拍卖数字显示：100万元！若有幸见上一面这“万金一蝶”，人就该高兴得翩翩起舞了。金斑喙凤蝶振翅优雅，嬉戏在山花烂漫间，被尊贵的它点一下眉头，花花草草做梦也会笑醒。金斑喙凤蝶位列世界八大名贵蝴蝶之首，是我国的“国蝶”。若非法捕杀1只要立案，3只属于重大案件，6只属于特大案件。蝶之重，重于泰山；蝶之美，自然馈赠。

There is a rare butterfly, the golden Kaiser-i-Hind[1] that lives in the Dayao Mountains of Guangxi. A specimen recently sold for one million Yuan! If you're lucky enough to see one in the wild, you should dance happily. It's a butterfly with beautiful, elegant wings that likes to flutter over mountain blossoms, a truly striking insect. It's one of the eight most valuable butterflies in the world and the "national butterfly" of China. If you illegally capture one, a case will be brought against you. Capturing three will result in a "major case" and six an "extraordinarily serious case".

茶族皇后

Empress of Tea

文：潘惠娟

物以稀为贵。全世界90%的野生金花茶分布于广西防城港市十万大山的兰山支脉一带。每到花开的季节，巡山的人走上几十公里的山路，也要护金花茶周全。宋徐致中《山茶》里提到，金花茶“黄香开最早，与菊为辈朋”。金花茶的花呈金黄色，温润如玉，晶莹如蜡膏，花冠或杯、或碗，惟妙惟肖。明李时珍《本草纲目》中称“山茶嫩叶炸熟，水淘、可食，亦可蒸晒作饮”。金花茶是广西的名片，国外称之为“神奇的东方魔茶”。

That which is rare is valuable. More than ninety percent of the world's wild yellow camellias (Camellia nitidissima C. W. Chi) grow in the Lanshan Mountain in Fangchenggang City. When these flowers bloom, mountain guardians often walk tens of kilometers to protect their surroundings. Xu Zhizhong of the Song dynasty mentioned them in Mountain Tea, calling them the "friends of the chrysanthemum". They are golden-yellow in color, have a warm character like jade, and a waxy luster. The blooms can be cup or bowl shaped. Li Shizhen of the Ming dynasty wrote in his Compendium of Materia Medica "the leaves can be fried, steeped, and eaten. They can also be steamed and then sunned to make a drink". The yellow camellia is the calling card of Guangxi, and abroad is called the "mysterious oriental magic tea".

1. *Teinopalpus aureus*

猿中君子

Noble Ape

文：潘惠娟

广西中越边境的喀斯特森林，晨曦轻拂群峰，忽然一声猿啸，穿透边界两岸。东黑冠长臂猿，仪态优雅地活跃于崇山峻岭间。它是全球 25 种最濒危灵长类之一。东黑冠长臂猿谦谦若君子，食不厌精，每一猿高歌，众猿必定和鸣，让人恍惚错觉，不知起伏的是山峦，还是气如长虹的猿鸣……

As the rising sun's rays brush over the tops of the karst forest on the border between China and Vietnam, one hears a monkey's howl that echoes between the mountains. The Eastern Black-crested Gibbon, Nomascus nasutus, elegantly leaps about the high peaks. It is one of the twenty-five most endangered primates in the world. This gibbon is a noble among primates. It eats fine food, and when it sings others resonate with it. When it calls out, one can be confused – is it the monkey's cries rising and falling, or the mountains themselves?

走在人行道，手可摘果食

Fruit on the Way

文：潘惠娟

以果树为行道树，“手可摘果食”，颇具南国风光。而以扁桃唱主角的理由是：不矫情，接地气。扁桃树冠幅大，易管护，亭亭如盖。到了扁桃垂挂枝头的季节，一阵风雨，大果小果滚滚落尘，喜了垂涎果实的欲，伤了硕果累累扑地的心。行道树的绿色小扁桃，是不可贪食的，涩酸，但尝个鲜儿还是能圆异乡游人的梦。

Here there are walkways lined with fruit trees, a real southern sight. Almonds are one of the main players. The trees have a large canopy and are easy to protect, and stand straight and strong. When the season comes, the fruit hang from the branches. When rain and wind come along, the fruit drop all over. Desires are satisfied as they pile upon the ground. The small fruit on the path resist gluttons – they're astringent and sour, but trying one of them is a path to fulfilling a traveler's dream.

南国春夏赏个秋

Autumn Appreciation

文：潘惠娟

人面果树，在广西是春夏时才换叶。风雨后，落叶纷飞，一条遮天蔽日的林荫道上，抬头是绿意盎然的天，低头是金黄软绵的地，入眼全是叶子，绿的、黄的。从街头到巷尾，叶子扫了，又掉了，掉了，又扫了，还掉，玩乐似的。人面果树的叶子还真讨了人厌，却装点了南方人的“秋天”。

The "Pacific walnut" (Dracontomelon dao) in Guangxi changes its leaves in spring and summer. After a rain, the leaves fly about, blocking out the sky on the tree-lined pedestrian walkways. Looking up, you see a green sky; looking down, you see a blanket of golden yellow. There are leaves everywhere, green and yellow. From the larger thoroughfares to smaller alleys, people sweep the leaves, and they fall again, and people sweep again. It's like some kind of game. It's a hassle for those responsible for keeping the ground clear but makes for a beautiful display of color in autumn in the South.

升官发财马

Lucky Horse

文：潘惠娟

德保有矮马，昵称“果下马”。矮马可人，它乘车不用买票，因为身高不够。德保矮马是世界两大矮马源流之一。相传，朱元璋称帝时，德保人不远万里，亲自骑着矮马进京朝见。朱元璋快步上前，果然，马儿袖珍，骑上它，果树变得高大起来。亲历这新奇事让他兴奋不已，给进献者授官晋爵，因此民间以德保矮马为“吉祥马”“升官发财马”。

Debao has a kind of pony that's known as the "horse under the tree". It's cute and short. It's one of the main two progenitors of modern ponies in the world. Legend has it that when the founder of the Ming dynasty Zhu Yuanzhang claimed the throne, a man from Debao, riding a pony in this kind, took the long journey to the capital to see the emperor. The emperor, upon seeing the horse, discovered that its small size made the fruit trees taller. He was very excited and awarded the visitor a title and promotion. For this reason, the ponies of Debao are known as "auspicious horses", or "lucky horses".

“小红伞”有脾性

Little Parasols

文：潘惠娟

广西浦北，五黄岭山脉的原始红椎次生林，每年的端午、中秋，一场豪雨过后，你会发现脚下突然冒出星星点点的“红”，大约经过 6~8 小时，它们就变成了一朵朵漂亮的“小红伞”。生长在浦北的红椎菌有脾性——过时不候。采摘的时候菌帽和菌杆不分离，动作轻柔，一鼓作气，过了须臾，它就不见了，要再等上一年。而采来的红椎菌入汤，色泽红亮，浮在汤面上，“小伞儿”又展了半闭半开娇羞的漂亮模样。

红椎菌　摄影：谢勇云

In the Wuhuangling Mountains in Pubei, there are secondary forests of Castanopsis hystrix, a broadleaved evergreen. Every year at the Dragon Boat and Mid-Autumn Festivals, after heavy rains, one will find the ground covered suddenly with little red dots. After six to eight, they will turn into "little red parasols". These fungi, the darkening brittlegrill[1], have quite a temperament. They appear as they want. When one picks them, the cap and stem do not separate. They come and go quickly. After a while, they're gone, and one must wait until the next year. When stewed in soup, they yield a bright red color as they float upon the broth, half-open, pretty and shy.

1.*Russula vinosa Lindblad*

一年好景君须记，最是收获橘红时

Tangerine Time

文：潘惠娟

融安的滑皮金橘，长在山坡上。金橘时节，葱茏的绿与金橘的红，拢了一个巨大的甜在果农的心里。收成若好，孩子该添置的衣物就置办了去。金红的橘果，皮滑无孔隙，薄皮裹满丰盈的汁水与果肉，咬上一口，啧啧声，甘甜如蜜。若是燥气喉涩，来三两颗，立马润喉生津。在融安，一年好景君须记，最是收获橘红时。

The smooth-skinned kumquats of Rong'an grow upon mountain slopes. When their season comes, the leaves are verdant green, and the fruit is red-orange, gladdening the hearts of the fruit growers. If the harvest is good, the children will get new clothes. The thin skin of golden-red fruit is smooth without dimples, enveloping a body full of juice and flesh. With a bite, the fruit makes a little popping sound. It is sweet as honey. If one's throat is dry, eating two or three of the fruit will immediately bring the moisture back. One of the most important sights and times is the season of these fruits.

天天吃火麻，活到九十八

Eat Weed Everyday

文：潘惠娟

在巴马，百岁的老人都爱吃火麻。巴马百岁的老人睡得轻浅，晨早便麻利地掀锅，上灶，把火麻磨制的粉，慢火煨糊，火麻糊入口绵延，身轻气定；到了晌午，家里用火麻油炒个油麦菜，简单吃食。“天天吃火麻，活到九十八”是火麻的功劳，抑或是百岁老人的生存之道？

In the Bama Yao Autonomous County, the centenarians enjoy eating the Cannabis sativa. They wake up after a light sleep, and in the morning skillfully work their woks, lighting a fire in an earthen oven, grinding the plant into powder and slowly stewing it into a paste. It has a nice texture, and calms and stabilizes the eater. At noon, the family uses Cannabis sativa oil to fry yau mak choi (Lactuca sativa L., a leafy green) for a simple meal. "Eat weed every day, live to ninety-eight" is a phrase well known here.

土味的“羊额籽”

Shatian Pomelo

文：潘惠娟

秋季，容县沙田柚成熟，黄澄澄的。从树上采摘下来，12度的甜度刚刚好，口蜜齿香，满口的晶莹颗粒蹦跳起舞，很是富足。虽然有个土味的名字——羊额籽，但土里土气长得丑的沙田柚，滋味最是甘甜。把沙田柚黄色表皮去除，留下包裹果实的白色棉絮嫩里，泡水去涩，再翻炒烹制，能出一道美味的菜肴。

In autumn, the Shatian pomelos of Rong County mature, glistening yellow all over. When one picks them at this time, their sugar content is around that of a papaya. They're sweet and have a nice texture; the juice vesicles yield a satisfying pop. The fruit isn't pretty, but it's very tasty. After removing the yellow peal, one finds a thick white mesocarp. Then it's immersed in water to remove the astringency. After that, it can be cooked and form a delicious dish.

树上结了个大菠萝

Jackfruit on the Tree

文：潘惠娟

南宁街道两边的木菠萝树不高，有老式楼房的三两层。叶子肥厚，落在地上够得上个孩子的脚印。夏季，几十斤的木菠萝很常见，外形不规则，大个子憨态可掬，吊抱在树干上，结盟似的一个个群挨着，像探头探脑的可爱娃娃。不采摘，熟透的木菠萝就会"砰"地强势落地，甜腻的果肉香裹着热气冒烟四溢。

There are jackfruit trees of medium height along the streets of Nanning, about two or three stories tall. The leaves are fat and thick, about the size of a child's footprint on the ground. During the summer, it's common to see a jackfruit that weighs tens of kilograms. They're irregular in shape, and funny to look at. They huddle together, like peeking babies. If they're not picked, the ripe fruit will fall to the ground with a "bang" as they land, spewing their fragrance all around.

木菠萝树　摄影：陈炜平

此罗汉非彼罗汉

Monk Fruit

文：潘惠娟

"一玻璃杯，捏碎果壳，不硌手，干制过的棉絮果肉涨满了水，细絮丝儿洋洋展开，吐出深褐黄的茶汤；嘬一口，清心寡欲，暑气尽散。"这里说的是永福罗汉果。若以茶论，其为果茶；若以果论，其为茶果。用手摸，用眼看，用嘴尝，品相好的永福罗汉果，在南方能管上一个四季。闲时，自个儿泡，慢品；燥时，街边凉茶铺，牛饮……其惬意恰似一罗汉。

When the dried flesh and pith of this fruit are soaked, the filaments will grow and emit a deep black liquid that can be drunk as a tea. Taking a sip, you'll feel full of satisfaction and forget the heat of the summer. This is the Yongfu monk fruit, known as the "arhat fruit" in Chinese. Talking about it in tea theory, it's fruit tea. Talking about it in terms of fruit, it's a tea fruit. One can feel it with the hand, observe it with the eye, and taste it with the mouth. The high-quality monk fruit of Yongfu is good year-round. When you're relaxing, you can slowly make a cup of tea; when you're in a hurry, you can find a tea stand and drink ravenously. You'll feel a little bit of enlightenment yourself.

流出的都是黄色的汗

Yellow Sweat

文：潘惠娟

六七月，田东的桂七芒上市了。成熟的桂七芒青黄皮，头尾小勾呈S形，凑近闻，隐隐清甜果香，沿着果核剖一刀，切下大半果肉，划菱形刀，一翻转果皮，嫩黄的果肉汁水充盈，入口细滑微脆。双手捧着果核舔舐，能吃到山林夏季葱茏味……蔡澜先生提及吃芒果，最后“流出的都是黄色的汗”。那黄色的汗，还充满了芒果香。

In June and July, Tiandong mangoes enter the market. The ripe fruits have green-yellow skin, and the head and tail form a slight "S" shape. When one smells them up close, there is a bit of a fruity fragrance. Slicing along the seed, one can lop off the larger half of the fruit, and cut it into rhomboid cubes, delicious and juicy. Holding the fruit in hand, licking the juice, one seems to be in the mountain forest. Famous food writer Chua Lam said of eating mango, "in the end, it's yellow sweat all over". That yellow sweat is full of mango scent.

百色芒果丰收了　摄影：陆杰　黄美玉

无法拒绝的邀约

Cordial Invitation

文：潘惠娟

小心翼翼地摘下柿子，“啪”，掉地，脆裂了半，捧起啃一口，甜！柿子上的方形果蒂如铜钱般。用棉线拴住果柄，晾起的柿子长长的，像串了万贯的钱币，排过天际。干制后的恭城月柿肉质棕红，拿在手上向阳看去，能透进一丝光，却不真切，柿皮上的雪白柿霜似糖，形如圆月，对于小孩儿那是无法拒绝的邀约：来吃我吧，甜丝丝的。

You carefully pick a persimmon, but "pop", it splits in half. You cup it in your hands and take a bite – so sweet. The square pedicle at the top of the fruit is like an old bronze coin. One can tie the stalks up with string and hang the fruit out to dry; it's like an ancient string of money. The dried Gongcheng persimmon cakes have brown-red flesh. They are half-transparent when you hold them up under the sun. The "frost" upon the fruit is sugar and looks like a full moon. For children, it's an invitation they can't refuse: eat me, I'm sweet.

恭城月柿　摄影：何运斌

啃着过瘾的竹蔗

That Sugar

文：潘惠娟

每年 11 月至翌年 3 月，广西的竹蔗长势惊人，南方人的小个头，走在蔗地里是要没进深处的，只有青黄的竹蔗瘦条条地挤挤挨挨，风过竹蔗只点个头，硬挺着。在广西的农村，种植竹蔗多成为家庭经济的主要来源。收获时，一卡车、一卡车的满满竹蔗往外拉，用于榨糖。紫黑皮的是果蔗，牙口好的可以啃着过瘾，还可以自己榨汁喝。

Every year from November until March of the next year, the growth of sugarcane in Guangxi progresses at a surprising rate. People here aren't very tall. When they walk among the plants, they can disappear. The thin stalks of the plants stand in the ground closely together; they only nod slightly when the wind blows. In the agricultural villages of Guangxi, planting sugarcane is the primary source of income for many families. When harvest time comes, trucks head out, each full of cane to be pressed for sugar. The purple-black skinned stalks are chewing cane. If your teeth are good, you can take bite after bite, feeding your addiction. The stems can also be skinned and juiced for a delicious drink.

糯香出南蛮

Fragrance of Rice

文：潘惠娟

自古中原多富庶，多半不知糯香出南蛮。明李时珍《本草纲目》中提到："香粳，长白如玉，可充御贡……"环江香粳，一年一季播种，占了节气的先机，饱染了天地的日月芳华，长成了米精儿，有异香。土灶，大锅，用柴火蒸，袅袅炊烟，灶火熏脸，糯香早已跑出十里八乡。若用红粳酿酒，酒水色泽透出女郎般的醉人粉红。南人蛮，善战；但黏糯的粳米却是温柔的。

From ancient times the south of China has been a region for excellent rice. Ming writer Li Shizhen mentions in his Compendium of Materia Medica: "The round-grained non-glutinous rice is white like jade, and suitable for imperial tribute". The Huanjiang round-grained rice has its own season. It takes in the essence of Nature and has a unique scent. A large pot sits over an earthen oven, fired by wood, the smoke of which wafts upwards. The fragrance can be smelled miles away. The red rice can be used to make liquor, which blushes like a young girl. The people of the south were known for their fiery temper, but their sweet rice is gentle.

评论

红光四射的太阳

Red Sun

文：潘惠娟

南方日照长，春季来得早，乐业当地自家的娃儿小口嘬红心猕猴桃的时候要比其他地方早一个月。“红心猕猴桃，果肉碧绿，中间果肉的纤维质是红色的，因此切面上像是有一个红光四射的太阳，特别奇异。”大嘴吃四方的人一上手就大半口，汁水没掉了下巴；碰上了小嘴巴的美人，小口吃也是香甜味美，浓情蜜意。

There is much sunlight in the south, and the spring comes early. The local children have the chance to bite into the red-hearted kiwifruit a month earlier than elsewhere. “The flesh of the red-hearted kiwifruit is green, but the core of fibers at the center is red. Thus, when you cut it open, you see a little red sun, rays radiating everywhere.” One can eat half of the small fruit in a single bite, with juice dripping down the chin. It’s a tender sight to see a small-mouthed beauty nibbling away at one of these delicious fruits.

欲与天公试比辣

Spice Contest

文：潘惠娟

天等的指天椒，个小肉厚，形似指头朝天生长，欲与天公试比辣，艳红扎眼般刷存在感；剁成碎末入菜、佐料，辣了眼睛，呛出一腔的吃食气，香郁浓厚，让人垂涎不已。若是以天等指天椒入南方的粉、汤、面，那个辣劲能让你涕流眼泪飞。花椒入不了桂林米粉，会水土不服。

The conical red peppers of Tiandeng, fat and round, look like little fingers pointing at the sky. One can chop the dazzlingly red peppers up into an addition to a dish, or as a garnish. In doing so, you may find your own eyes turning red as you begin to cough. The fragrance is thick and robust, and makes one salivate. They add flavors to the southern noodles and make a strong impact on your mouth, nose and eyes. Prickly ash can’t be used in Guilin rice noodles – it’s not a good fit.

好一个爽利无渣

Brisk and Neat

文：潘惠娟

鲁迅先生爱桂林马蹄，心切不得而憾，“桂林荸荠，亦早闻雷名，惜无福身临其境，一尝佳味，不得已……”临桂县四塘乡的桂林马蹄为最，洗净后扁圆鲜亮，“咔”的一声脆口，清甜得醍醐灌顶。巧手的桂林媳妇儿，多以没有渣的桂林马蹄做成糕，绵滑清爽，博了婆婆的一笑，赢了孩子的甜吻。婆婆也常用“桂林马蹄”夸媳妇儿——你这人（好得）没得说，爽利无渣。

Author Lu Xun was a big fan of the water chestnuts of Guilin and even wrote praises to the corm of the famous plant. The best water chestnuts come from Sitang Village in Lingui County. When washed clean, they’re oblate and bright. They crack with a refreshing sound in your mouth. The deft women of Guilin make them into smooth and refreshing cakes which are enjoyed by all the children. The name “water chestnut” can also be used as an affectionate name for a younger daughter-in-law, a way of praising their brisk and neat character.

神米
Divine Rice
文：潘惠娟

东兰的墨米，高人一头，谷穗青黑，次第排开，单独种植易倒伏，往往与其他稻种间种。墨米是东兰人几百年勤勉劳作向神农讨来的“药米”“神米”，吃了能让人长寿，煮起来却大有讲究：淘米入锅，水没过米面，浸泡，1~2 小时后与其他精细大米拼蒸煮，不过须臾，米香跑出了锅，呼啦地奔出几里地，唤回了百岁阿婆的小时光。

The black rice of Donglan grows taller than ordinary rice. The stalks are very deep in color. They are interspersed with other species of rice in rows to prevent lodging. This black rice is a medicinal, “divine” form of rice that’s been cultivated over centuries by the rice farmers here in Donglan – eating it leads to a long life. It’s carefully prepared: first, the rice is washed and placed in the pot, with the water-line above the rice. It’s soaked for an hour or two and steamed with other fine rice. The fragrant rice soon is ready, and as it’s taken out of the pot, the elderly recall the days of their youth.

珠本神物
Southern Pearl
文：潘惠娟

合浦南珠，“珠本神物”，自古珍贵，有“西珠不如东珠，东珠不如南珠”的美誉。豪门贵胄趋之若鹜，但珠光宝气无法满足权贵争相索取的欲望，却徒增了采珠人的苦泪。南珠亦称廉珠，“污吏贪则珠徙，太守廉则珠还”。古有还珠岭、还珠亭，今有还珠大道、还珠大厦。还或徙，一念之间，毫厘毕现。这也是人们至今仍深深怀念汉时孟尝太守的原因。

The “southern pearls” of Hepu have been prized since ancient times. It’s said that the pearls of the east are superior to those of the west, and the pearls of the south are superior to those of the east. The rich and the nobles scrambled for these treasures in times past, but there was no way to meet demand, which meant that the pearl harvesters were put under much pressure. The southern pearls are also called “honest pearls”. It’s said that they will leave when the officials are corrupt and will return if the officials are honest. There used to be a Huanzhu (“returning pearl”) Peak, and a Huanzhu Pagoda. Now there is a Huanzhu Boulevard, and a Huanzhu Building. The southern pearls are loved because they can tell apart honesty and corruption. For the same reason, the honest procurator Meng Chang of the Han dynasty is still respected today.

评论

好茶还需遇知音

Tea and Friends

文：潘惠娟

万承苦丁茶，产于大新。饮一口，蹙眉紧锁，苦味漫过头顶。鲁迅曾说："什么是好茶？小苦微甘即好茶！"不爱苦味的，多半受不了大新的苦丁，好茶还需遇知音。苦丁茶煮饮，明目消炎，能良药苦口利于病。多数人知道，常饮苦丁身体康健。再饮一口，慢慢地，苦尽开始回甘，确实好茶。

The bitter tea of Daxin is made from the leaves of broadleaf holly. It has a bitter character, and taking a sip causes you to furrow your brow. Lu Xun praised the slightly sweet tea as an example of "good tea". Only true tea-lovers can appreciate the good flavor of the bitter tea. The drink clarifies the vision and diminishes inflammation. Many people know that drinking the tea is healthy for the body. As you slowly take another sip, you'll feel the bitterness fade and slight sweetness emerge. This is indeed "good tea".

恰似你的温柔

Bamboo Shoots

文：潘惠娟

田林八渡乡，一场春雨，竹林浸染春风，笋尖冒头，手劲大点的可掐个嫩角儿尝鲜。夏日的笋，充盈了长势，笋粗如男人的健美臂膀，掰不动。鲜嫩的八渡笋切丝儿，大火爆炒，少许油盐，嫩爽、清脆，像捧着一片山林；有块头的切片，细嚼起来糯香四溢，像品着四野的丰盈。食八渡笋，闻香一回首，恰似你的温柔。

In Badu Village, when spring rain comes and the wind blows, fresh shoots of bamboo will emerge from the ground. You pick the tip and try the freshness if you are strong enough. The bamboo shoots grow quickly, and by the time the summer comes, they're thick enough that one can't break them off anymore. The tender and fresh Badu bamboo shoots can be chopped into strips and fried over a large fire. A bit of oil and salt makes for a delightful dish that's clear and crispy, as if one holds a stretch of forest in hand. Chopped into slices, they need more chewing to experience the natural taste.

结在草上的浆果

Fruit on the Herb

文：潘惠娟

南方多蕉，鸡蕉、芽蕉、芭蕉，似小孩子的嘴，甜糯糯。曾仕于广西的宋人周去非，在其《岭外代答·蕉子》中提："芭蕉，极大者凌冬不凋，中抽一干，节节有花如菡萏。花谢有实，一穗数枚，如肥皂，长数寸……"蕉树枝高叶大，却是草本植物。结在草上的浆果，一大串，几十斤，算是遂了南方人的口舌之欲。

There are many varieties of banana in the south: the Musaceae bananas, Cavendish bananas, hardy bananas, and more. They're sweet and gummy. Zhou Qufei, who served as an official in Guangxi during the Song dynasty wrote of the Chinese banana: "This is a plant that doesn't wilt even in the cold, with a central stock. The flowers that look like lotuses give way to bunches of fruits..." The banana "tree" is large, but it is, in fact, an herbaceous plant. The large bunches of fruits seek to satisfy the tastes of the people of the south.

长成大树的蕨类

Ferns and Forest

文：潘惠娟

广西的大深山，自然生态植被保持着最原始的状态。顺着山脚，拾岩而上，原始森林呈典型的垂直分布，有蕨类、裸子类及被子类植物百余种。转角不知名的溪谷边，一棵蕨类树形撑天，冠大如伞，叶若巨臂伸展，树干满是六角形斑纹。那是桫椤。知者以其为草，不知者以其为树。两亿年的桫椤，挡不住沧海桑田，时过境迁，但它亭亭玉立，风姿绰约，老当益壮——不以物喜，不以己悲。

The vegetative cover of the deep mountains of Guangxi has been preserved in its most original state. Climbing up the rocks from the base of the mountain, one sees the primary forest that has a typical vertical distribution, with ferns, gymnosperms and angiosperms of all kinds. Turning into an unknown river valley, one sees a large fern reaching up to the sky, with a vast canopy, leaves extending out like strong arms, the trunk covered in hexagonal patterns. This is an Alsophila spinulosa tree fern. The knowledgeable know it's an herb, whereas the unknowing think it's a tree. This two-hundred-million-year-old species witnesses changes but remains calm and elegant, like a sage.

书香，非墨香

Literary Life

文：潘惠娟

广西的大瑶山盛产灵香草。秋季收，带根茎小束烟熏烘干，覆以青叶，清水洒之，叶黄草香，香气浓郁醇厚，可藏书驱虫，置席去虱。古时，能用香草的，多是家有藏书的广识富贵之家，现多指书香门第。书香，非墨香，灵香草而已。

金秀灵香草　摄影：张小宁

Upon Dayao Mountains in Guangxi grows “Lingxiang herb”[1], with yellow flowers and broadly ovate to oblong alternate leaves. Harvested in the autumn, the stems with roots can be smoked and baked dry. Covered with leaves, sprinkled with water, they emit a grassy fragrance, a thick scent. It can be used to preserve volumes, drive away insects, and eliminate fleas. In ancient times, it was usually wealthy and knowledgeable families that used the grass to preserve their collections. Now it is a sign of book collection and literary pedigree.

1.*Lysimachia foenum-graecum Hance*

禾花落尽鲤鱼肥

Fish among the Grains

文：潘惠娟

桂北全州，在田里养禾花鱼，以乌肚鲤为最。风吹稻花，鲤鱼儿争食田间扬落的花粉、花瓣，长得肉嫩鲜美。待稻子成熟时，从田里挖出水道，鱼儿沿着水道流入田角水塘。水尽鱼跃，最是肥美。“禾花鱼送酒，碰不到对手。禾花鱼送饭，饭鼎锅刮烂。”种禾，除草，收稻，获鱼，实在是一种上好的生产方式。

Quanzhou in northern Guangxi is home to Procypris merus, a kind of cyprinid fish; the black-bellied carp is the most famous. When the wind blows upon the flowers, the fish forage for the fallen pollen and petals. They grow fat, full of tender flesh. When the rice matures and the trenches are dug up, the fish follow the path to a pond at the corner of the field and can be easily harvested. They make an excellent addition to other food and drink. Planting grains, cutting grasses, harvesting rice and getting free fish on the side is an excellent means of production.

可以喝的古董

Drinkable Antiques

文：潘惠娟

梧州六堡茶，黑茶之一，秉承古法制茶，曾乘西江里一叶扁舟下南洋，味醇隔宿不变，能解南洋水土疾患。喝过六堡茶的华工，能尝出茶里的槟榔味，醇和甜滑，甚至有“没有梧州六堡茶，南洋华人不开工”之说。但久藏的梧州六堡茶，最能打动人的是岁月的沧桑之味。

The Liubao tea of Wuzhou is a kind of black tea that is prepared by adopting traditional techniques. It came to Southeast Asia along the Xijiang River in ancient times. It had a lingering taste and was capable of curing diseases. Chinese laborers overseas who had drunk the tea could discern the taste of betel nut, a mellow sweetness. It was said that these laborers would not start work without this tea. Liubao tea that's been stored for a long time brims with the taste of history.

千金不换

Very Valuable

文：潘惠娟

靖西田七，黑棕色，周围瘤状突起，皱纹密布，极为难看。明李时珍的《本草纲目》中提到的“山漆”疑似“三七”，民间多以“三七”称“田七”。三七粉，生苦，研磨的粉细，生抹、入药、浸酒、熟食皆宜，多药到病除，千金不换。以三七炖鸡，鸡锅多药味，不苦，一勺田七的药草香，口腹饱足，病痛不药而愈，颇为神奇。

The pseudoginseng (Radix Notoginseng) of Jingxi is black-brown and ringed in striations and nodules. It's not pretty to look at. Li Shizhen in Compendium of Materia Medica mentioned that the "wax tree" resembled it in form. The powder of the rhizome can be ground finely, smeared raw, put into medicine, soaked in liquor, or cooked and eaten. It's said to cure diseases and is quite valued. It can also be used to braise chicken, giving it a medicinal flavor that's not bitter. A spoonful of the fragrant herb should cure the stomach and drive away diseases; it's quite a plant.

瑶医瑶药　摄影：张小宁

穿过百年的栗香

Chestnut

文：潘惠娟

种板栗，在广西东兰是一年种百年收的好差事。除了三餐，当地人夜里嘴巴要是痒了，就“咔哧”一声，掰了薄皮，吃个香甜，发个栗子梦。晚秋初冬，糖炒栗子是最好的零食。东兰的板栗，个大泛着乌光，用黑沙石翻炒，等上栗子香时，用纸袋包上一团，吃起来的感觉是粉红色的。梁实秋先生说：“栗子的记忆，多是甜的，冒着热气。”

Planting chestnuts has long been an important part of life for the people of Donglan, Guangxi. Aside from regular meals, when the locals have a craving, they crack open a chestnut and enjoy the fragrant, sweet fruit inside. At the end of autumn and the start of winter, stir-fried chestnuts are the best snack. The black sand and Donglan chestnuts are mixed in the pot and turned over until the fragrance emerges. They're packed in a paper bag for an excellent portable snack that warms and satisfies. Essayist Liang Shiqiu said, “Memories of chestnuts are all sweet, and full of warmth.”

红水河奇石

Hongshui Stones

文：潘惠娟

红水河奇石以大化彩玉夺目。其形端庄硕大，纹清色美，韵彩玉感，明艳动人。岭南奇石标准独特，主要看形、色、质、纹。“烛龙”出水于2002年，现估价在5000万元以上，为中华奇石园镇馆之宝，由著名藏石家高津龙先生以228万元搜购。据说当时有人在岩滩坝不到一公里的地方打捞到此石，“形似山沟里的蜥蜴，而且色彩丰富”。众人以之为奇，后得高先生慧眼，此石以“烛龙”之名出世……

Hongshui (“red water”) River is known for its curious stones, among which the most famous specimen is the Dahua Colored Jade. It's a large stone with beautiful colors and patterns, and has the texture of jade. It's a striking specimen. The curious stones of the Lingnan area have their own standards, in terms of form, color, texture and patterns. The “Dragon Candle” was plucked from the water in 2002, and has an estimated value of more than fifty million Yuan. It's a treasure of the Chinese Museum of Curious Stones, and was purchased by collector Gao Jinlong for 2.28 million Yuan. It's said the stone was found less than a kilometer away from the Yantan Dam. “Its form is like a lizard in a gulley, and its colors are rich.” Many people view it as a curiosity; Gao was clever enough to snap up this “dragon candle” when he had the chance, as it later went on to become famous.

评论

千金难买玉桂香

Pricey Bark

文：潘惠娟

广西的肉桂，又叫玉桂。肉桂薄薄的表皮下面，富含油脂，油珠渗出，香气浓烈。在古代，玉桂是南方的一味名贵药材，全身可入药。古罗马博物学家普林尼在其传世之作《博物志》中记录："桂皮油价格高达 1000~1500 便士每磅，这相当于一名罗马士兵 6 年的工钱。"当年秦在岭南设桂林郡，桂者，玉桂也。

The Chinese cinnamon of Guangxi is also known as "jade cinnamon". The thin bark of the tree is full of oil, droplets of which exude from it with great fragrance. In ancient times, it was a famous medicinal plant in the south, all parts of which could be used to make medicine. Roman historian Gaius Plinus Secundus thus wrote: "The oil of the cinnamon bark cost as much as 1,000-1,500 denarii, which is equivalent to six years' salary of a Roman soldier." When Guilin was established in the Qin dynasty, the "gui" referred to the local cinnamon.

桂出深山　摄影：何碧云

煨香了一碗汤

A Fragrant Bowl of Soup

文：潘惠娟

"他不回答，对柜里说，'温两碗酒，要一碟茴香豆。'"鲁迅笔下，孔乙己要的茴香豆里就有茴香。茴香即八角。宁明八角，属乔木，有木香，角瓣饱满、平直。广西西部和南部的八角产量几乎占到了全国产量的 90% 左右。新鲜的八角从树上采摘，烫水沥干晾晒，可佐料。南人爱煲汤，汤里会放八角调鲜，味美绵长；冬天一碗汤，煨香了一夜。

"He didn't respond, and said to the clerk over the counter: 'warm two bowls of liquor, and a plate of aniseed beans.'" Lu Xun thus wrote of Kong Yiji. The aniseed he was referring to is star anise. The star anise of Ningming County is a shrub with a wooden fragrance that grows lushly and straight. The western and southern parts of Guangxi account for almost ninety percent of star anise production in China. The fresh star anise is picked off the tree, treated in hot water and drip-dried before being sunned; it is a seasoning. The people of Nanning enjoy making soup and will add star anise to adjust its flavor for a lasting taste. Making a bowl soup in the winter means fragrance for the whole night.

莽草救众生

Lifesaving Plant

文：潘惠娟

四月栽苗，七八月的融安，一人多高的青蒿漫山遍野，发疯地长。风过，滚滚绿浪从山的这头到那头，喜上了草农的眉梢。簌簌地，刀过草落，收割好的青蒿草摞在路边，药草香铺满地，这时的青蒿素含量最高。目前，融安的青蒿草所提炼的青蒿素已经占了全国生产供应量的 1/3，占全球生产供应量的 1/4，被世界卫生组织指定为采购供应商。一把青蒿药草，既治疗疟疾，又能精准扶贫，妙哉！

Seedlings are planted in April, and by July and August fields of sweet wormwood[1] grow as high as a person is tall, covering the ground. The wind blows, and the plants ripple in waves. They rustle as they're cut down by the farmers' sickles. Harvested grass was bundled up on the sides of the road. The medicinal fragrance floats throughout the air. This is when the plants have the highest content of artemesinin, an antimalarial drug. Currently, the artemisinin refined from the plants here accounts for one-third of Chinese and one-quarter of world production and is bought up by the WHO. It's a great arrangement – it allows the world to combat malaria, and gives the people here an income.

花非春而常放

Blooming Year-round

文：朱燕

人们常用“半城绿树半城楼”来形容南宁，不过我更喜欢这句：“草经冬而不枯，花非春而常放。”漫步南宁街道，总有成串成片的三角梅映入眼帘。紫蓝色、朱红色、桃红色、绛紫色、橙黄色……火一般绽放在社区人家的庭院、墙头、阳台和绿地的草坡上，与南宁的绿叶繁枝共同搭建了一个五彩缤纷的大观园。三角梅的花期极长。从 3 月到 6 月一直盛放，到了 8 月，停歇喘息一阵，又再次盛开，这次花期更长，开得更烈，直到 11 月方结束。三角梅是没有花香的。为什么要香气呢？少一点粉饰，就多一份纯朴。无论近看，还是远观，那一树绚烂的三角梅艳而不媚、雅而不俗，正正当好。

People frequently describe Nanning as being "half green, half buildings", but I prefer the phrase "grasses don't wilt in the winter, and flowers bloom year-round". Walking around the streets of the city, you'll see paperflower (Bougainvillea glabra) all about. Purple-blue, crimson, peach-pink, and orange, they bloom like blazing fires in the communities, in gardens, upon walls, balconies, and green spaces. They add a whole palette of color to the green backdrop of the city. Their blossoms persist for a large part of the year. They're lit up between March and June, and take a bit of a rest in August, before springing back and holding out until November. These flowers have no fragrance. Why should they? They are more straightforward yet more intimate. Whether you view them from near or far, you'll be taken in by their beauty and charm.

1. *Artemisia carvifolia*

森林海

Ocean of Trees

文：潘惠娟

日照足，水生态充沛，葱茏笼盖四野，对于广西的守林人来说，满眼的绿，没有四季。广西的森林覆盖率达到 62.2%，位居全国第三位，西部地区第一位；各种乡土、珍贵树种，经济林、储备林、商品林基地拔得全国头筹。广西的树绿到了尽头，是林海；一呼一吸，满是绿色的味道，有点清澈的甜。

With abundant sunshine and water, green covers the fields everywhere. For the forest keepers of Guangxi, there are no four seasons, only green. Forest covers 62.2% of the land here, third in China, and first in western China. It leads China with all kind of local trees or rare trees, as well as the economic, storage and commodity forests. The forests grow as far as one can see, like an ocean of trees. Breathing in the air, one finds it is clear and sweet.

俯瞰红椎林　摄影：谢勇云

桂林三花的沉醉　摄影：邓霆

舌尖·忆锦
Tastes and Times

六月六，子鸭肉，炒苦瓜，浆血醋

Duck and Blood

文：廖珊

“六月六，子鸭肉，炒苦瓜，浆血醋。”桂林全州必吃的一道菜，是醋血鸭。取盛夏上市的仔鸭一只，杀鸭留血，注入酸醋。先用大火爆炒鸭子，再用文火焖熟。待鸭子出锅前，倒入醋血，起锅上桌。酸醋富含的乙酸分子与血浆完美结合，闻起来醋香扑鼻，再搭上绵软入味的鸭肉，酸辣鲜香，开胃可口，是酷暑时节最佳选择。

If there's one food you can't miss out on in Quanzhou, it's the vinegary duck with blood. At the height of summer, one buys a green duck, slaughters it and keeps the blood, adding vinegar. The duck is first stir-fried on high heat and then stewed on medium flame until ready. Before removing the duck from the wok, one adds the vinegar and blood, and serves it immediately. The acetic acid and the blood come together wonderfully for a mixture that's quite fragrant. The duck is tender, spicy and tasty. It gives an edge to your appetite and is the best choice for midsummer.

专属于高峰的鸭中美味

Lemon Duck

文：廖珊

和广东直接拿鲜果做配菜的烹饪形式不同，广西人更喜欢用腌制过的水果入菜，如柠檬鸭。做柠檬鸭最重要的调料，是腌制过的酸柠檬和酸姜、酸辣椒、酸藠头、山黄皮。它们共同组成丰富的酸料，经高温烹制后，再和鸭肉完美融合。南宁人一说柠檬鸭，必提高峰。他们宁愿花上几个小时，驾车穿越邕武高速，只为品尝这一专属高峰的鸭中美味。

Whereas the people of Guangdong like to use fresh fruit as a garnish in cooking, in Guangxi people prefer pickled fruits in their dishes: such is the case with lemon duck. The most important ingredients for this kind of duck are the pickled lemon, ginger, pepper, Chinese onion[1], and Clausena excavata. Together they form a robust pickled seasoning mixture. After being cooked at high heat, the duck meat is added to finish the dish. The people of Nanning will always mention Gaofeng when talking about the lemon duck. The locals are willing to spend hours on the road, navigating the Nanning-Wuming Expressway to get a taste of this exquisite meal.

柠檬鸭　摄影：张小宁

1. *Allium Chinense*

一方好水 腐乳香

Good Water, Good Curd

文：廖珊

几乎每个人都吃过家常豆腐乳，但桂林市临桂县四塘乡横山村的豆腐乳成为非物质文化遗产却是一件新鲜事。和用红曲制胚的红腐乳、用苦浆水腌制的青方腐乳不同，横山白腐乳好吃的秘诀，在于水。横山村，有一口深不见底的四方井。打上来的井水清冽甘甜。村里人用井水与黄豆混合发酵，制作腐乳。而一旦离开了横山村，离开了四方井，腐乳还是腐乳，却远没有横山的浓郁鲜香、入口即化。

豆腐乳发酵　摄影：邓霆

Fermented bean curd is ordinary to Chinese people, but the curd of Hengshan Village in Sitang Town, Guilin is not. It is newly listed as intangible cultural heritage. In contrast with the curd made with red yeast rice, or that made with bitter starch solution, the secret to the white fermented bean curd here is in the water. In Hengshan Village, there is very deep square well, the water of which is clear and sweet. The villagers mix it with the tofu and ferment it to make this product. If one leaves the village, leaves the well, he or she can still make fermented bean curd, but it won't have the fragrance and melt-in-your-mouth texture of the stuff produced here.

豆腐乳切块　摄影：邓霆

只能在阳朔吃的鱼
Yangshuo Fish

文：廖珊

有一种鱼，生于阳朔，长于阳朔，也被食客们簇拥于阳朔。没错，这就是大名鼎鼎的阳朔啤酒鱼。阳朔啤酒鱼大多取用漓江或遇龙河里鲜活的大鲤鱼。因清澈河水的常年滋养，鱼肉异常鲜嫩，却也必须承担易煮老的风险。因此，聪明的桂林人在烹饪过程中加入了啤酒。鱼肉与啤酒结合，更显滑嫩鲜美。这样一份佳肴，一旦移师别处，就大不一样。

There is a kind of fish that is native to Yangshuo and sought by the gourmands there. This is the famous Yangshuo Beer Fish. Most of the fish used are carp from the waters of the Lijiang and Yulong rivers. Nourished by the clear waters, the fish has especially tender flesh, but can easily be overcooked. For this reason, the intelligent people of Guilin add beer during the cooking process. The fish and beer come together for a smooth and fresh taste. This is an excellent dish that can only be appropriately enjoyed here – the flavor won't be the same if it is served elsewhere.

打油茶
Oil Tea

文：廖珊

“一杯苦，二杯夹（涩），三杯四杯好油茶。”作家彭匈这样描写他眼里的“油茶经”。在恭城，油茶不是煮出来的，也不是泡出来的，而是“打”出来的。这一击打的器物，为一根茶树天然生成，呈直角状，叫油茶槌。当炭炉熊熊燃烧，油茶锅支起，茶叶、葱头、姜段进入锅内，拿起油茶槌，在高温下混合击打，待出现黏稠状，注油再打，掌握火候，再注入滚滚沸水。且慢，还不是喝油茶的好时机。第一锅和第二锅，茶叶的苦涩刚被打出来，要到第三锅，这时的茶汤油褐清亮，姜葱暗香。寒冬时节，来上这么一碗，胃暖心顺，再好不过了。

“The first is bitter, the second astringent, and the third and fourth are true oil tea”. Author Peng Xiong thus described the drink in his “oil tea classic”. In Gongcheng, the tea isn't brewed or steeped, but rather “beaten” out. The implement is made out of a part of a tea tree, a kind of mallet with a right angle in it. When the charcoal fire is burning bright, the teapot is set up. Tea leaves, onions, and chunks of ginger are placed within, and then beaten with the mallet at high temperature. A sticky solution emerges, to which then is added oil. It's further beaten, and then boiling water is added. It's not done just quite yet, though. The first pot is bitter, and the second is astringent; after these flavors are removed, the third pot produces a soupy tea with a bright brown color. The subtle but persistent flavor of the ginger and onions is noticeable. During the cold winter months, a bowl of this tea warms the stomach and comforts the heart.

鸡包纸，纸包鸡

Paper-Wrapped Chicken

文：廖珊

据说“纸包鸡”是最早的外卖。时光倒流回1932年，粤军将领陈济棠就曾特派专机来梧州，空运纸包鸡回广州。食在岭南，不能不尝纸包鸡。这一历史悠久的“外卖”，当之无愧。作为梧州饮食文化的名片，梧州纸包鸡早在1983年人民大会堂举办的全国烹饪美食大赛上就赢得了“中国一绝”的美誉。

It's said that paper-wrapped chicken is the earliest form of takeaway in China. Back in 1932, general Chen Chi-tang sent a plane out to Wuzhou to bring the dish back to Guangzhou. It's said that one must try it if he or she goes to Lingnan Area. It's fully deserving of its reputation. As a culinary calling card for the city of Wuzhou, it won top title at the 1983 banquet contest in the Grand Hall of the People.

三天不吃酸，走路打倒窜

Gotta Have Vinegar

文：廖珊

“三天不吃酸，走路打倒窜。”在广西三江侗寨，有着流传千年的腌酸文化，而这一切，都和他们每天“上山下乡”的劳动习惯有关。人们每天越过山丘去开垦荒地，为节约时间，午饭就得随身携带。为保证午餐质量，人们于是想到了腌酸肉。将鸡、鸭去头和内脏，猪肉清理干净，放入木桶压紧后，再放一层糯米和盐做的圆饼。后压上木盖，木盖上灌水，隔绝空气。放置阴凉处，等待时间的发酵。一年后，逢良辰吉日，一家开桶，满村酸香。

In the Dong Village in Sanjiang, there is a culture of pickling with more than a millennium of history, one that's related to their lifestyle. Every day people go through the mountains and hills to reclaim wasteland for farming. In order to save time, they carry their lunches with them. To guarantee the quality of the meal, they invented pickled meat. After removing the head and innards from a chicken or duck, and cleaning some pork, people place these items into a wooden barrel and compressed. Glutinous rice and salt are added, and a round cake is formed. After a wooden lid is attached, water is poured on top to form an air-tight seal. Then it is placed in a dark, cold area for fermentation. A year later, on a nice day, the barrel is open, and the fragrance permeates the village.

评论

以假乱真豆腐鱼

Tofu Fish

文：廖珊

在武鸣县灵马圩有一道家家户户都会做的菜：豆腐鲶鱼。相传，菜的由来和“鱼不够”有关。以前，有一户朱姓穷苦人家。一天朱父捉回一条野生鲶鱼，准备给家人打个牙祭。但家里十几口人，一条鲶鱼不够吃呀。正巧，妻子带回一块邻居赠的豆腐，朱父眼前一亮：“豆腐口感和鱼肉接近，要不就让豆腐来代替鱼吧。”果不其然，豆腐的清醇和鲶鱼的鲜香完美融合，从此豆腐鲶鱼家家爱吃，便流传下来。

There is a dish in Lingmaxu, Wuming County that every family makes: tofu catfish. According to legend, it was invented because there was a shortage of fish meat. There was a Zhu family in times past that was poor. One day, Mr. Zhu caught a catfish and was preparing to take it home to make a feast for his family. However, there were more than ten members of the household; thus one fish wasn't enough. It just so happened that his wife brought home a block of tofu that given by neighbors. Looking upon it, he said, “The texture of fish and tofu are similar, so let's have one stand in for the other.” It turned out that the clear taste of the tofu and fragrance of the fish mixed well, and thus tofu catfish was born and became a classic dish here.

青龙过海

Green Dragon

文：廖珊

“席间一试青龙味，半夜醒来嘴犹香。”博白蕹菜既“接地气”又名扬四海。和一般蕹菜不同，博白蕹菜叶疏茎长，叶尾尖细，掐之即断，鲜绿脆嫩。“水烫”和“猛火”是博白人对待蕹菜最常见的两种烹饪方式。水必须要达到沸点，在其中加入几滴花生油，迅速将菜放至滚水中，翻动至八九成熟后起锅，淋上酱油即成。这一行云流水的烹调过程，又被称为“青龙过海”。“猛火”也不复杂，油锅加热，起烟时放入蒜末，与蕹菜猛火翻炒至九成熟即可起锅。

It's said that if you eat the “green dragon”, and awake in the middle of the night, you'll still feel the flavor. The “green dragon” refers to water spinach of Bobai, which is famous far and wide. Unlike normal water spinach, the plant here grows with long stems and leaves that will snap if you pinch them. They are tender and crunchy. There are two common methods of preparing it in Bobai: “water soup” and “roaring fire”. Water is brought to a boil, and then a few drops of peanut oil are added. The vegetable is quickly put in the boiling water, and then taken out when it's eight or nine-tenths done, sprinkled with soy sauce and served. This style is also referred to as the “dragon crossing the sea”. “Roaring fire” isn't complicated either. A wok with oil is heated, and as soon as it begins to smoke, ground garlic and water spinach are added and stir-fried to about nine-tenths done, and then served.

两片
Two Slices

文：廖珊

横县鱼生又被称为“两片”，历来被称为“县菜”，代表着横县烹饪技术最高水平。出水欲飞的郁江青竹鱼，去鳞，脱皮，起骨，一气呵成；再配上姜、葱、蒜、木瓜丝、萝卜丝、柠檬丝等，鱼片鲜而不腥，嫩而爽滑，满口清香。孔子主张“食不厌精，脍不厌细”。脍是什么？脍就是鱼生、肉生。脍的标准是细。细到什么程度？宋段成式《酉阳杂俎》载，有位“善斫脍”的人能将鱼片切得像绸缎那样薄，像丝线那样轻，吹一口气都能使它飘飞起来。有人称这是“中国刺身”。但鱼生的历史，可比刺身悠久得多。

The raw fish of Hengxian County is also called “two slices”, and in the past was known as “county food”. It’s representative of the high level of cookery in the county. The “green bamboo fish” is taken from the Yujiang River, descaled, skinned, and deboned quickly. Ginger, spring onions, garlic, and papaya, radish and lemon shreds are added. The fish meat is fresh without a strong smell, tender and clear. Confucius mentioned this food himself, saying that cooked dishes should be fine, and raw fish should be sliced thin. During the Song dynasty, some chefs could slice the fish as thin as silk, so light that one could blow it away with a breath. Some people say that this is “Chinese sashimi”, but the history of this dish extends back much further than sashimi.

一碗米饭待客，足矣
Fish-sauce Rice

文：廖珊

来京族三岛，阮三娘的“鱼露拌饭”是非去不可的。当你走进小店，会发现，这里没有海鲜大餐，没有小炒鲜肉，只有热气腾腾的大锅和一碗碗白米饭。但周围的食客却手捧饭碗，吃得特别香。米饭还是那个米饭，只因拌上了鱼露，就完全不一样。橙红清澈如玛瑙般透亮的鱼露，提取了鱼汁中的精华，经冷却的盐开水压滤，终成此佳酿。据说，一百斤鱼才能酿出 30 斤左右的“头漏汁”，这样的上品鱼露，更是一瓶难求。

Upon the Three Jing Islands[1], the “fish-sauce rice” is a must-try. When you enter a shop, you’ll find that there aren’t any fancy seafood dishes, or fried compositions, just large bubbling pot and bowls of plain white rice. The locals, however, really enjoy this scene. The ordinary rice, when mixed with the fish sauce, becomes completely different. That sauce, clear and orange-red like agate, is a distillate of fish. It is pressure filtered with cooled salted water to produce the end product. It’s said that fifty kilograms of fish can produce only fifteen kilograms of the first round of this “fish juice”, making it quite valuable.

1. *Wutou, Wanwei and Shanxin; three islands near the border with Vietnam administered as part of Fangchenggang City.*

鸡肉也古典

Classic Chicken

文：廖珊

“用作原料的三黄鸡不大，也就一斤上下，斩成五件，隔水清蒸，小木桶堆码上桌，佐蘸料食用。当地人为这道脱胎于岭南白切鸡的菜品，起了一个既文雅又似乎含有历史意味的名字：岑溪古典鸡。”美食作家曾小帆对岑溪古典鸡的描写，道尽了这道菜后面的古风意味。据说，岑溪人特别喜欢在夏天吃古典鸡，因为鸡肉的原味清甜缓解了他们在酷暑时节对肉类既渴望又担心油腻的纠结。

“It’s made with a small three-yellow chicken[1], maybe half a kilogram or so. It’s chopped into five pieces and steamed, piled in a little wooden barrel and served with dipping sauces. The locals gave this derivative of plain-cut chicken a historical-sounding name: Classic Chicken of Cenxi.” Food writer Zeng Xiaofan thus described “classic chicken”. It’s said that the people of Cenxi especially like eating this kind of chicken in summer, because the natural flavor of the chicken, clear and sweet, slakes their thirst for meat without introducing the problems of heavy, fatty cooking.

闻名天下的荔浦芋　摄影：邓霆

扣肉——荔浦芋的标配

Lipu Taro

文：廖珊

被《奇葩大会》誉为“全中国最让人流口水的男人”，《舌尖上的中国》第一、二季导演陈晓卿认为：广西菜品中，搭配最地道的是荔浦芋扣肉。“肉里有芋头香，芋头里充满‘动物性’，两种食材的味道融在一起，特别香。”

Chen Xiaoqing, awarded the title of “number one tempter of food in China” by “Who Can Who Up”, and director of the first two seasons of “A Bite of China” believes that of all the dishes in Guangxi, the most authentic is lipu taro[2] braised pork. “The flavor of the taro permeates the meat, and the taro is filled with ‘animal nature’; the two ingredients together form a fragrant combo.”

---

1. A Chicken with yellow feathers, claws, and beak.
2. Colocasia esculenta

十八酿

Eighteen Wrapped Dishes

文：廖珊

相传李商隐在昭平郡（今广西平乐）任郡守时，平乐乡贤请他到船家饮酒。李商隐第一次看到酿菜这一菜式，觉得很有趣，问船家能酿出几种花样。船家的回答也颇有底气：“你写出几首诗，我就能酿出几种！”李商隐一口气吟出了10首关于桂林的诗歌，船家也在第一时间内端出了豆腐酿、柚皮酿、苦瓜酿、茄子酿等10种酿菜。后来，平乐人在此基础上，创造出了更多的酿菜样式，因为种类实在多到难以统计，于是统称“十八酿”。平乐人的这一创意，直接把饮食提升到了艺术的高度。

It's said that when Li Shangyin was the magistrate of Shaoping County (now Pingle, Guangxi), the county sage invited him to his boat to drink. It was the first time that he saw the "wrapping" manner of cooking. He found it very interesting and asked the boatman to show him more examples of the technique. The boatman told him boldly: "I can make as many dishes as poems you can write!" Li Shangyin quickly recited ten poems relating to Guilin, and the boatman quickly brought out tofu, pomelo peel, bitter melon, eggplant and other dishes, ten in total. Later on, more "wrapped" dishes were created. It's hard to count them all, so they're known together as "the eighteen". This kind of cooking has become art.

顺着浓香找骨头

Hot Bones

文：廖珊

“新州镇圩日这一天，市场边上几个近一米高的大坛子格外引人注目，几名苗族妇女坐在大坛子后，边聊天边绣鞋垫。有人上前，一名妇女放下手中的针线活，揭开大坛子的盖子，一股浓香顿时在周围弥漫开来……”新华社记者熊红明闻到的这股浓香，来自隆林家家户户都会做的一道菜：隆林辣椒骨。首先须将骨头碾得粉碎，变成骨泥；再将干辣椒舂成粉末，混合生姜、料酒、花椒做成辣椒酱，最后将骨泥和辣椒酱一起封入坛内，吃时舀出来，隔水一蒸——嗯！就是这个味儿！

"On a market day in Xinzhou Town, there are several particularly noticeable jars at the market, almost a meter in height. Some Miao women sit behind it, chatting and stitching insoles. Somebody comes up, and the women put down her needlework, lifting the lid of the jar. A burst of fragrance appears in the surrounding air..." The fragrance recorded by Xinhua reporter Xiong Hongming is familiar to everyone in Longlin. It comes from the spicy bones. The bones are chopped into small chunks and then mixed with a spicy paste made of dried chili powder, fresh ginger, cooking alcohol and prickly-ash. Finally, the bone chunks and paste are put in a jar. When the time comes, the mixture is ladled out and steamed – and there it is! What a great flavor!

此“碗”绵绵无绝期

Stacks of Bowls

文：廖珊

“你千计莫讲，一讲口水就流。”著名桂剧表演艺术家兰魁先生每次一提到马肉米粉，就两眼放光。鲜美的马骨汤，香脆的腊马肉片，再配上芫荽、花生、芝麻油……真是光想想就口水横流。但马肉米粉最让人欲罢不能的还不在此，而在于它用一种很小很小的碗盛装，有的人一口就能吃下一碗。吃一次粉不是以一碗两碗论，而是以十碗甚至几十碗来算，以至于马肉米粉店的餐桌摆设很是与众不同，每张桌子都是靠墙而设，这样才便于依墙叠起成摞空碗，真是此“碗”绵绵无绝期！

“Just thinking about them makes your mouth water.” Famous Gui opera performer Lan Kui’s eyes light up when he mentions horse-meat rice noodles. Wonderful horse bones soup along with crisp slices of meat, coriander, peanuts, and sesame oil… the thought really makes your mouth water. However, the most enticing aspect is the style of serving with very small bowls, each about one mouthful in size. You don’t just have one or two, but dozens. The layout of these restaurants is different from others; each table abuts a wall, which allows customers to stack up the empty bowls against it. It really is an experience.

白先勇：天下美味莫过桂林米粉

Rice Noodles

文：朱燕

据说，著名作家白先勇最喜欢桂林米粉。他小时候在桂林花桥桥头吃过花桥米粉，从此一辈子也没有忘过。桂林米粉还真是一绝。因为桂林水质好，榨洗出来的米粉细滑又柔韧，很有嚼头。桂林米粉花样多，原汤米粉、冒热米粉，还有独家的马肉米粉，各有风味。一把炸黄豆撒在热腾腾的莹白粉条上，色香味俱全。每次，白先勇回到桂林，三餐都到处去找米粉吃，一吃就是三四碗。

Famous writer Bai Xianyong is said to love the rice noodles of Guilin. When he was young, he ate rice noodles at the head of the Flower Bridge and had a lifelong affinity for them. These are indeed a local specialty in Guilin. The noodles are thin, smooth, and pliable due to the wonderful water here. They have a nice chewy taste. They come in many varieties, such as Yuantang and Maore. There are also special horse-meat rice noodles. Each type has its own flavor. Sprinkling fried soybeans over the light white noodles completes the taste. Every time Bai heads back to Guilin, he goes to a rice noodle restaurant for each meal and has three or four bowls each time.

桂林米粉　摄影：陈炜平

北海人的万能蘸料

Beihai Dippings

文：廖珊

在广西北海，有一道传说中的“黑暗料理”，初闻带腥，一旦吃上了，就根本停不下来。它就是连《舌尖上的中国》都不忍心放过的沙蟹汁焖豆角。这道菜美味的重点在于沙蟹汁。新鲜的沙蟹捶碎后，和盐、蒜片、姜片封装在玻璃瓶中，在阳光下晒上几个小时后开盖，咸香腥鲜，简直就是北海人的万能蘸料。

In Beihai, there is a famous kind of “ugly cooking”, or bizarre cuisine, which is addictive once you try it. Its even blew the minds of the people on “A Bite of China”: ghost crab with green beans. The key to the flavor here is the ghost crab juice in the dish. Fresh ghost crabs are hammered up and stored in a glass bottle with salt, garlic, and ginger slices. The bottle is sunned for a few hours and then capped. The flavor is salty, fishy but tasty. It’s an absolute killer dipping sauce specific to Beihai.

没有螺蛳的螺蛳粉

Where are the Snails?

文：廖珊

“螺蛳粉里到底有没有螺蛳”已经和“老婆饼里究竟能不能找到老婆”列入了本世纪难题之列。事实上，正宗的螺蛳粉是没有螺蛳或螺蛳肉的。最早的螺蛳粉是煮螺蛳的衍生品。支起大锅，用酸笋、紫苏、辣椒和骨头汤熬制螺蛳高汤，其间“咕噜咕噜”冒泡的，是鲜美的田螺。同时，在旁边打一炉灶，支一小汤锅，将大锅里的螺蛳汤舀部分出来，放入米粉烫煮，这才有了螺蛳粉。和桂林米粉一样，这麻而不燥、辣而不火、香而不腻的螺蛳高汤，才是螺蛳粉的灵魂。

“Are there actually snails in snail noodles?” is one of those hard questions like “Is there any wife in wife cake?” In fact, authentic snail noodles don’t have snails or snail meat. The original snail noodles were a by-product of boiling snails. A large pot of soup was boiled with pickled bamboo sprouts, purple perilla, chilies and bones. Field snails were bubbled in the pot. A smaller soup pot was set up into which the snail soup was ladled. Rice noodles were added to make the authentic snail noodles. Just like rice noodles of Guilin, the essence of snail noodles is the soup, which has the right amount of spice and fragrance.

螺蛳粉　摄影：陈炜平

老友常临

Good Friends

文：廖珊

"'老友面'者，酸笋肉丝汆汤下面也，不知道为什么叫做'老友'。"汪曾祺在散文《五味》中这样写道。汪先生不知道，名为老友，其实和一份真挚的友情有关。20世纪30年代，南宁街头上有一周记茶馆，一老翁每日必去喝茶。有几日，老翁没有如约而至，茶馆老板去探望，才发现他感冒了。于是老板亲自下厨，将蒜末、豆豉、辣椒、酸笋、牛肉末、胡椒粉等加以爆炒，后加水沸腾，放入面条，直吃得老翁大汗淋漓，感冒也好了。老翁专门制作"老友常临"牌匾，赠与茶馆。那年作家贾平凹来南宁，东道主彭匈问他对南宁印象如何，贾脱口而出："老友面！"

Why are the "old friend noodles", with a soup of pickled bamboo shoots and meat shreds, thus called? Wang Zengqi asked this in his essay The Five Flavors. What he didn't know is that the name of these noodles actually comes from an old friendship. In the 1930s, there was a Chou Kee Teahouse in Nanning; an old man went there every day to drink tea. Once, he didn't show up for a few days, and the proprietor of the teahouse paid him a visit, finding that he'd come down with a cold. The proprietor himself went into the kitchen, taking ground garlic, fermented soya beans, chilies, pickled bamboo shoots, ground beef, and pepper powder, frying them together and then boiling them in water before adding noodles. The old man sweated heavily as he ate them, and then his cold was cured. The man made a plaque "your old friend will frequently visit" and gave it to the teahouse. When author Jia Pingwa came to Nanning, and his host Peng Xiong asked about his impression of the city, he said, "old friend noodles!"

老友粉　摄影：陈炜平

粉尖儿上荡秋千

Swinging upon Noodles

文：廖珊

有人做过一个有趣实验：将 150 根仅重 200 克的米粉挂在横木上，让一位 70 公斤重的小伙子在上面行走并荡秋千！这一有着逆天柔韧度的米粉就是罗秀米粉，因产于桂平市罗秀镇一带而得名，清末明初就已闻名海外。采用罗秀山区特用的水质，配以当地优质白米，历选、浸、磨、蒸、晒、摺、切、扎等流程，做出来的米粉洁白如雪，质地柔韧。

Someone did an interesting experiment: hang 150 rice noodles weighing only 200 grams upon a cross-beam, and it's strong enough for a man of seventy kilograms to walk and swing upon. These incredibly flexible noodles are the rice noodles of Luoxiu Town in Guiping City. At the end of the Qing dynasty, they became famous even abroad. The local water is excellent, and the rice is washed, soaked, ground, steamed, sunned, folded, cut and pulled to make these white noodles, strong and soft.

罗秀米粉的制造　摄影：张小宁

广西版水磨年糕

Guangxi Year Cake

文：廖珊

在广西，当米粉变成年糕，会是什么样？很简单，就是粉利的样子。用上好大米细磨成浆，做成面团，揉搓成小圆柱状，上锅蒸至八分熟，取出晾干即为粉利。保存颇有讲究，必须放入冷水中保存，并需要不时换水，以防止表皮皴裂。粉利可当菜可当饭，切丝和辣椒、芹菜、西红柿、肉片爆炒，或是切片氽汤，色鲜爽口，非常美味。粉利以平乐沙子镇的最为正宗。

When rice is turned into year cake in Guangxi, what does it look like? The answer is "fenli", the local variant. Rice is ground and made into a paste, and formed into a ball, then rolled out into little cylinders. It's steamed to about eighty percent done, and then taken out and dried. To preserve it, you must place it in cold water which is continually changed out to prevent cracking of the skin. "Fenli" can be eaten as a dish or staple food. It can be chopped and fried with chilies, celery, tomatoes and meat, or sliced and put in soup where it makes for a delicious component. The most authentic example of "fenli" comes from Shazi Town in Pingle.

薄饼在风中飘飞

Thin Cakes

文：朱千华

1962 年春天，国歌的词作者、著名诗人田汉来到京族三岛访问，看到村民家家户户都在制作一种薄薄的米饼，觉得好奇，就问老乡：“那是什么饼？”村民回答：“宾来。”田汉听不懂京族话，一时没弄明白。老乡拿一张饼请田汉品尝。田汉吃了一口，觉得很酥很香，回味之时，忽来一阵风，把手上的饼吹走了。田汉笑道：“这饼好薄，风一吹就飘，不如就叫风吹饼吧。”

In the spring of 1962, writer of the lyrics to the National Anthem and famous poet Tian Han visited the Three Jing Islands and saw that the residents were all making a kind of thin rice cake. He was curious and asked one of the locals what it was. The villager replied “binlai”. Tian didn’t understand the Jing language and was confused. The villager took out one of the cakes for him to try. He found that it was crispy and delicious. As he was reflecting upon it, a gust of wind came and blew the cake away. Tian laughed: “Such a thin cake, it can be blown away by the wind. It can be called cake-in-wind.”

冰井泉香，滴珠豆浆

Ice Spring

文：廖珊

早上五六点起床，梧州人通常会去做什么呢？到白云山脚下喝豆浆。梧州人爱吃的这种豆浆号称“冰泉”：“火山无火，冰泉无冰；唯彼泉源，甘寒可凝。”据《梧州文化》记载，唐朝大历三年，梧州城东白云山下，时任本管经略使的诗人元结发现了一口井。井水甘寒如冰、清冽香甜，与对岸的火山遥相对应。这就是“梧州八景”之一——冰井泉香。这一奇景，就连苏东坡也曾慕名前来，为之折服。

What do the people of Wuzhou do after they wake up at five or six in the morning? They go to the foot of Mount Baiyun to drink soy milk. The variety that they like is called “Ice Spring”. “There’s no fire on Fire Mountain and no ice in the Ice Spring. The spring water is cool and sweet.” According to Culture of Wuzhou, during the third year of the Dali Era in the Tang dynasty, poet Yuan Jie, who was temporarily dispatched there, discovered a well at the foot of Mount Baiyun. The water of the well was sweet and cold like ice, clear and fragrant, offsetting the “fire mountain” on the opposite bank. This is one of the eight sights of Wuzhou, the “sweet water from the icy spring”. Even Su Dongpo himself made a memorable visit here for the water.

评论

五谷丰登糯米饭
Five Grains

文：廖珊

壮族三月三，几乎家家户户都会煮一种5个颜色的糯米饭，或用作祭祖贡品，或用作赶圩干粮。除了白色是糯米本色，其余4种颜色，来自4种天然植物：枫叶、黄姜、紫饭叶、红蓝草。5种颜色象征五谷丰登。相传，这种食品是深得仙女们的赞赏后流传下来的，也有人说是祭祀歌仙刘三姐的。据说吃了这种饭，人丁兴旺，身体健壮。带着植物甘甜清香的糯米饭，就这样流传下来。

On the third day of the third lunar month, almost all Zhuang families will make five-colored rice. It can be used as an offering for ceremonies, or as a dry snack to take on market days. Aside from the plain white rice, there are four natural sources: maple leaves, yellow ginger, and the purple and red leaves of the magenta plant[1]. The five colors symbolize the plenty of the five major grains. According to legend, this kind of food was passed down after being appreciated by fairies; another legend says it's for paying tribute to Liu Sanjie. It is said people who eat this rice will have a big family and good composition. Each bite of the glutinous rice is the continuance of a long tradition.

壮乡五色饭　摄影：张小宁

粑粑中的贵族
High-Class Cakes

文：彭匆

桂林平乐印子粑可以说是粑粑中的贵族。首先在形状上它很有点讲究。糯米粉包了肚，放进一个粑粑印（木模）去压实了。粑粑印刻有精美的图案和花边，印出来的粑粑很漂亮。粑粑脱模后垫上两张柚子叶，蒸出来一屋喷香。外观上会用色彩来区分，甜的显淡黄色，染了黄栀子；咸的呈粉红色，用的是花红粉。印子粑有看相，是行村送礼的必备之物。

The "embossed" cakes of Pingle, Guilin can be regarded as the aristocracy of cakes. First, they have a beautiful form. Wrap the glutinous rice piece around the filling, impress it with a wooden mold with delicate patterns and borders, then put it between two citrus leaves, steam it, a puff of fragrance will come out. Colors are used to mark flavors: sweet cakes are dyed yellow with cape jasmine, and savor cakes are dyed red with pear-leaved crabapple extract. These cute little cakes are frequently given as gifts in the village.

1. *Peristrophe roxburghiana.*

驼背大粽 vs 三角小粽

Rice Dumpling Showdown

文：廖珊

广西人一年四季都包粽子。在横县，人们喜欢包一种庞大的粽子。因为要在有限的粽叶里，塞进尽可能多的糯米和馅料，于是就有了中间高两头低的造型。从侧面看，这种粽子特别像一个驼背老人在低头前行。到了桂林，人们喜欢一种小巧的三角粽。三片竹叶侧弯成圆锥形，放入糯米、香肉、绿豆、板栗，另一头的叶子包裹过来，形成一个三角体，如香囊般小巧可人，吃起来毫无压力。

The people of Guangxi make pyramid-shaped rice dumplings wrapped in bamboo leaves, or zongzi, all year round. In Hengxian County, the locals like making them large. As the supply of the leaves is limited, they stuff them with as much rice and filling as possible. A "hump" is formed where they're tied at the top, which makes them look like a camel from the side. In Guilin, people like making delicate, triangular dumplings. Three bamboo leaves are made into a conical shape, filled with glutinous rice, dog meat, mung beans, and Chinese chestnuts, and then sealed with a leaf on the other side for a triangular composition. They're cute and fun to eat.

三角粽　摄影：张小宁

坦坦荡荡大狗舌

Dog-tongue Cakes

文：彭匈

平乐、恭城一带的狗舌粑，制作上有些简单粗糙，糯米粉混了少许芝麻糖，用竹片划成一段一段，裹上蕉叶即成。蒸熟了的粑粑活像一条大狗舌，坦坦荡荡，不像西点的热狗那样羞羞答答。有的地方叫得文雅一些，叫褡裢粑，也像。

The dog-tongue cakes which are prominent in Pingle and Gongcheng are simple in production. Glutinous rice is mixed with a little bit of sesame candy, and then cut into segments with a piece of bamboo before being wrapped in a banana leaf. After being cooked, they look like a dog's tongue, large and broad, unlike the flimsy hot dogs of western cuisine. Some places give them a more elegant name, "cloth jacket cakes".

可以吃的木头
Edible Wood

文：朱燕

去崇左龙州，不可错过的是鸡肉粉，但带回家的特产则是桄榔粉。龙州桄榔粉是经过加工深山中生长的桄榔树干，提取其淀粉而成，所以又称“可以吃的木头”。由高大粗壮的桄榔树干变成细腻的桄榔粉，颇有一种“铁杵磨成针”的感觉。据《本草纲目》记载：“桄榔粉味甘平，无毒，作饼炙食腴美，令人不饥，补益虚羸损，腰脚乏力，久服轻身辟谷。”苏东坡也留下过“雪粉剖桄榔”的诗句，可见桄榔粉至今最少已有1000多年的历史。

When visiting Longzhou, in Chongzuo, one must try the chicken with rice noodles, but one must take gomuti[1] powder back home. This product is made from dried gomuti from deep forest, from which starch is extracted, and is thus called “edible wood”. Turning the strong trees into a fine powder is a bit like making a needle out of a baton. According to the Ming dynasty Compendium of Materia Medica, “Gomuti is of sweet taste and neutral nature, non-toxic, and makes for full, delicious cakes. It staves off hunger and revitalizes the body. Continued consumption leads to a light figure.” Su Dongpo also wrote a poem about the plant, which shows that its consumption has at least a millennium of history in China.

平淡中的好滋味
Salted Cakes

文：朱燕

不甚起眼的盐糕属于小众美食，常出没于老街、集市，外地游客较少见之，然而它却是宾阳当地最受欢迎的小吃之一，尤其受孩子们的喜爱。从前，卖盐糕的是走街串巷的担郎。沉甸甸的筐子晃晃悠悠，装满了令人垂涎的盐糕，一声响亮的吆喝便能引客而至。如今，经营盐糕的“老字号”也常客满盈门，大多是附近的街坊和镇上的居民，一两碗盐糕就能解决一顿早饭或午饭。狭小陈旧的店铺里，充满着市井烟火和寻常百姓的生活气息。

Salted cakes are a niche snack, which normally appear in old streets and at fair markets. Visitors from afar rarely see them, although they are one of the most popular snacks in Binyang, especially loved by children. Previously, they were mainly sold by hawkers carrying wares on a pole upon their soldiers. The heavy baskets swung back and forth, full of the delectable snacks, as the calls of the hawkers readily drew buyers. Today, “old shops” that sell these snacks are frequently packed and do brisk business. Most of them are located within residential areas. A bowl or two of the little cakes can serve as a breakfast or lunch. Within these old, small stores, one can see the life and activity of the old residents of the city.

1. *Arenga pinnate, the gomuti palm.*

大肚能容

Big Belly

文：彭匈

真正让人解馋觉着痛快的，是平乐、恭城一带的大肚粑。大肚粑真是大肚能容，肉丁、虾米、豆腐粒、芹菜、葱蒜等全部包容进去，大小如娃儿的拳头，一大锅煮熟，吃完四个差不多就饱了。大肚粑跟红烧肉一样，日子一精细，人们就不大吃它了。

The big belly cakes popular in Pingle and Gongcheng really are an enticing treat. They're thus called because they can contain a lot of filling: meat chunks, sea shrimp, tofu, celery, spring onions, garlic and more can all be stuffed into a cake the size of a child's fist, which is then steamed in a big pot. Eating four of them is enough to fill most people up. These cakes are like pork braised in brown sauce: on fine days people don't eat so much.

运盐途中腌牛肉

Beef on the Road

文：廖珊

玉林人对牛巴情有独钟，在广西是家喻户晓的，他们早、中、晚餐连宵夜都会与牛巴相遇。相传南宋开庆年间，有个姓邝的玉林盐贩子，他的牛累死在运盐途中。但结局并不悲伤：他舍不得将牛丢弃，只好将牛宰了，用盐腌起来，边往回走边晾晒成牛肉干。回到家，他支起大锅，将咸牛肉放进去，并佐以八角、桂皮等作料焖烧。牛肉出锅时，满街都是奇香，引无数街坊闻香而至。后世人将其称为“牛巴”。

The people of Yulin have an unusual affinity for preserved beef; people all over Guangxi know that they have it for breakfast, lunch, and dinner – even for late night munchies. Legend holds that during the Kaiqing Era of the Southern Song dynasty, there was a salt merchant surnamed Kuang in Yulin whose cow died from exhaustion on the road. The end to the story, however, isn't sad: he didn't want to leave the animal behind, so he butchered it, and preserved its meat with salt; he dried the meat in the sun as he made his way back, yielding jerky. When he reached home, he took out a big pot, and placed the meat within, adding star anise, cassia bark, and other spices as he slow-cooked it. When it was done, the entire street was full of a wonderful fragrance, and the product became widely known and appreciated here.

玉林牛巴　摄影：陈炜平

年年艾叶绿，岁岁粿泛香

Wormwood and Steamed Cake

文：廖珊

清明，不止是“雨纷纷”的时节，更是万物生长的季节。尤其是艾草，正值茂盛。人们将采摘回来的艾叶洗净、煮熟、剁碎，与糯米粉、黄糖和匀，捏成一个个墨绿色的圆形糍粑，在糍粑里可放香喷喷的芝麻花生馅，也可放咸香可人的头菜肉末馅……艾叶的清香混入糯米的弹劲，再加上美味的馅料，真是“年年艾叶绿，岁岁粿泛香”。这是广西人“三月三”必吃的美食哦。

The Qingming Festival isn't just a time when the rains fall continuously; it's also a time when all things grow, especially Asiatic wormwood, which flourishes at this time. People pick the leaves and wash, boil and chop them before mixing them with glutinous rice and brown sugar to make inky-green rice cakes. One can place fragrant peanut and sesame paste within, or opt for vegetables and meat. The soft flavor of the wormwood mixes with the chewy taste of the rice; together with the delicious filling, it makes for a snack people look forward to the whole year round. It's an essential food for Sanyuesan ("the third day of the third lunar month") in Guangxi.

瘦身成功的黄瓜

Thin Cucumbers

文：廖珊

我们说的黄瓜皮，不是物理意义上的黄瓜外皮，而是腌制后“瘦身成功”的黄瓜。在钦州，几乎人人都会腌黄瓜：先用筷子，在黄瓜上戳几个洞，再放入滚烫的开水锅里，10 分钟后取出，用布包好，压在一块大石头底下。三天后取出，这时的黄瓜皱皱巴巴，成了名副其实的黄瓜皮了。这一秘制风味，兴起于宋代，在清朝声名鹊起。相传粤籍御厨锦长青就用这道不起眼的小菜，赢得皇上的喜爱，从而坐稳了御膳房的第一把交椅。

When we talk about "cucumber skin", we don't mean the peel on the outside of the vegetable, but rather the cucumbers that have "lost weight" after pickling. In Qinzhou, almost everyone can make this. First, one punctures a few holes into the cucumber with a chopstick. Then, the cucumber is boiled for ten minutes. After wrapping it in cloth, one presses it under a large stone. After three days, it's taken out. The cucumber is covered in wrinkles, and is now the famous "cucumber skin". These were first popular in the Song dynasty and experienced a resurgence in the Qing. When a Cantonese chef in the imperial kitchen prepared them, the emperor became quite fond of them, and his place in the imperial kitchen was solidified.

瓜皮　摄影：陈炜平

竹筒里头烤米饭

Rice in the Bamboo

文：廖珊

米饭怎么煮更好吃？广西山民用古老的经验告诉你：放在香竹里烤过更好吃。选当季新鲜香竹，将米泡好，装入竹筒内，如果你想做出不同的风味，还可加入腊味等配菜。随后用鲜叶子将竹筒口塞紧，然后放在火上烧烤。竹筒表层烧焦时，就是米饭熟了的信号。用刀将竹皮剥开，被竹膜包裹着的米饭混合着竹子的清香，别有一番风味。

How can one make white rice taste even better? The people of the mountains in Guangxi will tell you from their old experience: put the rice in a bamboo stem to cook it, and you'll see an improvement in taste. Take a segment of fresh bamboo from the current season, and after soaking the rice, place it within. If you want to flavor it, you can add some preserved meats or garnishes. Stuff the opening of the bamboo with fresh leaves, and then place it on fire. As soon as the surface of the bamboo browns and starts to crack, the rice is done. Cut open the skin of the bamboo with a knife, and the rice within the bamboo membrane will be full of the fragrance of the plant.

中药小零食

Medicinal Snacks

文：廖珊

早在明末清初，就有一款“中药小零食”风靡宫廷。据《苍梧县志》记载，当时的苍梧郡（今广西梧州）制作售卖龟苓膏的店铺已有相当规模。龟苓膏店铺还会在店门口摆上一张八仙桌，放上一块巨大的龟壳，表示店不欺客，真材实料。龟苓膏中的“龟”，指的是名贵中药鹰嘴龟。它和土茯苓相结合，再配以生地黄、蒲公英、金银花、菊花等，制出的龟苓膏乌黑透明，药草清香，有清热解毒之效。

At the end of the Ming and beginning of the Qing dynasty, there was a kind of "medicinal snack" what was quite popular in the court. According to The Chronicles of Cangwu, the tortoise jelly of Cangwu (now Wuzhou) was selling quite well. The shops would position a square table at their entrance, upon which they would place a giant tortoise shell to show that the store was "for real" and used the exact ingredients. The "tortoise" in the jelly was an extract of the eagle-mouth tortoise, which was mixed with Tu Fu Ling (Rhizoma Smilacis Glabrae). Dried Rehamnia root, Herba Taraxaci, honeysuckle flower, chrysanthemum and other ingredients were added to produce a black, translucent jelly with a medicinal scent that was said to "reduce heat and remove toxins".

评论

美人难过“酸嘢”摊

Pickled Stuff

文：廖珊

新鲜的包菜、胡萝卜、木瓜、长豆角，放入清澈透亮、酸香扑鼻的酸水中，密封至陶罐或玻璃罐中。待到市集开市时，罐子一字排开，颇有排场。广西人热爱“酸嘢”，热爱到“英雄难过美人关，美人难过酸嘢摊”。而在广西，按照地域，“酸嘢”还分为都安（桂北）派和靖西（桂南）派。都安酸浓郁酸甜，靖西酸清新酸洌，都各自拥有数量庞大的粉丝群。

Fresh cabbage, carrots, papayas, and cowpea are placed in fresh vinegar water and then sealed in ceramic or glass jars. They stay there until it's time for the market; it's always an occasion when they're opened at the stands. The people of Guangxi love "pickled stuff", to the extent that one might say "even heroes fall for beauties, and even beauties fall for pickled stuff stands". Pickled stuff in Guangxi can be divided into two groups: the Du'an (northern) style, and the Jingxi (southern) style. The Du'an style is densely vinegary and sweet, whereas the Jingxi style is clearer and lighter; both have huge masses of fans.

酸嘢摊　摄影：陈炜平

一餐没豆豉，下饭总不香

Fermented Soybeans

文：廖珊

“县官爱豆豉，味道果然长。一餐没豆豉，下饭总不香。”相传清朝年间，出身黄姚镇的举人林作楫，去江西上任前，专门在自己的行李里放进了两坛豆豉。黄姚豆豉的特别在于，它可以随意搭配：与辣椒组合成豆豉辣椒酱；与姜丝合炒，是米粉的绝佳作料；与蒜瓣结合，焖排骨完全没问题。在黄姚镇，人们视它为万能调料。它也获得了“国家地理标志产品”称号。

"The county official loved fermented soybeans, which of course had a great flavor: a meal without them wasn't complete." It's said that during the Qing dynasty, Lin Zuoji, the successful candidate in the imperial examinations from Huangyao Town, before reporting to his post in Jiangxi, packed two jars of fermented soybeans in his luggage. What makes the fermented soybeans from Huangyao special is that they can go with anything. With chilies they can make soy chili sauce, with ginger shreds they can make a great accompaniment to rice noodle, with garlic cloves they can be used to slow-cook pork ribs. In Huangyao, people think of them as an all-purpose seasoning. They have been granted the status of a national product of geographical indication in China.

美食助推剂
Gourmet Propellant

文：唐晓燕

桂林人厨房里必备两个坛子——酸坛子和辣酱坛子。前者可以成就无数道菜，后者是众美食的“助推剂”。即便是清寡无油盐的白饭，亦或是白饭青菜“组合”，配上辣椒酱之后，那饭菜就多了色彩，味道也变得丰富。要问桂林辣椒酱的做法，随便找个桂林人都能说上一番：红辣椒、大蒜头剁碎，拌入豆豉，加入三花酒和细盐，密封入坛。看似简单的腌制，却各家有各家的味。辣椒酱还成了“桂林三宝”之一。

自制辣椒酱　摄影：陈炜平

You will always find two jars in every kitchen in Guangxi: a vinegar jar and a chili sauce jar. The former can be used for all kinds of dishes and the latter is a “gourmet propellant”. Whether it’s plain white rice or ordinary vegetable, the addition of some chili sauce makes for a full meal, one full of flavor. If you ask someone from Guilin how to make the chili sauce, anyone can tell you: red chilies and chopped garlic, mix in fermented soybeans, Sanhua (“three flowers”) Liquor and fine salt, and seal it in a jar. Even though the process is simple, each household has its own flavor. It’s one of the three treasures of Guilin.

全州剁剁茶
Quanzhou Chopped Tea

文：阳庆萍

广西全州的剁剁茶让人回味。饭后，女主人端出火盆，拿出平底铁锅、七字型木锤。浸泡过的茶叶伴着生姜，木锤起落，“剁剁”声中香味弥漫，加入一瓢水、一勺盐。女主人笑言：“盐出百味。”这时，茶水沸腾，倒入洁白小碗，茶汁如琥珀般闪亮，热气腾腾。喝上一口，既有茶香，更有姜味，回味无穷。

The chopped tea of Quanzhou in Guangxi is something that gives people lasting impressions. After a meal, the hostess will bring the fire basin and take out an iron pan and a wooden mallet. After being soaked, the tea is mixed with fresh ginger and pounded. A scoop of water and a spoon of salt are added, and it’s ready. The hostess smiles as she says: “The salt brings out all flavors.” The tea reaches a boil and is poured into a clean and clear white bowl. The tea flashes like amber. After a sip, the combined taste of tea and ginger leaves a lingering flavor in your mouth.

开海啦！

Sea Season

文：廖珊

每年8月，在经历了漫长的休渔期后，海鲜党们的福音来了！没错，一年一度的开海季（即捕捞季）终于拉开序幕。钦北防（钦州、北海、防城港）的高速路车堵为患，都是对海鲜口水流成河的向往。除了各种螃蟹、大虾，以及有"海上牛奶"之称的钦州大蚝，北海的沙虫要特书一笔。只生活在无污染浅滩的沙虫，自然有着最新鲜的海洋气息。每天清晨，渔民拿上小竹篓，在滩涂中寻找沙虫。别想依靠什么机械工具，只能用手捡，拾掇干净后白灼，再淋上蒜蓉拌的酱油，天然手作，是广西开海季最独特的美味。

Every year in August, after a long off-season, a joyous time rolls around for fans of seafood. Every year, the opening of the fishing season brings a lot of excitement. The highways to Qinzhou-Beihai-Fangchenggang are packed with cars, all of whom are heading towards the sea. Aside from all kinds of crabs, shrimp, and "seal milk" (that is, Qinzhou oysters), the peanut worms of Beihai are also quite sought after. They can only live in unpolluted beaches and have a naturally fresh flavor. Every morning, the fishers head out with small bamboo baskets in search of the worms. There aren't any machines or tools – they can only be caught by hand. After being cleaned up, they are boiled and then sprinkled with a bit of minced garlic mixed with soy sauce. Natural and prepared by hand – this is a unique taste of the fishing season in Guangxi.

肥美诱人的钦州生蚝　摄影：谢勇云

一股浓香，一缕温暖

Fragrance and Warmth

文：黄育娟

20 多年前，我还是个小孩子。那时，嘴特馋！每当听到街头大婶吆喝"芝麻糊咧！又香又甜的芝麻糊咧"，就会抓起零钱飞奔过去，喝了一碗又一碗。每次，都把碗沿舔得干干净净的。弹指一挥，20 多年过去了。前两年，在大婶摊前喝芝麻糊，走时把钱包和手机落下了。当我满头大汗回来找时，她笑着说："都在这，看看少了什么没有？"那一刻，感激之情无以言表，心里久久回味那句"南方黑芝麻糊"的经典广告词："一股浓香，一缕温暖！"

More than twenty years ago, I was still a child. At that time I loved to eat. Every time I'd hear the "yo-heave-ho" of a hawker on the street, I'd run over with my change. "Time for sesame paste! Fragrant and sweet sesame paste!" I'd drink bowl after bowl, licking the container clean each time. Now more than two decades have gone by. Two years ago, enjoying a bowl at an auntie's stand upon the street, I dropped my wallet and phone as I left. When I hurried back, sweating, she smiled and said, "Here you are. Please check if anything is missing." I was full of gratitude, and thought of the ad of "Southern Black Sesame Paste": it is "full of fragrance and warmth".

桂花香满桂林城

Osmanthus Everywhere

文：朱燕

桂花飘香，是桂林城最奇特的秋意。桂林人对桂花的热爱，经过岁月的积淀，已成为这座城市精神内涵所不可或缺的部分。桂花带给桂林人的，不仅是桂花香，桂林人还把自己这份桂花情结演绎到了更多领域，用桂花制成桂花茶、桂花酒、桂花糖、桂花糕、桂花酱等。这些各式各样的桂花制品在桂花的催化中也沉淀出了更丰富的味道。

In Guilin, it's a nice feeling to smell the drifting scent of osmanthus blossoms in autumn. The people here very much like these flowers, and over the passage of years they have become an essential part of the spirit of the city. People love the floral fragrance and bring the flower into other areas of their lives, such as osmanthus tea, liquor, candy, cakes, and paste. These various types of osmanthus products through the catalysis of the flower have formed even richer flavors.

评论

白切

Plain-Cut

文：廖珊

清代袁枚所著的《随园食单》中，关于鸡的佳肴就列了数十款，蒸、炮、煨、卤、糟，各种做法皆有，但在袁枚眼里，都不及“白片鸡”，说它有“太羹元酒之味”。这就是在两广盛行百年的“白切”。在广西陆川聚居着60万客家人。客家人向来追寻原汁原味，因此白切之法走入了千家万户，白切牛杂、白切猪手都是其中的经典菜式。

In Qing-dynasty author Yuan Mei's Suiyuan Recipes, he lists dozens of ways to prepare chicken – boiling, quick-frying, simmering, stewing, soaking in wine, and more. However, in his eyes, none of these compare to "plain-cut chicken", which he says has the flavor of "plain food for sacrifices". This "plain cut" chicken is popular in both Guangdong and Guangxi. More than 600,000 Hakka people live in Luchuan. Everyone here looks for original flavors, and for this reason, the plain-cut method of preparation is quite popular. Plain-cut beef tripe and pork trotters are also classic dishes.

白切鸡　摄影：陈炜平

桂林喀斯特地貌　摄影：许沂

山水·听音
Scenery and Sounds

通天佛道

The Way in the Sky

文：朱燕

桂平西山与佛有缘。说到佛道，最典型的就是西山上的120级台阶，相当于5层楼高，被誉为“通天道”。“通天道”一头在山上，一头却是连接着水，连接着西江，是有着桂平文化特色的码头，是佛道，也是人道。

Mount Xishan in Guiping has a connection with Buddhism. The most classic feature is the 120 steps, as high as a five-story building. They're referred to as the "stairway to the sky". One end is upon the mountain, and the other is at the Xijiang River. This is the way of the Buddha, and the way of people.

桂平西山通天佛道　摄影：陈炜平

青秀山之秀

Mount Qingxiu

文：朱燕

有人说青秀山是南宁青春洋溢、生机勃勃的“绿肺”，也有人说青秀山是南宁扬波荡漾的裙幅……青秀山秀美的内涵不仅在于自然天成，更在于开拓创新。她怡然安坐在南宁市郊，向南，温情脉脉地傍着邕江；向北，仪态大方地挽着东盟商务区、凤凰岭、铜鼓岭……她没有令人望而生畏的傲气，海拔仅289米，山不高可远足，林荫道好漫步。她植被繁茂，冬夏皆宜，草木共荣，四季常绿。

Some people say that Mount Qingxiu is the living "green lung" of Nanning, overflowing with spring; some people also say that it's a rippling skirt of the city. Mount Xingxiu's real beauty isn't just a matter of nature, but even more so one of opening up and innovation. It sits on the outskirts of Nanning; to the south is the flowing Yongjiang River; to the north is are ASEAN Business District, Phoenix Ridge, Tonggu Ridge... It doesn't have a formidable appearance. Being only 289 meters high; it's not tall but is a nice place for a hike. The forest path is nice to walk, the vegetative cover is dense, and the weather is nice in the winter and summer. Trees and grasses are always green.

桂林最神奇的“玉簪”

Most Mysterious Hairpin

文：朱燕

韩愈曾赞桂林山水：“江作青罗带，山如碧玉簪。”用“玉簪”比喻桂林山势再恰当不过。独秀峰，就是桂林最神奇的“玉簪”。1600年前始安（今广西桂林）郡守颜延之就写下“未若独秀者，峨峨郛邑间”。自唐代李靖在这里建子城开始，长达1400年的时间里，它都是桂林城的中心。“独秀挺立标地镇，千秋巍峙并华嵩”，道尽此峰作为桂林地标的权威地位。

Tang poet Han Yu once praised the scenery of Guilin: “The river runs here like a silk cord, and the mountain protrudes like a jade hairpin”. It couldn’t be more appropriate of a way to describe the mountain. The Duxiu Peak is the most mysterious “hairpin” in Guilin. One thousand six hundred years ago, the magistrate of the prefecture of Shi’an (now Guilin) wrote: “the Duxiu Peak towers over the wall and city”. From when Li Jing of the Tang dynasty started the construction of the inner city, over 1,400 years, it has been the center of Guilin. “The Duxiu Peak stands high and lofty upon the ground here.” The peak is a significant landmark and holds the most exalted position in Guilin.

象鼻山

Elephant’s Trunk

文：朱燕

桂林市桃花江和漓江汇合处，有一座因酷似巨象伸鼻吸水而得名的象鼻山。据说，这巨象原是玉帝的一位大将。一天，它来到美丽的桂林，玩得竟忘了吃饭睡觉，后来病倒，受到当地人的细心照顾。大象病好后帮助桂林人疏通水利，耕种良田，并想于此长留。玉帝得知后勃然大怒，派托塔李天王前去捉拿。正当大象在漓江边喝水时，不幸被李天王用箭射死，化为象鼻山。

Where the Taohuajiang and Lijiang rivers meet in Guilin, there is a mountain that looks very much like a giant elephant drinking water – Mount Xiangbi (“elephant’s trunk”). It’s said that this mountain was one of the Jade Emperor’s generals. One day, when he came to beautiful Guilin, he had such a good time that he forgot to eat and sleep. Later, he fell ill and was cared for by the locals. After his recovery, he helped the people with irrigation and agricultural work, and wanted to remain there. The Jade Emperor learned of this and became furious, and dispatched the Heavenly King with a Pagoda in Hand after him. As the elephant drank from the Lijiang River, he was shot with an arrow by the king and died, turning into the mountain.

桂林象鼻山　摄影：邓霆

舟游桂林，一日可遍至

Guilin Cruising

文：朱燕

两江四湖环城水系的建成改变了过去桂林市“东西一条街，南北一座桥”的市貌。今日之桂林，是景在城中、城在景中，堪称“东方威尼斯”。榕湖、杉湖、桂湖与木龙湖四湖相连，东接漓江，西通桃花江，恢复了始于宋代的“舟游桂林，一日可遍至”的环城水上游览线路。这里的灯光夜景或幽似春江诗话，或艳如火树银花……游船所到处，音乐喷泉或高亢激昂，或娓娓动听，让人流连忘返。

The round-the-city water system of two rivers and four lakes changed the former “a street from east to west, a bridge from north to south” appearance of Guilin. Today’s Guilin is a city within scenery, and a place of scenery within a city, almost like an “oriental Venice”. The Ronghu Lake, Shanhu Lake, Guihu Lake and Mulong Lake connect with each other, as well as the Lijiang River in the east and the Taohua Lake in the west. This brings back the Song dynasty situation: “One can travel all of Guilin on a boat in a single day.” The scenery of the lights at night is flamboyant or tranquil. Wherever these boats travel, there will be music and fountains, or great excitement, or a constant flow of pleasant sounds. It’s something to see and remember.

东郎西郎都是山

Donglang and Xilang

文：朱燕

福利古镇有一山于万顷田畴中拔起，山顶突出一巨石，酷似人像，又因其位于阳朔东部，故称“东郎山”。苏轼有诗云：“横看成岭侧成峰，远近高低各不同。”东郎山也如是：从东南面看，形似一柔情少女，美眉含笑；从正南面看，似一蹒跚老叟，信步闲游；从东面看，又似一戎装武士，肃立山野。东郎山附近有西郎山，还有大姑山、小姑山、月亮山、卓笔峰。诗人贺敬之游此，口占一绝：“东郎西郎江边望，大姑小姑情意长。望穿青峰成明月，诗仙卓笔写月光。”

In Fuli Old Town there is a mountain that rises in the middle of immense fields. On the peak there is a giant rock that looks like a person; as it’s situated in the eastern part of Yangshuo, it’s long been called Mount Donglang (“the man in the east”). Su Dongpo once wrote “It is a ridge when viewed at the front, and a peak viewed from its side. It changes its face when you change your position.” Mount Donglang is also like this. When you look at it from the southeast side, it resembles a gentle girl, smiling with beautiful eyebrows. From the direct south, it resembles a limping old man, strolling leisurely. From the east, it looks like a warrior in military attire, standing at attention in the fields. Near Donglang there is also Mount Xilang (“the man in the west”), Mount Dagu (“big aunt”), Mount Xiaogu (“little aunt”), Mount Yueliang (“moon”), and Zhuobi (“excellent brush pen”) Peak. Poet He Jingzhi traveled here and remarked: “Donglang and Xilang look over the river, and Dagu and Xiaogu stand there cordially. Looking past the green peak one sees the bright moon, which the Poet Master described with his excellent brush pen.”

鸳鸯秀水

Water Scene

文：朱燕

桂江、西江像两条彩带绕梧州城而过。放眼望去，只见西江浩淼，水流滔滔；桂江碧绿，波光粼粼。桂江清，西江浊，水旺时节，两江交汇处有着分明的清浊际线。宋代大诗人苏东坡当年获赦路经梧州，适逢中秋夜，面对清浊江水不禁吟诗赞道：“我爱清流频击楫，鸳鸯秀水世无双。”“鸳鸯秀水”之名也就从此传开。

The Guijiang and Xijiang rivers encircle Wuzhou like silk ribbons. Looking far out, one can see the torrents of the Xijiang River and the ripples of the Guijiang River. The Guijiang River is clear and the Xijiang muddy; when the waters are high, there is a clear line where the two come together and mix. When Song-dynasty poet Su Dongpo was pardoned, on his way back he passed Wuzhou, it happened to be an autumn night. He couldn't help but remark as he looked at the scene: “I seek to be an upright and clean person, and I love the two rivers joined together like male and female ducks.” This phrase became quite famous.

中越跨国大瀑布

Cross-Border Waterfall

文：朱燕

德天瀑布位于大新县硕龙镇德天村，横跨中越边境，又叫“中越跨国大瀑布”。瀑布由三大层景组合而成。第一层河水沿着绝壁山势俯冲落至一百多米下的深潭，其势震魂摄魄。第二层较低的山势造就了一个几十米的台阶，让第一层飞瀑冲下来有所喘息。第三层汇聚从源头流下的四散河水，串起一匹垂直的水幕，形成了一幅掩映在绿树怀抱之中的天然画卷，那雄壮、神奇与妖娆甚是令人拍案叫绝。

The Detian Waterfall is located in Detian Village, Shuolong Town, Daxin County, and straddles the border between China and Vietnam; it's also called the Sino-Vietnamese Cross-Border Waterfall. The site of the waterfall is made up of three layers of scenes. The first is the water passing over the precipice and plunging over 100 meters down to a deep pool; it's a stunning sight. The second is a lower part where the water takes a rest and flows over a step of a few dozen meters. The third is a curtain of water formed by the various streams from above, which looks like a natural painting among the green trees. It's a bold, mysterious and stunning scenery that makes one exclaim with approval.

德天瀑布　摄影：陈炜平

金子做的天梯

Golden Steps

文：朱燕

据说，有着“世界梯田之冠”美称的龙脊梯田的开凿始于元代。由于依山而建，所以梯田大者不过一亩，小者仅能插下两三行禾苗，故有“青蛙一跳三块田”“一床蓑衣盖过田”之说。数百年间，经过多少代人的劳作，龙脊梯田日臻形成从山脚一直盘绕到山顶、“小山如螺，大山成塔”的壮丽景观。收获时节，龙脊梯田中熟透的水稻色泽金黄，从山脚一直蜿蜒盘绕到山顶，仿佛一条金子做的天梯。

It's said the "best terraced fields in the world" are the Longji ("dragon's spine") terraces, first dug in the Yuan dynasty. As they're built on the mountains, the larger ones are less than 700 square meters, and the smaller ones sometimes only have two or three rows of rice. In the past, people said that "a frog could jump over three fields in a leap" and that "a single straw raincoat could cover one", among other things. Over the course of centuries, they have been worked by many people, and the terraces gradually came to encircle the entire mountains up to their peaks. It's a beautiful sight, with "small mountains like spiral shells and large mountains like pagodas". When the harvest season rolls around, the squashy paddies of the Longji terraces shine with gold luster, winding all the way from the foot to the top of the mountain, golden steps to the sky.

愿做桂林人，不愿做神仙

Better in Guilin

文：朱燕

叠彩山紧傍桂林漓江西岸，因其山石层层横断，如彩绸锦缎相叠而得名。古代因山上多桂树而称“桂山”；又由于山中有个四季生风的洞，又叫“风洞山”。叠彩山海拔不过 73 米。主峰明月峰有许多古今名人留下的脍炙人口的诗篇和名言，让人印象最深的是“愿做桂林人，不愿做神仙”。这是 1963 年陈毅陪同西哈努克亲王来桂林时留下的名言，它成为对“桂林山水甲天下”的最好诠释。

Mount Diecai ("folded brocade") is very close to the western bank of the Lijiang River in Guilin. Because of the layers upon layers of differently colored stone, it appears like a pile of folded silk brocade. In olden times many people called it "Mount Laurel" due to the number of laurel trees upon it. It also has a cave in it that makes wind year-round, and thus is also called "Windy Cave Mountain". Its total height is less than 73 meters. Its main peak, Mingyue ("bright moon") Peak has had many very popular poems written about it, one of the most famous containing the line "Better to be a person of Guilin than an immortal". This was written by the Minister of Foreign Affairs Chen Yi in 1963 when he accompanied former and later king of Cambodia Norodom Sihanouk to Guilin, and is one of the best lines penned extolling the virtues of the city.

花的山，花的海

Mountains and Seas of Flowers

文：朱燕

猫儿山因山形如猫而得名。其主峰为五岭之首越城岭山脉的最高峰神猫顶，海拔 2141.5 米，是华南第一高峰。猫儿山杜鹃科的植物品种多达 46 种，大多属于珍稀的高山杜鹃，其中猫儿山杜鹃、红瘦杜鹃、紫蓝花杜鹃、美丽杜鹃、子花杜鹃等为其特有。每到初夏，高山杜鹃漫山遍野地绽放，形成了猫儿山独有的“杜鹃的世界、花的海洋”的景致。

Mao’er Mountain is so named as it looks like a cat. Its primary peak is the highest in a series of five, Shenmao (“divine cat”) Peak. It has an elevation of 2141.5 meters above sea level, making it the highest peak in south China. There are 46 species of ericaceae on the mountain, most of which are rare high-mountain rhododendrons, such as the Rhododendron maoerense, named for the mountain itself, the many-petaled thin red flowers of Rhododendron simsii Planch, the purple Rhododendron russatum, Rhododendron bellum with its broad petals in soft colors, and the Rhododendron flosulum with dense, tightly packed petals on its blooms. Every year at the start of summer, the high mountain is covered with an explosion of blooms, making for the famous sight of “mountains and seas of flowers”.

华南第一峰——猫儿山　摄影：张小宁

归春河

Guichun River

文：朱燕

归春河源出靖西县，全长约 150 公里，途经越南迂回 35 公里后又折回广西，故当地边民叫它“归春河”，寓意为“归国遇春”。从德天村至硕龙镇那段河道就是天然的国界，河面宽 30 米。从河边看对岸村子，山下土路上停着一长溜花花绿绿的大货车，装着药材、咖啡、香烟、香水、农产品等，要到中国来……

The Guichun (“returning of spring”) River originates in Jingxi County, and is 150 kilometers in total length, meandering into Vietnam for 35 kilometers before returning to Guangxi. It’s so named by the locals because it “returns to China in spring”. From Detian Village to Shuolong Town, the river forms a natural national boundary. The river is 30 meters wide, and villagers across the way can see each other on the opposite bank. On a dirt mountain road waits a large lorry, full of medicinal materials, coffee, cigarettes, perfume, agricultural products and more. It’s coming to China.

会“变脸”的湖

Changing Lake

文：朱燕

隆安更望湖属季节湖，水来得快去得快，短短几天就蓄满水，短短几天又跑得无影踪，像“变脸”一般。冬季枯水时，村民便在湖底种上三角麦。每年冬春，三角麦花开正艳，白茫茫一片，置身其中，像走进了白雪皑皑的塞北天国。春风吹拂，绿色麦浪卷着白色浪花袭来，更兼四周青山如黛，牛群散落……那种闲逸，那种静谧，仿佛世外桃源、人间天堂。

The Gengwang Lake of Long'an is a seasonal lake; the water comes quickly and goes quickly. In just a few days it fills up, and just a few later it's gone without a trace, just like a "face changing" performance. During the winter when the lake is dry, the people of the village plant buckwheat on the bed of the lake. Every year in winter and spring the flowers of the plants are in bloom, forming a huge white sheet that makes you feel like you've stepped into a snowy field. The spring wind blows, and waves of white flowers undulate. The mountains all around are deep and dark in color, and groups of cattle graze around. This leisure and tranquil atmosphere makes one feels as if in paradise.

鹅泉

Goose Spring

文：朱燕

鹅泉，位于靖西市西南约6公里处，面积约两公顷。鹅泉水清如镜，四季不涸，为西南地区三大明泉之一。相传古时候，念安屯有一位姓杨的老妈妈在山上捡到两个鹅蛋，爱不释手，常温怀里。日子久了，竟孵出两只鹅来。一日，一对小鹅在水中游玩，忽然天昏地暗，雷雨大作，轰隆一声，池塘塌落，变成深潭！从此，泉水奔涌，浩浩荡荡……

Goose Spring is situated approximately six kilometers south-west to Jingxi City and covers about two hectares. The water is as clear as a mirror and never runs dry. It's one of the three most famous springs in southwest China. According to legend, an old woman surnamed Yang in Nian'an Village collected two goose eggs from the ground. She was fond of them and incubated them by holding them in her arms. Not long afterward, two geese hatched. One day, the two goslings were playing in the water when suddenly the sky turned dark, and great rains came about. Thunder cracked out, and the shallow bond collapsed, forming a deep pool. After this, spring water has continuously flowed out.

评论

防城港金滩彩虹　摄影：陈炜平

那坡风光　摄影：张小宁

圣堂山　摄影：张小宁

圣堂杜鹃

Shengtang Blossoms

文：朱燕

圣堂山在广西金秀，那里生长的高山杜鹃天下闻名。每年四月，圣堂山杜鹃花开得热烈。花海从半山腰起，一直绵延到山顶。当那漫山遍野的山花开放时，油画般的世界便铺张开来，仿佛只用了一种浑然天成的写意，就让全天下的色彩彻底臣服，渲染了人世间少有的神奇或不可思议。

Mount Shengtang ("sanctuary") is located in Jinxiu, Guangxi. The high-mountain rhododendrons that grow there are famous. Every year in April, they bloom with great energy. The sea of flowers extends from the mid-reaches to the very top of the mountain. When these wildflowers are all in bloom, a world like an oil painting opens up extravagantly, as if the natural world has been filled with color by brushwork, making for a wonderful and mystifying scene.

神秘大龙湖

Big Dragon

文：朱燕

上林大龙湖景区以山奇水秀而著称。大龙湖因传说中的壮族短尾龙"特掘"留于此处生活而得名。大龙洞内有"钟乳石林""万年神龟""大象饮水""七仙女晒裙""六十大罗汉""雄狮相斗""牛郎织女银河相会""点兵台"等景点。它的神奇在于，你在黑暗的山洞里摸索着每走一段路，都能看见一个明亮的天窗直通天穹，那是关于黑暗的惊喜，又是人与上苍的对话。

The Dalong ("big dragon") Lake Scenic Site on Shanglin County is famous for its beautiful mountains and waters. According to the legends of the Zhuang people, Dalong Lake was the place where "Tejue", a famous short-tailed dragon chose to stay. The Dalong Cave has many interesting sites, such as the "stalactite forest", "ancient turtle", "drinking elephant", "seven fairies sunning dresses", "sixty great arhats", "battling lions", "meeting of the Cowherd and Weaving Maid at the Milky Way", "roll call platform". What makes it so fascinating is that within the darkness wherever you go, you can find a bright skylight in the high vaulting. These are surprises in the dark, and dialogues of humans with the sky.

一条河流的边关情

Border Feelings

文：严风华

水口河河面不宽，约20来米，是条中越界河。一撑竹排，水面起澜，就可到对岸去了。两岸竹林青翠，蕉叶、果树茂盛。农舍隐约其中，炊烟相织，鸡犬相闻。每逢圩日，或红白喜事，两国边民便穿梭于林荫道上，只要跳上竹排，就可到对岸聚在一起了。大家穿的都是同样的服饰，越南人可以讲壮话，壮族人可以讲越语，分不出彼此。

The surface of the Shuikou River isn't wide, at approximately twenty meters. This is a border between China and Vietnam. One can float to the other side on a bamboo raft. The bamboo forests on both banks are verdant, and farmhouses are hidden among the dense woods of fruit trees. Smoke from kitchens floats upwards as the chickens and dogs call out. On market days or those of weddings and funerals, people go through the woods, hop on bamboo rafts and gather together at the opposite bank. Everyone wears the same kinds of clothing, the Vietnamese can speak Zhuang, and the Zhuang can speak Vietnamese; they can't be told apart.

百里漓江，美甲天下

River Site, River Sight

文：彭匈

漓江的美名，早在1000多年前的唐代就已传到了都城长安，杜甫、韩愈、白居易皆留下咏桂林的佳作。美国前总统尼克松说："我们所访问过的城市中，没有一个比得上桂林美丽。"而对于漓江山水的神韵，现代诗人贺敬之写下的《桂林山水歌》最为动人，诗的开头两句就韵味十足："云中的神啊雾中的仙，神姿仙态桂林的山；情一样的深啊梦一样的美，如情似梦漓江的水。"

More than a thousand years ago during the Tang dynasty, the Lijiang River was already known in the capital, Chang'an; great poets such as Du Fu, Han Yu and Bai Juyi wrote praises to its beauty. Former US president Richard Nixon said, "Of all the cities we have visited, none compare with Guilin." The romantic features of the river have been best captured by "Song of the Scenery of Guilin" by contemporary poet He Jingzhi; the first two lines of the poem are full of charm: "Deity in the clouds and sages in the mist; the fairy-like mountains of Guilin. Deep like love and beautiful like a dream, is the Lijiang River."

漓江秀色　摄影：张小宁

龙首翘望的湘楚之地

The Blessed Land

文：朱燕

集丹霞地貌精华于一身的八角寨又名云台山，以其主峰生出八个翘角并常年云蒸霞蔚而得名。八角寨好些山岭都以“龙”命名。龙脊岭，逶迤延伸，形若弄雾拨云；龙头山，威风凛凛，意欲掀天揭地；二龙戏珠，悠荡神怡，傲视天下无敌。相传很久以前，有人预测，八角寨龙首翘望的湘楚之地，会因龙的灵气造就一代伟人。如今在朦胧弥漫中，人们可见山岗内居高仰卧一巨大身躯，形态酷似巨人于斯安详长眠。明代著名旅行家徐霞客于崇祯十年（1637 年）游至此地，面对此景，曾赞叹不已。

An excellent example of the unusual Danxia landforms is in Bajiaozhai (“fort with eight bulges”), which has eight bulges on its main peak. It is also known as Mount Yuntai (“platform in clouds”) as rose clouds rise year round. A number of ridges here have “long” (“dragon”) in their name, such as Longji (“dragon’s spine”) Ridge which meanders as it stretches on, as if creating mist and scattering clouds, Mount Longtou (“dragon’s head”) which inspires awe with its earth-shaking appearance. The dragons play with each other, swing, sway, and look down at the earth below. It’s said that long ago someone predicted that a certain place in Hunan and Hubei, where the dragon is gazing at, would give birth to a great person. Today, people can see that a huge body lies within a hillock, as if it is in the midst of a very long slumber. When the Ming-dynasty traveler Xu Xiake visited here in 1637, facing this site, he was struck with awe.

老山界的之字路

Laoshanjie

文：朱燕

老山界，一个扣人心弦的名字，它是中央红军 1934 年离开江西开始二万五千里长征途中翻越的第一座险峻难走的大山。“在‘之’字拐的路上一步步地上去。向上看，火把在头顶上一点点排到天空；向下看，简直是绝壁。”每次走进山里，总会情不自禁想起陆定一写下的著名篇章《老山界》，想起当年红军长征翻越老山界时惊心动魄的情景。

Laoshanjie (“old mountain zone”) is a name that plucks at ones’ heartstrings. It was the first precipitous and hard-to-cross mountain encountered by the Central Red Army in their Long March. “We had to cross over switchback roads slowly. Looking upwards, there were lines of torches snaking along the slope; looking downwards, it was practically a cliff.” Every time one walks upon the mountain, one can’t help thinking of these words written by Lu Dingyi in Laoshanjie, the harrowing ordeal the Red Army endured when crossing the mountain.

万山群中河都高速公路特大桥——聋竹坪大桥　摄影：周军

田东棋盘滩，等你来对弈　摄影：张小宁

广西庐山

Another Mount Lushan

文：朱燕

用“飞流直下三千尺，疑是银河落九天”形容有着“广西庐山”之称的大明山瀑布，也很恰当。进得山来，到处可以听到“哗啦哗啦”的水声，越往深处，水声也越大。峰回路转，便看见天抛银链的飞泉穿空腾跃，从两山的缺口冲下万丈松崖，悬水丰盈，飞珠四溅，水声震荡峡谷。飞瀑击打在周边山石和地面上，使得云雾弥漫，迎面扑来，气势磅礴，蔚为壮观。

“Water falls through four thousand feet; it makes one think that maybe the Milky Way has fallen from the sky”. It is very appropriate to use these lines by Li Bai to describe the Damingshan Waterfall which is compared to Mount Lushan in Guangxi. When one enters the mountain area, one can hear the roaring of the water; the closer one approaches, the louder it gets. After summiting and turning back, one sees the flow crashing down between the gap in the two mountains, flying through the air, throwing pearls of water all about. The waterfall pounds the rocks and ground, making a scene cloudy and misty. It’s a powerful and moving sight.

古井喷乳

Milky Spring

文：朱燕

在桂平西山上，一棵根须裸露的大榕树下有碑刻一块，楷书“乳泉”二字笔力雄健深厚，为清道光年间浔州知府胡南藩所写。据清同治年间的《浔州府志》云：乳泉“清冽如杭州龙井，而甘美过之。时有汁喷出，白如乳，故名乳泉”。有人说，古井喷乳，十年难遇，每冒一次“白乳”即意味着桂平兴旺。乳泉喷汁现象最近一次发生在 1981 年夏天一场大雨过后，泉井恰似一锅煮沸的牛奶，持续四五分钟后才渐渐消散、净尽。

Upon Mount Xishan in Guiping there is a stone stele among the exposed roots of a large banyan tree, with the two words “milky spring” written in strong regular script upon it. This is the writing of Hu Nanfan, the magistrate of Xunzhou during the Daoguang reign of the Qing dynasty. In the Provincial Documentation of Xunzhou, the spring water is described as “clear like the Dragon Well of Hangzhou but even sweeter. Occasionally it will spew up broth which is white like milk; for this reason, it’s called the Milky Spring.” Some people say that this rare occurrence that happens less than once a decade signals that things will go well in Guiping. The last time the phenomenon occurred was after heavy rain in 1981. It was as if boiling milk shot forth from the spring for four or five minutes before slowly dying out.

桂平乳泉古井　摄影：陈炜平

潭蓬古运河

Tanpeng Ancient Canal

文：朱燕

防城港市江山半岛的潭蓬运河古道是中国古代唯一一条海上运河。因为在岩石上开凿一条运河无异于天方夜谭，以致后人难以相信祖先留下的这条泽被后世的运河是人工开凿的，于是称它为“仙人泷”。潭蓬运河古道水清澈，山翠绿，石碑后有个壁台，石坪有青苔，常有水流下。水库两岸，林木茂盛，树上野果鲜艳欲滴。据说，这里每年还会有许多白鹭翩然而过。

Situated in Fangchenggang City, the Tanpeng Canal upon the Jiangshan Peninsula boasts the only sea canal in ancient China. Carving a canal out of the rock is like something out of Arabian Nights; people who benefit a lot from the canal find it unbelievable that it was really made by their ancestors. For this reason, it's referred to as the "divine watercourse". The water in the canal is clear, the mountains are green, behind the stone steles there are platforms, and moss grows upon the stones where water flows continuously. On the two banks of the reservoir, trees and shrubs grow thickly, with wild fresh fruit upon them. It's said that every year a large number of egrets fly by.

壮族的神山圣地

Sacred Place

文：朱燕

“山不在高，有仙则名。”应该说，先有仙人，后有圣地。敢壮山的圣人就是布罗陀和姆六甲。传说，为繁衍人类，他们受大帝委派下凡。启程那天，他们挑着一对大箩筐，一头装着 5 个小孩，一头装着被褥、农具。飘到田阳上空时，暴风雨骤来，担子忽从布罗陀肩上脱落，装被褥的箩筐滑下，就成了敢壮山；5 个孩子散落周边，就成了五指（子）山。锄头坠落之处，撞出一道弯弯的大裂沟，形成了右江河。布罗陀和姆六甲就住在敢壮山上，繁衍出了壮族后人。

"A mountain is famous not for its height, but for the immortals living in it." One should say that immortal comes first, and then the sacred place. Mount Ganzhuang's immortals are Buluotuo and Muliujia, the ancestors of the Zhuang people. In order to propagate the human race, they were sent down to the world of mortals. When they set out, they carried a pair of big bamboo baskets, with five children in one, and bedding and agricultural tools in the other. When they were floating downwards, a great storm came about, and the carrying pole that Buluotuo had on his shoulders fell down. The basket of bedclothes formed Mount Ganzhuang. The five children fell near it formed Mount Wuzhi ("five fingers" or "five kids"). When the hoe fell, a huge ditch was dug, which became the Youjiang River. Buluotuo and Muliujia lived upon Mount Ganzhuang and gave birth to the Zhuang people.

道家第二十洞天——容县都峤山　摄影：陈炜平

道家第二十洞天
Twentieth Cave

文：朱燕

容县都峤山是丹霞地貌，形状奇特，气势恢宏，山中植被丰富，沟壑幽深。当年大学士苏东坡被贬海南，来回走的就是北流水路。在都峤山中修道的邵彦甫道士是苏东坡的同窗好友，更是他的铁杆粉丝，下山追随他到海南生活了三年。苏东坡获赦从海南归来，邵彦甫又陪他到藤州玩乐了十来天。苏学士给他写了不少诗，其中一首是《送邵道士归都峤洞天》。

Mount Duqiao in Rong County has a Danxia landscape; it's special in its form, and is extensive and deep. When scholar Su Dongpo was sent down to Hainan, he took the water route of Beiliu River. The Taoist priest Shao Yanfu who practiced in the mountain was a classmate and friend of Su Dongpo, as well as a great fan of his. He went down from the mountain and followed Su to Hainan, living there for three years. When Su was pardoned and came back, Shao accompanied him to Tengzhou to have fun for ten or so days. Su wrote him many poems, one of which was Shao's Return to Duqiao.

岩石连，出状元
Zhuangyuan Stone

文：朱燕

桂林漓江之滨的伏波山，是一座依水傍水的孤峰，汉时伏波将军马援南征曾经过此地，故得名。还珠洞里有一悬挂的巨石，离地一寸许。有传说伏波将军马援在此巨石旁试剑，一剑断巨石，故名“试剑石”。民间相传试剑石能伸缩，若“岩石连，出状元”，因而又叫“状元石”。

Mount Fubo is on the bank of the Lijiang River in Guilin; it's a single peak near the waterway. During the time of the Han dynasty when General Fubo went south conducting military action, he passed by here. The Huanzhu (“returning pearl”) Cave has a hanging stone within, suspended about an inch over the ground. Legend says that when General Fubo practiced his sword next to this giant stone, it was split with a single stroke of the blade. Thus it is named the “sword-testing stone”. It's said it could expand and contract; every time it touches the ground, Guilin will produce a zhuangyuan (“scholar of the highest grade, placing first in the imperial examinations”), and thus it is also known as the “zhuangyuan stone”.

桂东南第一峰

First Peak in South-eastern Guangxi

文：朱燕

广西北流市城区北面，因“其迴阔无所不容”而得名的大容山，林木终年常绿，四季花开果熟，山涧瀑布飞溅，鸟兽啾啾争鸣。海拔 1100 多米的莲花峰一带，形成了世界罕见的高山草甸、高山湖泊、高山飞瀑、高山圣诞林的综合景观，被誉为“华夏欧景”。山上珍稀动植物繁多，除了“活化石”老桫椤、“花中之王”金茶花，还有黄猄、松鼠、千年龟……还有一种“恐怖”的山蚂蟥，饮血海量，咬人不觉，久驱不去……

In the north of Beiliu City in Guangxi, Mount Darong (“great contents”) is said to encompass vastness. The trees are always green, and flowers bloom and fruits ripen year round. Waterfalls cascade, and birds and beasts compete with their calls. Upon the 1,100-meter Lotus Peak, there are unusual high-altitude grassy marshlands, lakes, waterfalls, and forests which have a kind of European feel. There are many rare animals and plants upon the mountain; aside from the “living fossil” of the spinulose tree fern, there are also the “king of flowers” golden camellia, Indian muntjacs, squirrels, and old tortoises. There are also terrifying mountain leeches that have a huge appetite for blood, bite stealthily, and are hard to drive off…

玉林大容山　摄影：陈炜平

天下第一滩

First Beach

文：朱燕

被誉为“天下第一滩”的北海银滩属于典型的亚热带海洋性气候，年平均气温为 23 度左右。到了银滩，你可以不游泳、不冲浪，但绝不可以不玩赏那些颗粒分明的浪沙。这些沙粒细腻致密，若是人在潮水刚退去的海滩上漫步，甚至连脚印都不会留下。

Lauded as the “first beach”, the Silver Beach at Beihai has a subtropical marine climate.The average yearly temperature is 23 degrees. When you come here, you don’t have to swim or surf, but you must play upon the sands. The sand grains are so fine and dense that even footprints will not be left after you walking on the beach where the tide has just receded.

巴马命河　摄影：陈炜平

巴马命河

Minghe River

文：朱燕

巴马命河位于巴马母亲河盘阳河源头之一的那社乡。命河在那社乡田垌里左拐右弯，从高处俯视，酷似一个巨型草书体“命”字镶嵌在广袤的田野间，让人称奇。命河孕育了许多寿星。沿岸百岁以上的老寿星多达80余人，占巴马寿乡百岁老人比例的三分之二以上，八九十岁的长者更是不足为奇。神奇独特的命河，是寿星南极仙翁恩赐寿乡巴马的印鉴，保佑着一代又一代的巴马人健康长寿。

The Minghe River is at Nashe Village, which is the source of the Panyang River, the mother river of Bama. It winds through the fields in the village left and right. Viewed from above it looks like the word 命 (“fate” or “life”) inlaid into the vast landscape. The Minghe River has raised many people of longevity; more than 80 centenarians are living along this river, two-thirds of all the in Bama. People in their eighties and nineties are quite normal here. The special and mysterious Minghe River is a gift from Longevity God to the Bama people, protecting generation after generation into their late years.

金鸡山古炮台

Mountaintop Batteries

文：朱燕

海拔 596 米的金鸡山位于友谊关西侧。金鸡山三座山头鼎足而立，各有炮台一座，分别为镇北、镇中、镇南炮台。每座炮台装有德国克虏伯兵工厂制造的 120 毫米要塞巨炮一门，每门重达数万斤。1907 年 12 月，孙中山、黄兴等发动镇南关起义，孙中山亲自在镇北炮台放炮轰击清兵。如今，伫立山顶，那历经了一百多年风雨的大炮仍傲视群山，虎威依旧……

The 596-meter Mount Jinji ("golden chicken") is located on the west side of the Youyi ("friendship") Fort. Its three heads stand tall with a battery on the top of each. They're known as the Zhenbei ("pacifying the north"), Zhenzhong ("pacifying the center") and Zhennan ("pacifying the south") batteries. Each battery has a 120-mm fortress cannon made by the Krupp Arsenal of Germany, weighing tens of thousands of kilograms. In December 1907, Sun Yat-Sen and Huang Hsing started an uprising at Zhennan Fort, and Sun himself bombarded the Qing troops from the Zhenbei Battery. Today, they still stand there, looking over the mountains after more than a century, still as frightful as grand tigers.

"环保菜"遍开澄江河

Environmental Consciousness

文：朱燕

有别于其他湿地公园，都安澄江国家湿地公园是目前国内唯一集河流湿地、城市湿地、农耕湿地于一体的喀斯特湿地公园。值得一提的是，公园里有一条会开花的河，名叫澄江河。一年四季，河面上都会大面积盛开白色的海菜花，美不胜收。海菜花是我国特有的一种濒危水生植物，对水质很敏感，一旦水质受到污染便不能生长。所以，当地人又亲切地称它为"环保菜"。

Unlike other wetland parks, the Chengjiang National Wetlands Park in Du'an is the only karst wetland park in China to comprise river wetlands, urban wetlands, and agricultural wetlands. It's worth noting that the park has a river with flowers in it, the Chengjiang River. All year long, white flowers of the Ottelia acuminata bloom upon the surface of the lake; it's quite a beautiful sight. The endangered plant is only found in China and is very sensitive to water quality. If the water is polluted at all, it won't grow. For this reason, the people here call it the "environmentally conscious vegetable".

评论

南方天险——昆仑关
Kunlun Fort

文：朱燕

踏上那331级台阶，站在素有“南方天险”之称的昆仑关山顶，中国军人在民族危亡之际的大气和凛然盖天而降。阵亡将士纪念塔碑主体为正三棱型，如枪似剑直指苍穹，塔上竖刻着“陆军第五军昆仑关战役阵亡将士纪念塔”，塔座正面刻有“碧血千秋”四字。为纪念这一千年古关和缅怀抗日阵亡的将士，每逢农历五月十三，昆仑关一带的群众就会自发组织开展各种形式的祭拜活动，并渐渐形成一个传统节日——关公磨刀节。

Walking up the 331 steps and standing upon the “natural barrier of the south” – Kunlun Fort, one will feel the tremendous courage of Chinese soldiers trying to save their country. The stele that stands in honor of those who died in the battle has three sides, like a sword or spear pointed at the sky. Upon it is written “Memorial Tower to the Soldiers of the Fifth Army Who Gave their Lives at the Kunlun Fort Battle”. The front face of the base has the words “In Memory of the Blood Shed for Justice”. To commemorate the millennium-old fort and those soldiers who perished fighting the Japanese, every year on the thirteenth day of the fifth lunar month, groups of people organize all kinds of memorial services, which have gradually formed a traditional holiday – “the day of the god of war sharpening his sword”.

从太阳里流出的河
River out of the Sun

文：朱燕

红水河是珠江流域西江水系干流，因洪水期河水呈红色得名。红水河滩多流急，礁石林立，暗流漩涡密布，水态复杂却丰富，水能巨大。其所孕育的百越文化，与自然恩赐呈现出一种互为滋养的生存状态。红水河生生不息，“这不是神话，也不是传说，壮乡有一条从太阳里流出的河……”

The Hongshui (“red water”) River is a trunk river in the Xijiang River water system; it gets its name from the fact that it turns red in times of flood. The river has many rapids and flows quickly; it has many reefs and hidden whirlpools, complicated but rich in hydro energy. It nurtured the Baiyue Culture, which is in harmony with the nature. It constantly flows: “This is not a myth, this is not a legend; this is a river in the Zhuang region that flows out of the sun…”

天峨红水河泛舟　摄影：张小宁

涠洲岛地貌　摄影：陈炜平

海神胸前的翡翠玉

Sea and Jade

文：朱燕

太阳越升越高，海面极目处与天空连到一起，像一张广阔无边的蓝色幕布，柔软而平静地舒展开来。涠洲岛，这个弓形小岛正如海神胸前的一块翡翠玉，在北部湾湛蓝的海面上凸起。斑斓的火山岩和多姿的海蚀地貌，是大自然鬼斧神工的艺术创造。此时，它正吸引着众多游人的惊叹目光。

As the sun rises higher and higher, the endless surface of the sea seems to join with the sky, like a vast, seamless curtain of blue, softly and calmly unfurling. Weizhou Island, rising from the blue ocean of Beibu Gulf, looks like a crescent jade in front of the chest of the "sea god". It attracts many visitors to marvel at the colorful igneous rocks and marine abrasion landform, a masterpiece of the Great Nature.

广西第三高峰

Third Peak in Guangxi

文：朱燕

融水元宝山为广西第三高峰，其山体就像个巨大元宝巍然耸立在万山间，故名“元宝山”。此峰山顶平坦，常年积雪，雪水汇集成一汪碧池。山中还有新发现的200余株生长于第四纪冰川时期的珍稀树种——冷杉，其千年不倒之风范，令人感怀。清澈的贝江穿流于峰峦间。每年“放排”季节，大批竹、木排顺江而下，破浪飞驰，篙师的勇敢和智慧令人惊叹不已。

Mount Yuanbao ("ingot") is the third-highest peak in Guangxi. The body of the mountain resembles a giant ingot towering between the other mountains, thus the name. The peak of the mountain is flat and gathers snow all year round. The snow melts and forms a lake. In the mountain, more than 200 fir trees from the Quaternary Ice Age have been discovered. These trees, standing there after a millennium, are imposing. The clear Beijiang River passes through the ridges. Every year during the "rafting season", a large number of bamboo rafts and timber rafts float down the river, flying along as they break the waves, skilled punters bravely and cleverly working their trade.

金秀六巷瑶族婚礼　摄影：张小宇

民俗·遍观

Customs and Views

姑妈“挂白”

Auntie's White

文：翟香丽

那坡县彝族尚白。每当新屋落成，姑妈就会带上长长的白布，从神堂开始，越过中梁和上梁，一直伸延至大门口，布尾还连着一米来长的白穗子。有些人家姑妈多，堂屋不够挂，就扩展到左右两边的房间。通屋的银白如雪，是姑妈们洁白美好的祝愿，也是屋主至高无上的荣耀。

The Yi People of Napo County hold the color white in high esteem. Whenever a new dwelling is constructed, the married sisters of the head of the household will bring long strips of white cloth, hanging them from the alcove to the middle and then upper rafter, all the way to the main entrance of the house. These strips of fabric have tassels a meter long. Some households have many sisters, and in these cases, the main hall hasn't enough room. Thus the area is expanded to the rooms on either side. These pure snow-white strips of cloths are wishes for cleanliness and beauty from the women, as well as the greatest glory of the homeowner.

锦上花开会有时

Brocade

文：翟香丽

青山绿水间，古镇人家里，木制织机上，轻拢慢打，浅吟低唱，姑娘们开始织壮锦啦。“那朵朵盛开在锦上的繁花，那寸寸织就出灿烂民族文化的光阴，就这样在壮乡女子纤巧的十指中”倾泻而出，凝刻了时光的味道，鲜艳而不张扬，仿佛轻轻推开了千年时光的门扉。

Amidst beautiful landscapes of verdant mountains and azure streams, in the homes of the people of the old villages, women sing as they work slowly making Zhuang brocade on wooden looms. They work meticulously, bringing the intricate designs of the brocade to life with care and deft skill. The product is a crystallization of the time and place, beautiful and reserved; it's almost like opening up a door to a time a thousand years ago.

织锦　摄影：张小宁

给树喂肉

Feeding the Trees

文：翟香丽

树是隆林仡佬族人生生不息的依靠，所以他们会拜树。跪拜完毕，会有一位德高望重的老者主持“喂树”仪式。在老者指挥下，一男子执刀在树皮上砍三个口子，另一男子将肉饭酒菜“喂”于刀口之中。喂食之时，对不同的树要说不同的话，比如对果树，要说：“喂你饭，结串串；喂你肉，结坨坨。”最后老者用红纸把刀口封住，众人给树除草培土，仪式结束。

The Gelao people of Longlin have a close connection to trees throughout their lives, and for this reason, they worship them. After kneeling in front of them, an anointed elder will conduct the “tree feeding” ceremony. Under his direction, a man will cut three holes into the tree’s bark with a knife, and another man will put meat, rice, alcohol, and vegetables into the holes to “feed” the tree. There are different songs sung to different trees when feeding them, such as “I feed you rice so you may grow tall; I feed you meat so you may grow strong.” Finally, the elder seals these holes with red paper, and the gathered people weed around and earth up the tree.

惜发如命红瑶女

Cherishing Hair

文：翟香丽

在桂林龙脊的山涧溪边，常可见三五成群的红衣女子临溪梳洗，一头乌黑的长发如同瀑布般倾泻而下。红瑶女子视头发为生命的一部分，一生只在 18 岁时剪一次头发，标志着长大成人，而且剪掉的头发要保存好，出嫁时要盘在新娘的长发里，作为嫁妆的一部分。通过长发的盘法，可以辨别红瑶女子的身份：盘圆型又包头巾的是未婚女子；盘圆型不包头巾，前面没有发髻的是已婚未育的少妇；盘圆型不包头巾，前有一个发髻的是已婚已育的妇女。

In the river valleys around Guilin, one can see groups of women washing up alongside rivers. Their hair spills down like a waterfall. The women of the Red Yao people view hair as part of their lives; it is only cut once at 18 years of age, showing that the girl has grown up. The cut hair is saved, and when a woman marries it is wound in the bride’s hair as part of her bridal makeup. Looking at the style, one can differentiate the identities of these Red Yao women: a coil with a scarf is an unmarried girl, a coil with a scarf but no bun is a young married woman who has not had children, and a coil with no scarf and a bun is for a woman who has married and had children.

评论

有情赠你小花帽

Flowered Hat for Love

文：翟香丽

传说很久以前，一个青年带着自己精心编织的花竹帽去赶圩，半路遇雨，他见一位姑娘没有雨具，便将花竹帽给她遮雨。雨中，姑娘发现竹帽上织有许多漂亮花纹，赞叹织帽人心灵手巧。当她知道青年就是织帽人时，顿生爱慕之情，两人结为夫妻。花帽作为有情人的信物，从此便在毛南山乡流传开了。每逢佳节，盛装的青年以歌谈情。遇上意中人，男青年将花竹帽送上，如女方也有意，便会接过花竹帽，并将亲手缝制的布鞋送给男青年以作答谢，一片真情尤可见。

There is a legend that long ago a young man took a flowered bamboo hat that he had woven himself to the market; on the way there, it started to rain, and he saw a girl without an umbrella, and thus gave her the hat to protect her from the rain. In the rain, the girl found that the hat was decorated with beautiful floral patterns, and the artistry wowed her. She fell in love with the young man when she found out he was the one who crafted it, and they were married. The flowered hat functioned as a token of trust between lovers, and thus the custom became popular in areas where Maonan people live. At each festival, youths express their love with songs. When he finds someone he fancies, a young man will give a hat as a gift; if the recipient reciprocates the feelings, she will keep the hat, and provide a pair of cloth shoes in return as a sign of gratitude.

踢沙示恋

Kicking Sand

文：覃兰

每逢喜庆节日，这里的青年男女便成群结队，欢聚一起，引吭高歌，托物寄情，物色佳偶。每每歌罢，他们就三三两两踏着月光，来到海边的沙滩上或丛林中游逛，寻觅自己的意中人。一旦发现中意的人儿，小伙儿便向对方步步靠近，脚尖将沙子撩向对方或折下一根树枝，掷到姑娘身上。如果男有情来女有意，那么她就照样用脚尖把沙子踢回对方，或把树枝掷到对方身上，以表示接受小伙儿的追求。这便是京族特有的“踢沙示恋”。

At each festival, the young men and women here form groups, in which they revel and sing together, exchanging tokens of affection and pairing off. At the end of the singing, they'll head over to the beach or the forest to walk around, looking for the ones they fancy. If a young man finds a woman he likes, he'll come close to her and kick a little bit of sand at her, or snap a twig and throw it at her. If the woman returns his affections, she'll return the gesture to signify that she accepts his advances. This is how a kick of sand is a sign of love among the Jing people.

柳州苗山芦笙踩堂　摄影：谌贻照

芦笙踩堂

Lusheng

文：朱燕

“滴——滴——滴哩——滴哩——滴——”一把插着锦鸡羽毛的小芦笙领了头，跟着，几十队芦笙瞬间“呜——拉拉——嗡”地齐鸣了。后生们歪头晃脑地摇晃着手中的芦笙，笙歌或粗或细、或轻或重、或缓或急地从笙管里倾泻而出，响彻云霄。穿着盛装的苗族姑娘踩着节奏，愉悦地跳起了芦笙踩堂舞。银的帽子、银的项圈、银的手镯一时间叮当作响，飘扬的衣带、漂亮的花边、层层叠叠的千褶裙随歌翻动，亮了芦笙堂，亮了围观人们的眼睛。

“Di-di-dili-dili-di...” This is the sound of “lusheng”, a kind of reed pipe instrument popular here. As the first player plays with a golden pheasant feather in his lusheng, suddenly dozens of others join in – “wuu-lala-weng” goes the sound. The younger players shake their heads as they hold their lusheng in their hands; the sound may be coarse or fine, soft or strong, languid or hurried as it rings out towards the clouds. Miao girls in rich dress follow the rhythm, happily dancing the Caitang Dance. Silver hats, silver necklaces and silver bracelets jangle. Fluttering belts, beautiful laces and pleated skirts move with the music, brightening the area as well as the eyes of observers.

评论

别致的幽会方式

Trysting

文：覃兰

夜幕降临，月华洒在吊脚楼上，年轻的小伙儿正借着吊脚楼突出的梁头向上攀爬，原来这是要去跟心爱的姑娘幽会呢。在广西金秀，茶山瑶族有种独特的婚恋习俗——爬楼。茶山瑶居住的房屋皆为木结构干栏式，在房屋一侧会设一间距地面有一定高度的吊脚楼。瑶族历来崇尚婚恋自由，所以当家中的姑娘到了谈恋爱的年纪就会到吊脚楼居住，以方便与“爬楼”来的小伙儿幽会。

When night comes, and the moonlight spills over the stilted buildings, young men climb the buildings upon the protruding beam heads – this is how they sneakily meet their girls. The Yao people of Tea Mountain, Jinxiu have a unique marriage custom – climbing buildings. The houses here are all built out of wood, on stilts. There will be a building on stilts of a certain height to the side of the house. The Yao people respect the freedom to choose one's own spouse, and thus when a girl is of marriageable age she will move to the building on stilts so that her lover can climb up to meet her.

腰带上的爱情花

Flowers of Love

文：覃兰

古往今来，定情信物可谓五花八门。不同于其他，红河两岸的彝家定情信物就很别致了，居然是腰带。当彝家姑娘爱上一个小伙儿后，便会用五颜六色的丝线，用心绣上一条精致的花腰带，悄悄在约会时把腰带送给心上人。所以要是看到小伙儿腰上缠有漂亮的花腰带，那就表示已经心有所属啦。当然小伙儿也会将手镯或耳环之类的回赠给姑娘。

Since long ago, there have been tokens of love. Those of the Yi people who live along the banks of the Red River are different from others – their tokens of loves are waistbands. When a Yi girl likes a boy, she'll use all kinds of colored thread to embroider a beautiful waistband, and then secretly slip it to him when they meet. This means that if you see a young man wearing a beautiful waistband, you know that he is in love. The boys, of course, will give bracelets, earrings or something similar to the girls.

评论

瑶家“嫁郎”

Wedding the Groom

文：朱燕

瑶家群众习惯把一种“上门入赘”的婚俗称为“嫁郎”。上门入赘被视为尊敬同族老人、顾及民族兴衰的美德。当男子嫁到女家之后，仍可保持一家之主的地位，但同时又在婚前和女方商量约定好，婚后生下的小孩可跟父姓也可随母姓。结婚后，如果男方家庭有困难，夫妇便一同回去，住上一段时间，帮助解决生产生活上的困难，然后再回到女方家。瑶家人把这种做法叫“两边顶”。

Yao families have a tradition of the man marrying into the bride's family called "wedding the groom". These customs are seen as a sign of respect for elders, as well as the history of the tribe. When the groom marries into the bride's family, he remains the head-of-household, but his children can have his or her surname according to their previous agreement. After the wedding, if the husband's family has difficulties, the couple will go to live with them for some time, helping them with their problems before returning to the wife's family. The Yao people call this "stepping on two peaks".

瑶族婚俗——嫁郎　摄影：张小宁

居不可无枫

Maple Scouts

文：翟香丽

行走在桂北的苗寨，不时会碰到高大挺拔的枫树，枫叶棱角分明又纤巧清秀。一入深秋，变红的枫叶便把苗寨点缀得抒情而秀美。过去，苗人每迁一处会先种枫树，如果枫树活了，则说明可以安寨。据说，苗寨中用于踩芦笙的芦笙柱顶上的脊宇鸟，是枫树树梢变出来的。

When walking among the stockade Miao villages of northern Guangxi, occasionally you will encounter a stalwart maple tree that has clear and beautiful angles to its leaves. In late autumn, the red leaves will add emotion and beauty to the village. In the past, when Miao people were to migrate, they would plant a maple tree at the site of their destination. If it lived, it was a sign that it was the right place to construct a stockade. It's said that the decoration at the top of the Miao reed flutes is an evolution of these treetops.

凤兮仫佬

Phoenixes

文：翟香丽

在广西罗城，凤凰是仫佬族的图腾。山为凤凰山，村为凤梧村，屯为凤立屯；在墙壁上画凤凰和凤尾，在石头上刻凤凰，在神龛下的香儿桌上雕凤凰，在镜屏上印凤凰，在衣服、背带、枕头、钱包、帽子、头勒上绣凤凰；婚礼上的公鸡为“凤凰公鸡”，鸡蛋为“凤凰喜天蛋”……恐怕没有哪个民族像仫佬族那样喜欢凤凰。

In Luocheng, the Mulao people use the phoenix as their totem. The mountain is "Phoenix Mountain", the village is Fengwu ("Phoenix Tree") Village, and the town is Fengli ("Standing Phoenix") Town. On the walls, there are phoenixes and phoenix tales. Phoenixes are carved into the rocks and the shrines table, printed on the mirror screens, and embroidered on clothing, suspenders, wallets, pillows, hats, and straps. The cock served at weddings is the "phoenix cock" and the eggs are "phoenix eggs". These may be the people most into phoenixes in the world.

评论

三江侗族妇女在程阳桥景区展示传统纺纱技艺　摄影：谌贻照

梅林侗族赶歌圩　摄影：张小宁

踩高跷捕鱼

Fishing on Stilts

文：覃兰

俗话说，站得高看得远。广西东兴的京族有种独特的捕鱼技巧——踩高跷捕鱼。脚踩高跷，肩扛三角渔网，一步步走向浅海，估摸着位置看着合适就把渔网放到海里，让渔网贴着海底浅滩平行移动，看准时机一把操起渔网……哎嘿！鱼虾就在里面啦！别看这捕鱼技术难度系数颇高，据说年景好时，一个捕捞季收获的鱼虾竟达 500 多吨。

It's commonly said the higher you stand, the farther you can see. The Jing people of Dongxing in Guangxi have a special method of fishing – they stand on stilts. They wade into the shallow waters upon them with a triangular fishing net, feeling out a place that's suitable to cast it. They run the net over the seafloor, and at the proper time whip it up – and there it is! A full net of fish and shrimp. Although it's difficult, it's worth the effort – a good season can yield a catch of 500 tonnes.

爱她就勇敢地抢过来

Take her if you love her

文：覃兰

广西毛南族有个很“霸道”的婚庆传统：“爱她就勇敢地抢过来！”这说的是毛南族未婚男女的“抢帽”。在赶圩或者集会活动时，小伙儿要是看上了哪个姑娘，就会想方设法去把姑娘头上的花竹帽给抢过来。若是姑娘也对小伙儿有意思，那就半推半就让小伙儿拿走，然后有来有往终成眷属。反之，姑娘便强势夺回，小伙儿也就知道姑娘对他没意思了。

The Maonan people of Guangxi have a very "overbearing" marital custom: "Take her if you love her!" This refers to the custom of "stealing hats" among unmarried men and women of the Maonan people. During market time or at group activities, if a boy fancies a girl, he'll try to find a way to steal the hat off her head. If the girl is interested, she'll make a weak display of resisting, and they will form a family. If she resists forcefully, however, this means that she's not interested.

评论

坡会
Gathering on the Slope

文：朱燕

到了坡会这一天，青年男女便会精心打扮一番自己，穿上节日的盛装，结伴而来。一路上，村道旁、田野边都摆满了摊位，各种民族饰品琳琅满目，令人眼花缭乱。山坡上，坡会节的活动热闹非凡，有寨民祭祀、芦笙踩堂，还有斗马、耍狮……站在田埂上，看着眼前的场景，很容易触摸到苗家文化所蕴藏的丰富内涵。

On the day of the gathering, young men and women dress up with festival clothing and come out. On the sides of the thoroughfares and by the fields there are all kinds of booths in which all sorts of ethnic accessories are on sale; it's a dazzling site. On the mountain slope, bustling activities take place. There are offerings to ancestors, Caitang Dance, horse fights, lion dances... Standing on the field ridges, looking upon the spectacle, you will feel the richness of the culture of the Miao people.

赶坡会 摄影：谌贻照

古老的美容术
Beauty Treatment

文：覃兰

姑娘出嫁前，请人开脸、开背，意为让新娘“别开生面”，祝愿她婚姻幸福美满。这其实是流传在广西地区的一种古老美容术。高超的手艺人，借助双手和牙齿，用一粗一细两根棉线形成的交叉三角在皮肤上绞动，就能让皮肤变得光洁且富有弹性。而且这门技艺可是闺房手艺，“传女不传男”。

Before girls married, they have a beautifying treatment performed upon them as part of the well-wishing activities for their new life. There is a set of processes that have been passed down since ancient times in Guangxi. Skilled beauticians use their hands and teeth as well as one thick and one thin thread that they hold in the shape of a triangle to clean the girl's skin, making it lustrous and supple. These techniques are the domain of the women, passed down from generation to generation without the involvement of the men.

热热闹闹赶街去

Bustling Market

文：覃兰

东村的豆沙油团，西村的凉茶糖水，小时总是期待每个“街日子”。广西很多地方都有赶圩文化，叫“赶集”或“赶街”。那是在以前物质匮乏、交通不便的年代，十里八乡的村民们为方便贸易而约定俗成的集市交易日。地方不同，约定的日子也不同，若是来旅游，别忘了跟当地人问问这儿的“街日子”是哪天，也凑凑热闹去。

The bean-paste filled buns of this village, the sweet water of that village – as children everyone always looked forward to the market day. There is a culture of a market day at many places in Guangxi. In previous times when items were scarce and transportation was difficult, people would come from villages and avenues all over to exchange goods at the market. In different regions, the market happens on different days. If you come here to travel, don't forget to ask on which day the market is – it's a lively affair.

打磨秋

Twirling Wood

文：朱燕

每逢春节、火把节，广西隆林的彝族群众都会在寨中平地或场坝上竖起一根粗如碗口、高约 3 米的木桩，桩顶上横放一根 9 至 12 米的坚木，两人各在坚木一端，手扶且腹贴坚木，通过用脚使劲蹬地的方式让坚木高低起伏，不断旋转。场外，孩子追逐戏闹，老人喝酒取乐，青年男女则围成圈子跳起竹棍舞、乐作舞……一时间，“磨秋”翻飞人闹腾，场里场外欢声笑语交织在一起，在群山间一阵阵回荡开来。

On Spring Festival or Torchlight Festival, the Yi peoples of Longlin will erect a wood post about 3 meters high upon the flat ground or an embankment, on top of the post a twirling piece of about 9-12 meters long is placed. Two people push their feet against the ground and turn it around, making the rotary part go up and down. Further out, children run around and play, the elder drink and celebrate, and young men and women form a ring and dance the Bamboo Pole Dance and Lezuo Dance. Everyone laughs and chats as they enjoy themselves.

隆林彝族打磨秋　摄影：张小宁

新年十天初，不租借火种

New Year Fire

文：覃兰

正月里，对于靖西壮族人而言，从初一到初十是不能借火种给别人的。他们认为这会使来年家门火气下降，发不起家，故有“新年十天初，不租借火种”的说法。为解决新春自家用火问题，即使是穷得无米下锅的人，都必先找一根大而坚硬的木头来做“连岁火种”。要绝对地保证年三十晚到正月初一天亮时火种不断，香火不断，明灯不熄，否则寓意日子不好过。

For the Zhuang people of Jingxi City, it's taboo to loan a source of fire to people from the first to tenth days of the first lunar month. They believe that it will dampen the spirit of the household and make for a difficult year. In order to solve the problem of maintaining fire, even the most impoverished families will find a large wooden log to tide them over for the period. They make sure to keep the fire burning all the way from the last day of the last lunar month to the next day; incense must burn, and lights must be kept on continuously. Otherwise, the next year will not be a time of prosperity.

壮乡迎客酒

Welcome Wine

文：沈世良

壮乡人热情好客，纯朴善良。每当到主人家里做客，客人要先喝三碗米酒。这一习俗，对于我这个生性好酒的外乡人而言，真是天大的美事。那会儿刚毕业不久，工作安定下来后，无论哪家有酒，逢叫必到，而且是屡喝屡醉，屡醉屡喝，非常痛快。醉了多少回，已记不清了。幸运的是，屡喝屡醉后，还当上了壮家姑爷。

The Zhuang people are ardent and welcoming and have a pure and benevolent character. When you go to a Zhuang household as a guest, you'll be invited first to drink three bowls of rice liquor. This is a custom which really moved me as an outsider since I am naturally inclined to enjoy liquor. I had just graduated and got a stable job. I found that wherever I went, it was time to drink. I was tipsy all the time, always drunk, and it was great. I have no idea how many times I got intoxicated. What's even better is that after all this drinking I married a Zhuang girl.

壮乡迎客酒　摄影：陈炜平

三更的婚礼

Midnight Wedding

文：覃兰

“夜半三更，对镜梳妆，长发轻挽，双眸含笑，穿上红妆，坐在床上，妹等哥来接新娘。”黑衣壮的婚礼在夜间进行。新娘出家门时，其父兄不能看；新娘出门后，不得回头看娘家，更不能往回走，否则被视为不吉之兆。新娘到了男方家，过门入洞房后，至午夜鸡叫头遍时，新娘又会悄悄地和伴娘返回娘家。女方婚后大部分时间仍是住在娘家，直到怀孕生子后才会在男方家定居下来。

“At midnight, facing the mirror, the girl does her toilet and gathers up her hair. Her eyes smile as she puts on her makeup. She sits on the bed, and waits for her groom to come.” The Heiyizhuang people (literally means Zhuang people who wear black clothing) conduct their weddings at night. When the bride leaves her house, her father and brothers are not allowed to look upon her. After she goes, she can’t turn her head or walk back; either of the two would be viewed as a bad omen. When she arrives at the groom’s house and enters the bridal chamber, she waits until the cock first crows, and then secretly heads back to her home with her bridesmaids. After she’s married, she’ll spend most of the time at her father’s house, and will not move to the husband’s home until she has a child.

雷神的女儿

Lightning God’s Daughter

文：翟香丽

田野里到处都是人，一个个都弯着腰，低着头，手里拿着一截小木棍。突然间，人群中有人大喊一声，紧接着周边的人就围了过去，也跟着呼喊起来。不用说，第一只蚂拐找到了。每年春节期间，这一幕都会在红水河流域一带的壮族地区出现，原来他们在过“蚂拐节”。蚂拐就是青蛙。在当地人心目中，蚂拐是掌管雨水的雷神的女儿，所以他们找蚂拐、孝蚂拐、葬蚂拐，以祈求风调雨顺。

There are people everywhere in the fields, bending at the waist and dipping their heads, with small wooden batons in their hands. Suddenly, someone in the sea of people calls out, and a circle of people forms, also crying out as they head over – everyone knows what this is about. The first Maguai (pong frog) has been found. Every year at the time of the spring festival, this scene occurs in Zhuang areas around the Hongshui River – they’re holding the “Maguai festival”. The common Maguai is to these people the daughter of the Lightning God, who controls the winds and rain. Thus, they look for, respect and even inter these frogs in the hope of favorable weather conditions in the coming year.

东兰蚂拐节上的竹鼓表演　摄影：韦鹏雁

京族哈节
Ha Festival

文：翟香丽

9时30分，鼓声响起，彩旗飘展，一年一度的京族哈节隆重开幕。长长的迎神队伍自哈亭出发，在锣鼓鞭炮声中，一路浩浩荡荡来到海边恭请“海神”。依照古老的祭海习俗，年长的主祭人庄严地面对大海宣读祭文，人们上高香、敬五谷五果，祭海神，祈求风调雨顺。哈节将持续七天七夜，京族群众通宵达旦唱歌跳舞，迎神、祭神、万人餐、山歌会、乡饮、祝酒、送神，场面蔚为壮观。

At 9:30 the sound of drums arises, colored banners are unfurled, and the annual Ha Festival of the Jing people begins. A line of people started from the Ha Pagoda to welcome the “sea god”, winding towards the sea amidst the sounds of drums, gongs, and firecrackers. Following their ancient maritime ceremony customs, the old officiator solemnly reads a text facing the waters. People offer tall and slender joss sticks, grains and fruits to the sea god, asking for favorable rains and winds. The Ha Festival goes on for seven days, with the Jing people singing and dancing throughout the night, welcoming the god, making offerings, having huge banquets, singing, drinking, and celebrating in a magnificent scene.

彝族跳弓节
Bow Jumping Festival

文：翟香丽

舞坪中间的金竹丛旁，早已摆上了香甜的糯米酒、五色糯米饭和肉类食品，众人静候令人振奋的枪响。随着一声令下，持枪手把枪指向苍天，抠动板机，“砰砰砰……”缕缕硝烟腾空；铜鼓手擂起铜鼓，在缓缓响起的鼓声中，全寨男女老少进入舞坪，排成两队，麻公巴（领舞者。据说是祖先打仗时首领的化身）走在舞蹈人群的前面，人们手牵着手蹁跹起舞。传说当年金竹帮助彝族先祖击败了敌人，彝族人在广场中央种金竹一蔸以示纪念，并把金竹看作神圣的吉祥物，世代相传，后形成那坡地区彝族人民的传统节日——跳弓节。

Next to the thicket of golden bamboo upon the dancing area there has already been placed glutinous rice liquor, multi-colored rice, and various meat products. The gathered people quietly await the “boom”. A signal is given, triggers are pulled, and pistols fire out towards the sky. “Pop, pop, pop...” Gun smoke floats into the air and the drumming starts. As the beat of the drums continues slowly, all the men and women in the village move onto the dancing area, forming two lines. Magongba (the incarnation, it’s said, of the leader of the ancestors at war) walks in front of all the people, and people link hands and spin as they dance. It’s said that in times back then the golden bamboo helped the ancestors of the Yi people defeat their enemies. Thus, they place some roots and stems of the plant in the center of the plaza as a memorial, and view them as a symbol of lucks. The custom has been passed down through the generations as what is now a traditional celebration, the Bow Jumping Festival, of the Yi people of this region.

醉倒在苗年　摄影：陈炜平

醉倒在苗年
Miao New Year

文：翟香丽

秋收过后，天气转凉，新鲜的稻米吃着吃着，融水苗族自治县的苗年就来了。男人们做一伙，灰黑一片；女人们成一帮，红绿一团。置办碗筷、锅头、香烛、纸钱、粉丝、水果，酿了酒，备了菜，制了衣，扫了地，祭了祖，吃了饭，好戏就该开始了：吹芦笙、踩歌堂、跳苗舞，斗牛、斗马，射击、爬竿……赢了可以“得意忘形”，输了依旧哈哈大笑。如果还品百家宴，那就只好醉倒在苗年了。

After the autumn harvest, the weather turns cold; people eat the fresh rice as the Miao New Year begins in Rongshui. The men dress in black, and the women in green. They set out bowls, chopsticks, woks, fragrant candles, joss paper, glass noodles, fruits, and home-distilled liquor. Meals are prepared, clothes are made, the ground has been swept, offerings have been made to ancestors, the meal has been eaten… The fun is just starting. Songs are played in on reed flutes as people dance, conduct bullfights and horsefights, and compete in archery and pole climbing. Winners bask in their glory and losers laugh. If you visit these large banquets, you’ll become intoxicated in the Miao New Year.

瑶族盘王节
King Pan

文：翟香丽

农历十月十六，初冬，微寒，高大威严的盘王像前供奉着猪头、糯米粑、鸡肉、酒等祭品，随着鞭炮、火枪的齐鸣，瑶族盘王节隆重的祭祀大典便开始了。在鞭炮声中，瑶族师公们唱着盘王歌，跳着盘王舞，忽而上跳，忽而下蹲，忽而左转，忽而右旋，再现了瑶族先民耕种狩猎、出征杀敌的一幅幅画面，表达对先祖的敬仰与怀念。

On the sixteenth day of the tenth lunar month, winter is just beginning, and it’s slightly chilly. Offerings are placed in front of the colossal statue of King Pan

– a pig's head, glutinous rice cakes, chicken, liquor and so on. Firecrackers go off along with muskets, and the grand festival to King Pan of the Yao people begins. Amidst the sound of the firecrackers, the grandmasters of the Yao sing the King Pan song, and dance the King Pan dance, hopping and kneeling, turning left and right, recreating the scenes of agriculture and hunting, and setting out on expeditions to slaughter enemies, showing their respect and love for ancestors.

等待很多年的鼓声响了

Waiting for the Drum

文：翟香丽

广西作家严风华说："没有哪个节需要等待这么久，一等就是七年，一等就是十三年。"没错，这是融水、三江一带苗族的拉鼓节。大鼓，13 年举行一次，拉一丈三尺长的大鼓；小鼓，7 年举行一次，拉五尺长的小鼓。均在农历十月。三天三夜，人们纵情歌舞。看拉鼓的人啊满山坡，拉鼓踩堂啊奏笙歌，共祝来年好运到，林粮丰收有吃喝！

Guangxi Author Yan Fenghua says: "These are festivals you have to wait a long time for; one you must wait seven years for, and another you must wait thirteen." That's right: these are the Drum-Pulling Festivals of the Miao people of Rongshui and Sanjiang. The big drum comes around once every thirteen years and involves a drum four and one-third meters long. The small drum comes around once every seven years and consists of a drum one and two-thirds meters long. They occur during the tenth lunar month, and last for three days and three nights. People have a great time singing and dancing. The slopes of the mountain are covered in revelers, with drumming, dancing and flute playing. It's a time for people to come together to wish for a year of good luck and a good harvest as they enjoy food and drink.

芒哥来了

Mang Bro is Here

文：翟香丽

融水安陲乡，每年的正月十七，身披芒草、戴着假面具的芒哥就左右摇摆着，跳起芒哥舞，通过各种有趣的动作向人们表达着敬意，憨态可掬又不失粗犷豪放。芒哥属于娱乐神，芒哥舞用于驱邪镇妖。据说，小孩的头被芒哥摸了，会平安长大；老人的手被芒哥摸了，会健康长寿；与芒哥拥抱的青年，会平安丰收，还会收获爱情。或许，该去会会芒哥了。

In Anchui Village, Rongshui on the seventeenth day of the first lunar month each year, Mang Bro wears a garment of silvergrass and puts on a mask, rocking about as he dances the Mang Bro dance. Through all sorts of interesting movements, he shows respect for the people in a manner that's both silly and forceful. Mang Bro is the god of entertainment, and his dance is used to ward off evil spirits. It's said that if he rubs a children's head, the child will grow up peacefully; if an old person touches his hand, he will enjoy a long life; and if the Bro embraces a youth, that person will enjoy good harvests and find love. Maybe we should meet him.

龙炮不伤人的奥秘

Firecracker Mystery

文：朱燕

宾阳人向来认为鞭炮代表“红火吉利”，放炮的和被炸的人是“一个愿打一个愿挨”。令人惊奇的是，在每年农历正月十一举行的宾阳炮龙节上，数十万乃至上百万人的狂欢却狂而不乱，多年来鲜有安全事故发生。其奥秘是炮龙节当晚所燃放的“龙炮”是特制鞭炮。每响“龙炮”装药不超过 0.02 克，威力有限，且含有的硫磺等物质有药效，即使炸伤了皮肉也不会很疼，3 天后就会神奇痊愈。

The people of Binyang believe the fire of firecrackers brings prosperity. Setting them off and getting blasted are two sides of exchange here. What's surprising is that with the hundreds of thousands of people going to the carnival every year, very few incidents occur. The key to the mystery is the special "dragon firecrackers" set off on the night of the Dragon Cannon Festival. Each cartridge has no more than 0.02 grams of explosive, limiting their power. They also contain other compounds such as sulfur. Even if people are injured, it isn't painful, and the wounds will heal magically within three days.

农家老牛过生日

Bovine Birthday

文：覃兰

每年农历四月初八的“牛魂节”又称“牛生日”“牛王诞”等，是壮、汉、瑶、侗、仫佬、布依、土家等民族的传统节日。传说在壮族山村举行“牛魂节”这一天，农家会给牛放假一天，各家各户把牛栏修整一新。村老们对全村的牛评头品足，并告诫各家要爱护耕牛。家家蒸制五色糯米饭，用枇杷叶包裹后喂牛。有的地方还在堂屋摆上酒肉、瓜果供品，由家长牵一头老牛绕着供品行走，边走边唱，以赞颂和酬谢牛的功德。

Every year on the eighth day of the fourth lunar month the "Cow Soul Festival", also known as "Bovine Birthday", takes place. The Zhuang, Han, Yao, Dong, Mulao, Buyi, Tujia and other peoples all celebrate this traditional holiday. It's said that on the day of this festival in Zhuang villages the cattle are given a day off, with all families repairing their enclosures upon this day. The elders will inspect all the cattle of the village, and remind everyone to love and care for their beasts of burden. Households will make five-colored rice, and wrap it in loquat leaves to feed the cows. Some places also lay out liquor, meat, nuts, and fruits, and lead the cow around these offerings as they sing, praising the merits and virtues of the animals.

评论

红瑶有个晒衣节

Sunning Festival

文：六少爷

以晾晒衣物为主题的节庆，恐怕要数龙胜各族自治县的红瑶最为独特。红瑶是瑶族的一个支系，崇尚红色，因女性经常穿着色泽红艳的服装而得名。每年的六月初六，家家户户都会把一年四季所穿的衣服拿出来晾晒，意在杀毒灭菌去霉。届时满寨子都是红衣裳，远远望去，片片红裙与竹楼绿水相映成趣，构成一幅优美的田园风情画。

Concerning the sunning festival, which centers around sunning one's clothes, that of the Red Yao people in Longsheng is special. The Red Yao is a branch of the Yao that admire the color red. Women of this group frequently wear bright red clothing. Every year on the sixth day of the sixth lunar month, families bring out all their clothes to sun them, killing bacteria and eliminating mold. At this time the village is full of red clothing; the red of the skirts contrasts with the green of the bamboo and water, forming a beautiful countryside scene.

旧的去了新的来

Out with the Old, in with the New

文：朱燕

每年农历八月，从四面八方赶来的宾客便云集隆林德峨镇么基村大水井屯，与当地仡佬族同胞一起欢庆一年一度的尝新节。人们身着民族盛装，一大早便到田里收割新的粮食和瓜菜回来煮熟，接着宰杀黄牯牛，分发牛肉、牛心，以示族人同心；然后祭拜“祖宗树”，唱起《采新祈祷词》：“冷的去了热的来，旧的去了新的来，苦的去了甜的来……”祈祷来年风调雨顺，五谷丰登，六畜兴旺。祭祀完毕，人们便围着象征丰收的粮垛载歌载舞，沉浸在一片欢乐中。

Every year during the eighth lunar month, people come and gather at Dashuijing ("big well") Village of Longlin to celebrate the "New Produce Festival" with the Gelao people. Everyone wears wonderful ethnic clothing and heads out early into the field to harvest fresh grain, fruits, and vegetables to take back and boil. Yellow bulls are slaughtered, and the meat and pieces of the heart are distributed, to symbolize they have a common heart. People go to worship at the "ancestor tree" and sing the prayer poem: "Out with the cold, in with the hot; out with the old, in with the new; out with the bitter and in with the sweet..." They pray for good weather, plentiful harvest, and healthy livestock. After the ceremony, everyone sings and dances around grain pile which symbolizes a fruitful harvest.

评论

侗家人祭萨

Progenitor

文：朱燕

每逢农历二月十五，素有“八百里侗乡南大门”之称的桂林龙胜各族自治县乐江乡宝赠村迎来一年一度的祭萨节。侗族最敬仰女神萨岁（“萨岁”为侗语音，意为至高无上的大祖母、始祖母），她为保卫侗寨在战斗中英勇牺牲。祭萨节时，巡游队伍挑着谷物挨家送福，身着节日盛装的侗族女子载歌载舞，有歌颂萨岁恩德、祈求赐福的耶歌，有模拟十二道农活的春牛舞，还有多姿多彩的侗族民风民俗走秀。

Every year on the fifteenth day of the second lunar month, at Baozeng Village in Lejiang, a place full of various ethnic groups, the Offering Festival is held. The Dong people worship a goddess known as Sasui, which in their language means most exalted ancestor. She was a heroine who sacrificed herself protecting a Dong village during the war. At the time of the festival, people parade and deliver grain house to house, and the Dong women sing and dance in costumes, extolling Sasui's virtues, and asking for blessings. The “spring cow dance” has movements mimicking twelve agricultural activities, and there are interesting shows of Dong folk clothing.

古老的东方情人节

Oriental Valentine's Day

文：覃兰

水族中有“过端不过卯，过卯不过端”的说法。在广西南丹、宜州等地的水族过的便是卯节。这天，青年男女身着节日盛装，结伴来到卯坡上对歌，用歌声传情达意、互诉衷肠。对歌一般从午后开始，男青年手牵手组成人墙将女青年围在中间，开始以歌试探。如果女青年中意，便留在人墙里对唱；如果不中意，便拼命突围，双方则在卯坡上重新物色意中人。年轻人赶卯坡谈情说爱是卯节活动的主题，所以卯节又被称为“古老的东方情人节”。

The Shui people celebrate either Duan Festival or Mao Festival in a year. In Nandan, Yizhou and other areas, the Shui people there choose Mao Festival. On that day, young women deck themselves out in nice clothing and come with companions to sing antiphonal songs upon the “Mao slope”, using lyrics to convey their feelings and emotions. The singing generally starts after noon; the boys link arms to form a human wall, encircling the girls. They use songs to make passes; if a girl is interested, she will stay within the wall and sing back; if she isn't, she'll try her hardest to bust out, and the two parties will try again with someone else. The pairing up on the slope is the main activity of the festival; thus the festival has been called the “ancient oriental Valentine's Day”.

一苇渡江 独竹漂

Reed Crossing

文：覃兰

只见数人赤脚踏在漂浮于水面的一根楠竹（或形似材料）上，手拿一根细竹竿为“桨”，依靠小竹竿划动，实现水上漂行，展现“一苇渡江”之妙。这不是在拍武侠片，这是在进行“独竹漂”比赛。这么别致的民族竞技，是每年农历夏至后的第一个辰日（龙日）前后环江毛南族分龙节上举行的一项赛事。“独竹漂”距今有上千年历史，被誉为“中华水上一绝”。

One can see something interesting here: people stand barelegged upon pieces of giant green moso bamboo or a similar material that floats upon the surface, using a long thin bamboo pole as an “oar” as they paddle across the water. This is “river-crossing on a reed”. This special competition happens on the first “dragon day” after the summer solstice, and is one of the activities for the Dragon Festival of the Maonan people. It has more than a thousand years of history, and indeed something to watch.

隆林彝族 火把节

Torch Festival

文：朱燕

入夜后，男女老少成群结队，手执火把先绕着各家各户转，后从四面八方往田间地头走去，进行巡游，并不时将火把插在田埂和路旁，远远望去，山岭、田埂火龙映天，蜿蜒起伏，动人万分。之后，全寨人在寨中的一块空地上汇聚，将火把集中起来烧成一大堆，熊熊火焰照亮整个寨子，人们围成一圈，唱歌跳舞，饮酒作乐，一片欢腾，通宵达旦。

As night falls, the men and women, holding torches, wind through the village in groups. They come out from all over into the fields, roaming around and occasionally planting torches in the ground on ridges within the field or beside the roads. The flames look like fire dragons snaking out over the terrain. The sight is magnificent and moving. Afterward, all the people of the village gather in a clearing and pile the torches up into a large fire which illuminates the entire village. They encircle it, sing and dance, drinking and reveling throughout the night.

隆林彝族火把节　摄影：张小宁

“偷瓜群众”不犯法

Pumpkin Poaching

文：覃兰

恰逢环江毛南族南瓜节，形状各异、金黄饱满的大南瓜摆满了各家楼板，年轻小伙们忙着走街串巷给大南瓜们量腰围、称体重。历经层层选拔，“南瓜王”脱颖而出。尔后，主人一刀将南瓜劈成两半，掏出瓜籽，以做来年的种子；然后将切好的南瓜拌进小米煮，熟了盛一碗供在香火堂前敬奉“南瓜神”，之后众人共餐同享，庆贺南瓜丰收。据说这天，全村秒变“偷瓜群众”都不算犯法，就看谁偷的大而多，谁就是获胜者。

During the time of the Pumpkin Festival of the Maonan people in Huanjiang, you’ll see pumpkins on the floor slabs of every house, in all shapes and sizes as the place is orange all about. Young people will go around the streets measuring the size of the pumpkins and weighing them. After a long series of selections, the “pumpkin king” will be found. Later, its owner will slice it in two with a single stroke of the knife, and scoop the seeds out to be used for planting in the next year. Then, the pumpkin meat will be cut up and mixed with millet to cook for a meal to be presented to the “pumpkin god”. Later, people gather and eat together, celebrating the pumpkin harvest. It’s said that on this date stealing a pumpkin isn’t illegal; whoever takes the most and biggest is the winner.

百花的生日

Flower Birthday

文：朱燕

“一年春事说今朝”，说的是农历二月举办的“花朝节”——俗称“百花的生日”，流行于东北、华北、华东、中南等地。崇左市宁明、龙州等地以农历二月初二为“花朝节”。旧俗记载，在这一天，男女青年从四面八方汇集在长有高大木棉树的地方对唱山歌，在真挚的歌声中赠花定情，抛掷绣球和互赠礼物。日落时分，人们按照传统习俗，从四周把绣球向木棉树高枝抛去，挂到木棉树上，以求百花仙子保佑爱情永结。

“This is the day when the spring flourishes”. The “Birthday of All Flowers” is celebrated in the second lunar month. It’s popular in many areas in China. In Ningming and Longzhou counties of Chongzuo city, the festival is held on the second day of the second lunar month. According to the old custom, on this day, young men and women come from all over to gather at a place that has large kapok trees, singing songs and looking for love. They throw cloth balls and exchange gifts. When the sun is setting, in accordance with traditions, they throw the balls high into the branches of the kapok trees – when they catch there, the flower fairy will protect the long-lasting love.

霜降时节 娅莫巡游

Yamo Patrol

文：朱燕

每年农历九月，广西晚稻收割结束后，壮族霜降节就来了。这一天，人们先拿着糍粑、肉、香烛等祭品到娅莫庙祭拜进香。娅莫庙是人们为纪念抗倭英雄岑玉音夫妇所建。玉音夫人凯旋之日正逢霜降节，因此民众逢霜降节就举行游神活动。只见一些人打扮成士兵模样，举着牙旗敲锣打鼓，在醒狮的开道下把娅莫画像抬出来巡游。巡到哪家，哪家就要放鞭炮。

Every year during the ninth lunar month, after the late harvest in Guangxi is finished, Frost's Descent (the eighteenth solar term) Festival comes for the Zhuang people. On this day, people take glutinous rice cakes, meat, incense, candles, and other offerings to the temple of Yamo. The temple was built to commemorate Cen Yuyin and his wife who fought against the Japanese pirates. When Mrs. Cen won the victory and returned, it happened to be the date of Frost's Descent, and for this reason, the people give praise to her on this day. One will see people dressed up like soldiers carrying pennants and beating gongs and drums. Led by a lion dance, they will take the statue of Yamo out and parade it around. As this happens, people are setting off firecrackers everywhere.

壮美磅礴的大地飞歌

Grand Songs

文：朱燕

丝路山水，画里民歌。一年一度的南宁国际民歌艺术节在广西体育中心体育馆隆重拉开帷幕。欢乐的铜鼓敲起来，七彩的绣球抛起来，在壮乡山坡屋檐造型的恢宏舞台上，来自亚洲、欧洲、非洲、美洲、大洋洲等多个国家的歌手和艺术家，以民歌的名义再次相约在壮乡。万众期待中，人气女团 GNZ48 闪亮登场，用她们特有的方式演唱了开场曲《大地飞歌》。民族和时尚旋律碰撞的强烈对比，瞬间点燃了这场壮美磅礴的民歌盛宴。

The scenery of the Silk Road, the songs in the paintings... Every year the Nanning International Folk Song Festival is held at the Nanning Stadium. The joyous sounds of copper drums ring out, and colorful cloth balls fly everywhere. Upon the large stage constructed in the style of a Zhuang village dwelling, singers and artists from Asia, Europe, Africa, the Americas, and Oceania all gather in the name of folk songs. The popular girl group GNZ48 shows up, using their own style to sing Flying Song of Earth. Pop and folk, modern and traditional, all elements combine and collide with each other, illuminating this beautiful Zhuang folk gala in an instant.

浴佛节的朝拜之旅

Washing the Buddha

文：朱燕

桂平西山鲶鱼坑的一棵大槐树下，前来参观的信众、游人将这里围得水泄不通。龙华寺大师诵经完毕，僧尼手捧香花灯烛，置铜佛于用紫檀、郁金、龙脑、沉香、麝香、丁香等配制成的香汤中，舀汤浴佛。礼佛浴佛毕，千人长队在僧侣的引领下，从鲶鱼坑三步一叩，一路朝拜上山，直至观音岩。整整用了两个半小时，才完成了每年一度浴佛盛会无比虔诚的朝拜之旅。

At the “Catfish Pit” in Guiping, under a large pagoda tree, the Buddha Washing Festival pucks in believers and travelers. After a master from the Longhua Temple finishes reading a scripture, monks and nuns come with incense, flowers, lamps, and candles. The statue of the Buddha is put in a soup made of rosewood, tulips, eaglewood, agarwood, musk, cloves, etc. The soup is ladled to bathe the statue. When the washing is complete, monks lead the crowd in a line, kowtowing every three steps all the way to the Guanyin (Avalokiteśvara) Rock. It takes two and a half hours to complete the yearly religious pilgrimage.

三月三，壮家欢

Zhuang Celebration

文：禤盈秋

每年三月三，是壮家人最隆重的传统节日。这一天，家家户户杀鸡宰羊，邀请亲朋好友，一同把酒言欢，共话幸福生活。这一天，也是壮家青年男女挑选意中人的甜蜜时刻。各村各寨的后生，集中在山坡上一起对山歌，一同跳民族舞，一块抛绣球，场面非常热闹，让人看着眼馋。明年客来，阿妹手中的绣球该抛给哪个阿哥呢？

Every year on the third day of the third lunar month, the most important festival of the Zhuang people arrives. On this day every family slaughters chicken and lamb, and invites friends and family to drink and celebrate, sharing tales of their lives. This is also a day of matchmaking for the young Zhuang people. Boys and girls gather upon the slopes of the hills and sing songs to each other, dance traditional dances, and throw cloth balls at each other. It’s a vivacious and attractive scene. Next year, who will be lucky enough to get the cloth ball from the pretty girl?

欢庆三月三 摄影：陈炜平

喜庆（布努瑶） 摄影：张小宁

布努瑶的感恩节

Bunu Yao Thanksgiving

文：翟香丽

农历五月二十九日，盛夏，巴马东山乡一个寨子中央的平地上，身着盛装的布努瑶孩童们手拉着手围成一圈，圈中央摆放着红鸡蛋、糯米饭等供品，他们一边跳着“陀番舞”一边唱：“糯饭还未吃，鸡蛋还未碰，父母来才吃，等密洛陀来分享……”祭祀之后，节庆娱乐活动才开始，但对布努瑶来说，祝著节是他们的感恩节，是给他们的始祖母密洛陀祝寿，意在提醒后人敬重祖先，孝顺父母。

On the twenty-ninth day of the fifth lunar month, at the height of the summer, upon the flat ground in the middle of a stockaded village at Bama, Bunu Yao children dressed in traditional clothing hold hands as they form a ring. Within the rings, there are red eggs, glutinous rice, and other offerings. Together they dance the “Tuofan Dance” and sing: “The rice is yet to be eaten, the eggs haven’t been touched. We’ll wait father and mother come to eat, and share with Miluotuo.” After the ceremony, the celebrations commence. For the Bunu Yao, this “Zhuzhu Festival” is their Thanksgiving holiday, in memory of their original ancestor mother Miluotuo, and reminding everyone to be respectful of ancestors and parents.

评论

容县“慈堂大屋” 摄影：罗劲松

建筑·品韵

Construction and Charm

一飞冲天 燕窝楼

A Flying Building

文：翟香丽

全州有一传说：清乾隆年间，有一天，石岗头村来了一位气度不凡的老者，他指着一座牌楼说，这是学风之楼，是正气之楼，应香火不断。老者所说的牌楼，就是闻名遐迩的燕窝楼。燕窝楼是广西全州县永岁乡石岗头村蒋氏宗祠的门楼，也是目前为止广西发现的最古老的木质牌楼。远远望去，燕窝楼牌楼上的如意斗拱形似燕窝，又如雄鹰展翅，仿佛随时都可冲天而去。

There is a legend in Quanzhou: during the reign of the Emperor Qianlong in the Qing dynasty, an exceptional old man came to Shigangtou Village. He pointed to a decorative archway and said: this is a building of academy and justice, and incense should always burn here. The structure about which the old man talked is Yanlanlou (literally means "Swallow's Nest Building"), the gateway to the Jiang-clan Family Shrine in Quanzhou. Looking upon it from afar, one would marvel at the bucket arches that look like a bird's nest, or the spreading wings of a fierce eagle, which seems ready to fly off into the sky at any time.

天下第一立交桥

The First Overpass

文：翟香丽

"夕阳西下，你荷着锄头，我赶着牲口，各行其道走过岜团桥，伴着木板的吱呀声，奏响了一曲侗乡暮歌。"三江岜团风雨桥上部桥面宽大，供行人通行；下部较窄，供牵着家畜的人通过。这是世界上首座人畜分道的木制立交桥，与现代都市的双层立交桥有异曲同工之妙，堪称人类立交桥的鼻祖，被赞为"天下第一立交桥"。

"As the sun sets, you carry your hoe, I drive the animals, and we take our own path over the Batuan Bridge. The boards creak under our feet, making a dusk song of Dong People." The upper layer of the Batuan Bridge in Sanjiang is wide, for groups of people to walk over, whereas the lower layer is narrow, for people leading livestock. This is the first wooden "overpass" in the world that separates people and livestock. It has a similar function as the overpass in modern cities, although in a different form. Thus it is called "the first overpass in the world".

三江岜团风雨桥　摄影：陈炜平

程阳永济风雨桥　摄影：陈炜平

百年风雨桥

The Century Bridge

文：翟香丽

广西风雨桥，不能不看程阳桥。1965年郭沫若曾赋诗盛赞程阳永济风雨桥："艳说林溪风雨桥，桥长廿丈四寻高。重瓴联阁怡神巧，列砥横流入望遥。竹木一身坚胜铁，茶林万载茁新苗。何时得上三江道，学把犁锄事体劳。"1911年春末夏初，程阳村的寨民们在杨唐富等12首士的带领下，从募集资金到启动造桥，从桥梁奠基到桥面铺板，供材不分贫富，服工不计日月，男女老少，惟力是尽，历十余寒暑而遹济，取名"永济桥"，又名"百年风雨桥"。

When talking about the historic bridges in Guangxi, you can't miss the Chengyang Bridge. Guo Moruo, a famous contemporary poet, once wrote a poem in tribute to it in 1965, in which he describes its dimensions, quality, strength and surrounding tea trees. At the end of the summer of 1911, the people of Chengyang Village, under the leadership of Yang Tangfu and other 11 volunteers, gathered resources to start the construction. Rich or poor, they gave what they could offer; day and night, they devoted their energies. During a period of over ten years, every villager exerted himself for it until the bridge was finally built. It was named the "Yongji Bridge" (literally means "bridge of constant connection"), also known as the "Century Bridge".

雁山园　摄影：罗劲松

桂林雁山园

Yanshan Garden

文：朱燕

雁山园位于桂林市雁山镇。公园西面有三座小山峰，远看形如一只展翅的大雁，园中钟乳山内有神秘溶洞，藏蝙蝠无数，是岭南仅有的“青山藏福”之地。雁山园最早曾是南明王朱由榔的行宫。园中有圆锥形的日山与半弯形的月山，园外的雁山像一把龙椅，南明王就坐在龙椅中，将日月、江山统揽怀中。

Yanshan Garden is located in the town of the same name in Guilin. There are three small peaks to the west of the park. If one looks upon them from afar, they appear like a wild goose. There is a wondrous cave in Zhongru Hill within the park, where numerous bats hide, a unique scene in Lingnan area. It once was a palace of Zhu Youlang, king of the Southern Ming. The Sun Hill within is round, whereas the Moon Hill is semi-circular; the Yanshan Hill outside the garden resembles an emperor's chair. The Southern Ming king sat in the chair and embraced the moon and the sun, dominating the scenery.

千年守孝为三王

Millennium of Respect

文：翟香丽

远远一瞥，就可以看到三江三王宫那别致的屋檐，像一个巨大的黑边“几”字扣在灰白的外墙顶上。巍峨的青鹅岭就雄踞在宫前，门前的“人和桥”则横卧溪上。庙因桥而居地利，桥因庙而占人和，融合了古代汉族宫廷风格与侗族建筑的精华。一到庙会，宫内的戏台前就会挤满头缠白布看侗戏的人儿。据说，侗民们头上的白布，是对古夜郎国三王子的千年守孝。

Looking far out, one can see the eaves of the Three Princes Palace in Sanjiang County, like the shape of a lowercase "n" on the grey-white walls of the structure. In front of it were the lofty Qing'e Ridge and Renhe Bridge. The temple is in a good position because of the bridge, and the bridge is harmonious because of the temple. The two exquisite structures combine Han imperial style and Dong tradition. When the temple fair comes around, the palace will be full of Dong people with white head coverings; these are a sign of their more than a thousand years of respect for the third prince of the ancient Yelang Kingdom.

正德年间的斜拉索桥

Old Bridge

文：翟香丽

波光粼粼的合浦西门江上，跨度26米的惠爱桥是一位三角形的敦厚君子。只有远远地驻足凝望，才可以领略到始建于明正德年间合浦惠爱桥的巧夺天工。印尼坤甸木质、三铰拱人架结构，与现代斜拉索桥神似。人字头顶覆盖了瓦面，以防雨水从各主要杆件上端渗入，各个环节匠心独具，堪称经典。

Light spills over the rippling waves upon the Ximen River in Hepu; the triangular Huiai Bridge stands upon it like an upright gentleman. Only when you take a close look at it can you see the marvelous workmanship of those who constructed it in the Zhengde period of the Ming dynasty. Made of ironwood from Indonesia, with a three-hinged frame, it looks like the cable-stayed bridges of modern times. The top of the triangle is covered with a glazed tile roof, which prevents rainwater from seeping into the main crossbar. The crafting of the bridge is precise and classic in each facet.

百柱立林古庙堂

Temple on the Pillars

文：翟香丽

富川福溪的濂溪河畔，百柱庙里百柱林立，120根各类圆木稳稳地立在莲花礅、兰花墩、麒麟礅、龙凤祥云礅等大小不一的石墩上。令人惊叹的是设计者就地取材，将一个大型生根奇石直接辟为托柱石墩。百柱庙本为纪念五代十国时期南楚开国君主马殷而建，却成为建筑史上的传奇，也成为楚文化沿着贺州古道南传的重要历史遗迹。

Baizhu (literally means “one hundred columns”) Temple is located by Lianxi River, Fuxi Villiage, Fuchuan County. One hundred twenty wood columns of different kinds stand on different stone bases, such as lotus, orchid, kylin, dragon, and phoenix. It’s impressive to see so many types of designs formed out of local resources. The temple was constructed to commemorate Ma Yin of the Southern Chu in the period of the Five Dynasties and Ten Kingdoms, but in the end became a miracle in architectural history, and a testament to the history of Chu culture in Hezhou.

富川福溪百柱庙　摄影：陈炜平

马胖鼓楼

Mapang Drum Tower

文：翟香丽

马胖鼓楼庄严肃穆地矗立在三江马胖寨的中央，高约30米，共27层重瓴飞檐。下部是由四根大杉木柱组成的中心框架，周边配以24根杉木为副柱，组成一个正方形厅堂。门两旁是用木柱和镂空菱形的木板砌成的“窗墙”；门上方是一幅占了3层重檐、雕工精美的双龙戏珠图。1至3层采用的是龙形飞檐，其余24层皆为飞角斗拱亭檐。顶部两层亭檐上绘饰着花草鱼鸟彩图。远望去，整个鼓楼由下往上渐小渐圆，壮观非常。

The Mapang Drum Tower rises mightily from the ground in the center of the Mapangzhai. It's 30 meters tall, and has 27 tiers of upturn eaves. At the bottom are four large fir pillars as the central framework and 24 smaller pillars as the support, forming a square chamber. To the sides of the door is the "window wall" made of wooden columns and hollowed-out wooden boards of diamond shape. Above the entrance is an image of two dragons playing with an orb that takes up three tiers of double-eaved roofs. The first to fourth rows are made in upturn eaves in dragon shape, and the rest twenty-four rows in a bracketed system known as "dougong". The top two rows are decorated with images of flowers, grasses, birds and fish painted in colors. The whole structure is a wonderful view to behold.

土木干栏

Stockade Structure

文：翟香丽

在密密匝匝的石块垒筑的地基平台上，一米多高的石柱再撑着木柱，一座座硬朗中带着几分古朴的土木干栏掩映于那坡一带苍茫的黑衣壮村寨中。在架空的底层前半部分，各种农用工具、杂物等摆放井然有序，后半部分圈养着的牲畜偶尔憨憨地叫着，中层里的主人们则用心经营着属于他们的年岁。人与自然就那样和谐共生，安详而美好！

黑衣壮村寨的土木干栏　摄影：陈炜平

Upon a solid platform of piled stones, wooden columns are erected above one-meter-high stone columns. This is the typical structure of Heiyizhuang people in Napo Village. In front of the ground floor are all kinds of agricultural tools and items arranged orderly; in the back, some of the livestock in pens call out softly. In the middle floor the owners live out their lives. People and nature here flourish together; it's serene and beautiful.

“久”九萦绕

Number Nine and Longevity

文：翟香丽

一个小门，二重围墙，三层主体，四方大门，五处假山，六幢房屋，七口池塘，八座亭子，九曲巷道。周边开十二个游门，意指十二个时辰运转不息；又有长廊曲径五千米，象征华夏五千年的历史与文明。私人山庄中，论设计的巧妙，陆川谢鲁山庄可谓少见。其所有景点贯以“一至九”的数字设计，并重“久”字，意为“天长地久”。

A small door, two encircling walls, a three-story building, four main gates, five artificial hills, six houses, seven pools, eight pavilions, and nine-curve lanes... Around there are twelve gates to pass through, representing the procession of the twelve constellations. There is a five-kilometer long corridor, which symbolizes the five thousand years of Chinese culture. With regard to stylish design, Xilu Garden is unparallel in private gardens. All the feature spots are designed with the concept of numbers one to nine, among which nine is emphasized in particular because it sounds the same as longevity in Chinese.

陆川谢鲁山庄　摄影：陈炜平

武风凛凛三宣堂

Stern and Cold

文：翟香丽

三宣堂是刘永福故居，语出钦州民谣：“年冬失收毋须慌，肚饿去找三宣堂。”三宣堂没有幽幽庭院，但有防盗门“拖龙门”、天井“拒贿庭”、祖厅“请缨堂”，还有密集的枪眼、威武的炮楼、高高的围墙和秘密通道，进可攻，退可守。这里的墙很厚，手榴弹都炸不开。瓦也特别，有三层。整座建筑俨然一座巨大的碉堡，武风尽显。

The Sanxuan Hall is the former residence of Liu Yongfu, a famous general who had fought against foreign aggressors; it's described in a folk song of Qinzhou: "If the harvest fails, don't panic in the winter; if you're hungry, go to the Sanxuan Hall." There have no tranquil gardens, but "dragon's door", "no-bribe courtyard" and "hall of military service" instead. There are also some bullet holes, an imposing cannon tower, a tall encircling wall, and numerous secret passages that can be used for attack and defense. The walls here are thick and can resist a grenade blast. The tiles are also unusual, in layers of three. The entire structure is a fort; its military character is evident.

400 多年前的模样
400 Years of Excellence

文：朱燕

经略台真武阁位于容城东面，被鉴为“天南杰构”。全阁通高 13.2 米，面宽 13.8 米，进深 11.2 米。全阁不用一件铁器，用近 3000 条格木构件，以杠杆结构原理，串联吻合，彼此扶持，相互制约，组成一个优美稳固的统一整体。2 层的 4 根大内柱，虽承受上层楼板、梁架、配柱和阁瓦、脊饰的重荷，柱脚却悬空不落地，是全阁结构中最精巧、最奇特的部分。真武阁经历了 5 次地震、3 次特大台风，仍安然无恙。今天人们看到的仍是它 400 多年前的模样。

The Zhenwu Pavilion, located in the east of Rongcheng Town, is praised as an excellent architecture in South China. It is 13.2 meter high, 13.8 meters wide and 11.2 meters deep. There is no metal used in its construction at all; rather it's built of almost 3,000 pieces of wood. The wood pieces pass through each other and interlock tightly for a strong and beautiful unified whole. Although the four large internal columns bear the weight of the boards, columns, tiles, and decorative spines of the upper stories, they hang in the air without touching the ground, forming the most delicate and interesting part of the entire structure. The pavilion has withstood five major earthquakes and three large typhoons and still stands stalwart. This is a model of architecture that has held strong for more than 400 years.

容县经略台真武阁　摄影：陈炜平

让人捉摸不透的花屋
Flower House

文：朱燕

横县笔山村的花屋，是1757年清乾隆年间始建的古民居建筑群。花屋拥有大小房屋72间，占地面积4000平方米，因整座古建筑雕梁画栋、工艺考究而得名。花屋布局紧凑复杂，左右走廊四通八达，每处回廊都与一个主屋相接，屋群的几处回廊环环相套，使得原本就带有神秘色彩的花屋更让人捉摸不透。村外的人走进来都会在古屋群里迷路。据说抗日战争时期，日本鬼子走进去后就出不来了。

The "flower house" of Bishan Village in Heng County is a group of old buildings, the construction of which commenced in 1757, during the Qianlong period of the Qing dynasty. It comprises 72 houses large and small and covers 4,000 square meters. All the structures have carved pillars and painted ridgepoles; the artistic workmanship here is famous. The layout is complicated as well as compact, with ambulatories going in every direction. Each ambulatory is connected with a main building, and many of these ambulatories encircle and intersect with one another, making for an enticing compound so confusing that people from elsewhere often lose their way here. It's said that after Japanese troops entered during the War, they couldn't find their way out.

梧州龙母太庙
Longmu Temple

文：朱燕

梧州龙母太庙始建于北宋，占地5000多平方米，因纪念战国时期百越地带仓吾族首领——龙母而得名。龙母太庙枕山面水、舆地通灵，原由山门、前殿、后殿、左右廊房、交亭组成。后因战乱，部分建筑遭损毁。经过多次修缮，如今庙宇又增添了牌坊、行宫、龟池、观音亭等主要建筑。庙内陈列有明代石龟和两广状元伦文叙题写的碑刻"总府题名记"。龟池上的大型雕塑"五龙喷水壁"，是明代著名画家鲁恭卿的作品，极具艺术魅力。

Longmu (literally means "dragon's mother") Temple in Wuzhou, first built during the time of the Northern Song dynasty, covers more than 5,000 square meters. It was constructed to commemorate Longmu, the leader of the Cangwu People in the Baiyue Region during the Warring States Period. The temple rests at a perfect site, against mountains and abuts water. Originally it had a front gate, front hall, rear hall, two smaller structures to the left and right, as well as a series of pavilions. As a result of later wars, a portion of these structures was destroyed. Through a series of renovations and repairs, the area now has a memorial archway, a small palace, a turtle pond, an Avalokiteśvara pavilion, and other main structures. Within the temple, there are displayed Ming dynasty stone turtles and a stele that was written by a famous ancient scholar. There is a "five dragon fountain wall" carved in stone above the turtle pond, a work of the famous Ming painter Lu Gongqing, which is full of artistic allure.

一百年的活色生香

Life of a Century

文：朱燕

骑楼，不过是旧时梧州城里最普通的一种建筑。临街两侧店铺二楼以上部分伸出来，用两根大柱子牢牢支撑着，远远看去，整个楼房就像“骑”在一条人行道上，因此人称“骑楼”。“骑楼骑你头，翻风落雨永不忧。”有骑楼的庇护，不论是烈日炎炎，还是刮风下雨，摩罗街上裙裾飘摆的鲜亮女子都是旧骑楼城最为美妙的风景。

There is a special type of building that is common in Wuzhou from times past – the “riding building”, an arcade in the front. The ground floor is recessed, and the first floor overhangs, supported by columns at the edge of the pavement. These buildings appear to “ride” the street. “The riding building rides your head, and thus you won’t be bothered by rain or wind”. With the protection of these buildings, whether it’s intense heat, strong wind, or heavy rains, one will still see pretty girls in fine dresses walking along Moluo Street.

梧州骑楼街　摄影：陈炜平

南宁国际会展中心

Nanning International Exposition Center

文：朱燕

南宁国际会展中心气势恢宏地矗立在一座山上，占地面积850亩。其设计巧妙，充分利用地形地貌，依山就势逐层升高。会展中心主体建筑的灵魂——大穹顶以南宁市花朱槿花为造型，直径60米，其12片白色的“花瓣”象征着广西12个世居少数民族，在阳光照耀下洁白无瑕，熠熠生辉。每年一届的中国—东盟博览会就在这儿举行。

The extensive exposition center is built upon a mountain, occupying almost 60 hectares. Its design is clever, using the natural contours of the land, rising along the mountain face. The soul of the main construction of the center is a large arched roof that represents the Nanning’s city flower, the hibiscus, with a diameter of 60 meters. Its twelve white “petals” symbolize the twelve ethnic minorities of Guangxi. The flawless surface of the structure sparkles underneath the sunlight. The China-ASEAN Exposition is held here every year.

宾阳县古辣镇蔡村　摄影：罗劲松

蔡氏古院书香深

Fragrance of Books

文：朱燕

宾阳古辣镇蔡氏古院是一组具有岭南乡村风格的明清民居。建筑群规模庞大，气势恢宏，集建筑、雕刻、绘画、书法艺术于一体，体现了蔡家官宦世家的庄严气派和书香门第的诗风书韵，被称为南方的“乔家大院”。至今，古院依然留传着蔡氏家族缭绕不绝的书香，县里不少读书人仍会自发到此拜祭。

In the Gula Town of Binyang lies the Old Cai Compound; it's a collection of Lingnan-style residences typical in Ming and Qing dynasties. The construction of the group is grand, with a great feel, an entity comprising buildings, carvings, paintings and calligraphy. It gives expression to the stately manner and literary character of the Cai official family. It's been called the Qiao Compound of the South. Even now, the fragrance of the books of the Cai family wafts through the air; many learners of the county will still come here to pay respects.

评论

文武双全 恭城庙

Two Temples

文：李慧

在恭城，孔子和关公比邻而居，打破了历来“文武庙不并存”的惯例。恭城文庙位于印山南麓，武庙位于文庙右侧，一山两脊，文为阳，武为阴，阴阳相合，一张一弛，正合“文能治国，武可安邦，文武双全”之意。恭城当地在道光年间曾推两名举人专程赴山东曲阜考察孔庙并将图样带回依图施工，建成了当时广西规模最大、最气派的孔庙。至今恭城每年都有盛大的“祭孔”仪式，从 2017 年开始正式举办“孔子文化节”。

In Gongcheng County, the Confucius (the master of culture) Temple and Guan Yu (the master of war) Temple stand next to each other; this breaks with the historical custom that “letters and swords are not neighbors”. The Confucius Temple is situated at the southern base of Mount Yin, and the Guan Yu Temple is to its right. They are different, but in harmony, just like Yin and Yang, as the phrase goes “culture can rule a country and might can keep it safe”. During the Daoguang period in Qing dynasty, two scholars were sent to Qufu in Shandong to observe the Confucian Temple there are bring back plans, according to which they built the premier and largest temple to Confucius in Guangxi. Every year a grand ceremony is performed in memory of Confucius, and the “Confucius Cultural Festival” is held since 2017.

回风塔

Whirlwind Pagoda

文：朱燕

芦圩古镇的回风塔与大桥镇的秀峰塔一起，称为宾阳两大古塔。宝塔共 7 层，由青砖砌成，距今已 120 多年。每层塔檐外伸，略上翘，造型古雅。檐下饰有各种图案。塔顶 8 个檐角各系 1 个铜铃，风吹铃响，清脆动听。清南海张中武题书“回风塔”三个大字刻于塔门上。塔门两侧为宝塔建成时知州叶茂松题书石刻的“秀气凌云天上星辰俱动；祥光耀日人间将相迭兴”。

The Whirlwind Pagoda in Luxu Old Town is a counterpart to the Xiufeng (literally means “beautiful hilltop” in Daqiao Village. They’re together known as the “two grand towers of Binyang”. Seven stories in height, it’s built of dark bricks and has stood for more than 120 years. Each story has eaves that extend outward and curve slightly upward for an elegant look. Under the eaves are all kinds of designs. Each of the eight eaves of the top story has a copper bell at the end. When the wind blows, a clear sound rings out. The tower has a plaque reading “Whirlwind Pagoda” at the entrance, and a couplet to the sides of the gateway, which was written by an official when the tower was constructed.

评论

宾阳回风塔　摄影：罗劲松

归龙斜塔
Leaning Tower

文：李慧

归龙塔，世界八大斜塔之一，位于左江归龙滩边的江心急流小岛上。在江心建塔，据建筑专家考证，在中国古塔建筑史上乃孤例。不同于其他几座斜塔因客观原因造成的倾斜，归龙塔自建造时起就是倾斜的。塔顶到塔底中心偏移 1.42 米，专家认为是当年工匠为了让归龙塔能长期抵御江风和激流，故意让它迎水流方向倾斜。事实证明这种设计极具科学性。将近400年的风吹雨打、洪水冲刷，归龙塔仍屹立不倒。

The Guilong ("returning dragon") Tower is one of the eight greatest leaning towers of the world, located upon an islet off the Guilong Coast of the Zuo River. Archaeological experts have determined that it's the only old leaning tower in China. What makes it different from other leaning towers is the fact that it was purposely designed and built this way. The tip of the tower is offset from the center of its base by 1.42 meters; experts believe that this is due to the desire of the constructors to combat the strong winds and currents on this river; for this reason, they constructed it to lean into the flow of the currents. Over the course of almost four hundred years, although battered by rain and winds as well as surging ties, it still stands tall and strong, as a proof of the scientific design.

归龙斜塔　摄影：罗劲松

武鸣明秀园

Mingxiu Garden

文：朱燕

明秀园是广西三大古典名园之一，位于武鸣县城西。明秀园三面环水，呈葫芦状半岛，面积约40多亩，嘉庆年间为乡宦梁姓举人私园，名为“富春园”。民国初年，两广巡阅使、耀武上将军陆荣廷购下此园，改称“明秀园”。民国初期，胡汉民、章太炎和梁启超等人曾到园中与陆荣廷共商讨袁大事。古榕合抱的龙眼双生树下的天然岩石刻成的石椅、石凳以及有百年树龄荔枝树的荔枝园，便成了他们商议军机大事之地。

Mingxiu Garden is one of the three classically famous gardens in Guangxi. West to Wuming County, the garden is ringed on three sides by water, forming a gourd-shaped peninsula. It has an area of more than 26,000 square meters, and was a private garden of an official in the Jiaqing Era, when it was known as “Fuchun Garden”. In 1910s general Lu Rongting bought the garden and renamed it “Mingxiu Garden”. Hu Hanmin, Zhang Taiyan and Liang Qichao and others once visited the garden and planned to overthrow dictator Yuan Shikai. The stone stools under the old banyans and the centuries-old lychee grove witnessed their discussion.

明秀园　摄影：罗劲松

千年浴火不倒的智慧

Fire Resistance

文：朱燕

桂林大圩古镇老街两旁一路都是民居、祠堂、店铺，多为木制建筑。据说，这些建筑历经千余年，且多次浴火不倒，是得益于其建造者的智慧。它是典型的二层三进、四进“官帽式”砖木结构建筑，每进之间距离开阔，用现在的话说——防火间距大。古街上那些高大、状若马头的马头墙就是这些建筑的封火墙，近在咫尺的漓江则是消防水源。

In the Daxu Old Town of Guilin, there are residences, shrines, and shops along the sides of the road, most of which are made of wood. It's said that these structures have stood for more than a millennium, and have been bathed in fire numerous times without toppling. This is due to the wisdom of their builders. These are classic brick-and-wood compounds with two layers of buildings of three or four rows; each row has a wide space separating it from the next, which functions as a fire compartment. The tall, corbel-stepped walls function as fire barriers, and the close-by Lijiang River provides water for firefighting.

大圩古镇　摄影：罗劲松

长安古镇骑楼街

Riding Building Street

文：朱燕

广西融安的长安古镇上，全长 1.5 公里的骑楼街是目前广西规模最大、保存最完好的骑楼街之一。徜徉其中，犹如步入时间隧道。这些颇具岭南特色的砖木结构建筑将中西方美学有机结合。楼高均为二三层，哥特式、法式、古希腊式风格的建筑或整齐或弧形排列一起。长廊有遮阳挡雨功能，楼上壁瓦雕檐，龙凤雕窗，极为精巧雅致。

In the Chang'an Old Town of Rong'an, the "Riding Building Street" is one of the largest and best-preserved streets of this style in all of Guangxi. Wandering through it, you seem to step into a tunnel through time. These brick-and-wood structures of Lingnan combine Chinese and Western architecture styles perfectly. The buildings are all two or three stories, in Gothic, French and Hellenic styles, arranged in arcs or straight rows. The corridor protects from rain, and the carved eaves and windows are exquisitely crafted.

合浦大士阁　摄影：罗劲松

傲然风姿楼阁起

Graceful Buildings

文：潘惠娟

合浦大士阁，广西北部湾畔，始建于明万历年间，历数次天灾，仍傲然屹立，被誉为“抗震阁”。主体为两幢阁楼相接，重檐歇山顶式磅礴大气；穿斗式与台梁式结合的木梁架，榫卯连接，无一钉一铁；各式浮雕珍奇入画；尤为精巧奇特的是，柱脚不入土，支承宝莲花石垫，其中1根立柱柱脚悬空翘起。诗云：“明代风情遗艳丽，良工斧藻意斯乎？”其是南方古建筑遗存的实例，有重要价值。

The Dashi Pavilion of Hepu stands beside the Beibu Gulf. It was built during the Wanli era of the Ming dynasty. It's stood strong through successive natural disasters, and is known as the "earthquake-proof pavilion". Its main structure consists of two connected pavilions with double hilltop eaves. The beams and pillars are arranged in two ways and connect by tenon-and-mortise work. No nails were used in the construction, and there are all kinds of relief carvings. The columns rest upon stone lotus pedestals rather than being anchored in the earth, and one of them floats. The cleverness of this architecture has been remarked upon in poems, impressing people of later dynasties. This site is a real example of southern classical architecture with significant value.

春风笑，海棠依旧

Smiling Spring

文：潘惠娟

横县海棠桥，地处郁江畔香稻溪，为土石结构，因秦观贬谪横州（今广西横县）在桥畔设馆讲学，留诗赋词驰名："瘴雨过，海棠开，春色又添多少。"旧时，暮春初夏，桥旁海棠花盛放，云雾缭绕，烟雨习习，转瞬即逝，美不胜收，即为"海棠暮雨"，"横州古八景"之一。

The Haitang[1] Bridge lies in Hengxian County, where Xiangdao ("fragrant rice") Creek flows into Yujiang River. It is an earth-rock structure. When famous poet Qin Guan was banished to Hengzhou (today's Hengxian), he established a school and gave lectures. Here he penned a line that became famous: "The hazy rains pass and the Chinese flowering apple trees bloom, adding color to the spring." In times past, at the end of spring and start of summer, many such trees blossomed at the sides of the bridge as mists flowed about and wispy rains fell. This sight persists today, and the "Dusk Rains at Haitang Bridge" is one of the eight famous sights of Hengzhou.

横县伏波庙　摄影：罗劲松

横县伏波庙

Fubo Temple

文：朱燕

伏波庙位于横县郁江乌蛮滩北岸，是为纪念东汉伏波将军马援而建的一座祭祀性建筑。伏波庙依山傍水，庙后天堂山连绵起伏，古木婆娑；庙前乌蛮滩礁石林立，浪溅水飞。雨后放晴，庙宇清新洁净，绿叶青翠欲滴，与滩上绿水浑然一体，山水一色，织成了一幅"乌蛮积翠"（"横州古八景"之一）的绚丽美景。

Situated on the northern bank of the Wuman Shoal of Yujiang River, Hengxian County, Fubo Temple was constructed as a monument to the Fubo General, Ma Yuan. The Tiantang peak behind the compound rises towards the sky, with old trees thriving. The shoal in front has rocks and torrents. When the sky clears up after rain, the temple is fresh and clean; the leaves drip with fine drops, forming a beautiful scene of green tiers; truly deserving a place in the "Eight Sights of Hengzhou".

1. *Malus spectabilis, the Chinese flowering crabapple*

百色粤东会馆　摄影：罗劲松

百色粤东会馆

Yuedong Guild Hall

文：朱燕

粤东会馆坐落在百色市繁华的解放街中心，面临碧波如画的右江。这座建筑物始建于清康熙末年，道光和同治年间先后两次重修，乃粤籍豪商巨贾醵资兴建。粤东会馆体现了南方古建筑的风格和思想文化。大殿前的石柱分别以花篮、南瓜、佛珠为柱础，表达了人们迎宾、多子多孙、虔心拜佛的美好愿望。会馆藏有15块珍贵的铁木牌匾，上书“与汉无极”“天地正气”等，280年来承载着粤商的精神追求、文化寄托以及生活梦想。

The Yuedong Guild Hall is located in the Jiefang Street in Baise City; it faces the beautiful Youjiang River. It was first built during the later years of the Kangxi Era and redone twice in the Daoguang and Tongzhi Eras. Funds were donated by wealthy merchants. The building is a realization of ancient architectural style and culture. There are flower pots, pumpkins and Buddhist beads on the column bases of the main hall, which show the wishes of the people to welcome guests, have more offspring and worship Buddha. There are fifteen precious ironwood plaques within the hall carved with traditional sayings, a showcase of 280 years of Cantonese merchant culture.

评论

刘三姐山歌唱响北京梅兰芳大剧院　摄影：邓华

艺术·显影
Art and Appearances

快乐的剧种
Happy Dramas

文：莫喜生

“哪嚯咿嚯嗨……”在广西，特别是桂北，有人的地方就有它。生老病死，满月做寿，大厦落成，婚丧娶嫁……兴奋的时候唱它，沮丧的时候唱它，得意的时候唱它，失意的时候也唱它……它，就是广西有名的剧种——彩调。临桂是广西彩调的主要发源地之一。早在清代，彩调已在广西境内风行。因其诙谐幽默，活泼欢快，彩调被当地群众称为“快乐的剧种”。

“Na Ho Yi Ho Hey…” In Guangxi, especially in the north of the region, there are dramas wherever there are people. For birthdays, groundbreaking, weddings, funerals, and the like, happy events and sad ones are always accompanied by the songs. People sing when satisfied and when disappointed. These are the caidiao, or “colored melodies” – the songs and performances that originated mainly in Lingui. During the Qing dynasty, they were already popular throughout Guangxi. Because they’re fun and humorous, active and upbeat, they’re known locally as “happy dramas”.

最美瑶族蝴蝶歌
Butterfly Song

文：翟香丽

“富川山歌有几多，出门三步歌绊脚；田里种禾又种歌，一颗谷子一首歌。”在广西富川，几乎每个村寨、圩镇都流传着各类民间歌谣，尤以蝴蝶歌最负盛名。因为在歌的衬字词中，常出现“蝴的蝶”“蝶的蝶”“黄蜂”之类，故得名“蝴蝶歌”。每逢瑶族重大节日，各村的群众便精心打扮，成群结队地聚在一起，以歌会友、以歌定情。那清亮、美妙的蝴蝶歌经久缭绕于瑶族美丽的大山里，有着不可言说的韵味。

“The mountain songs of Fuchuan are numerous; setting foot outside you’ll soon hear them. They sing and they plant, and each grain accompanies a note.” All kinds of folk songs can be heard in the villages and towns of Fuchuan in Guangxi; the butterfly song is the most famous kind, which is thus called because of its numerous references to the insects. On major Yao holidays, people from the villages dress up and gather in groups, greeting friends with songs and pairing out. The sound of these butterfly songs drifting throughout the Yao villages and over the mountains is a beautiful one indeed.

贺州富川古戏台和老观众　摄影：陈炜平

只有一根弦的乐器

Single String

文：翟香丽

对于广西京族特有的民族乐器——独弦琴，有人曾这样形容它的声音："泛音从手指的似弹非弹之间柔柔而出，那种乐感，虽不是个个喜欢的枕边细语骨边肉，但齐白石所言那种妙在似与不似之间的意境。说不定听着听着耳油就出来了。"在京族三岛的海风和涛声里常可听到它的清音，那一刻，你会沉浸入不同的音乐境界：或风平浪静，海阔天空；或潮起潮落，波逐浪涌；或柔情似水，袅绕动人。

The Jing people of Guangxi have a special instrument, the Duxianqin or "single-stringed zither". Someone once described its sound, "The overtone comes with the seemingly unnoticeable plucking movement. The feeling of the sound isn't that kind of universally-appreciated softness, but it has a soothing and clarifying effect, one of wonder between the similarity and dissimilarity, just like famous painter Qi Baishi put it." One can hear the sound of the instruments against the backdrop of the sea breeze and the crashing waves upon the Three Jing Islands on the border with Vietnam. It's an experience that brings you into a different musical realm, one that may be of calm wind and a deep sky, or maybe one of surging tides and churning water, or even one of the soft and uplifting feelings.

壮族人迷壮剧

Zhuang Operas

文：翟香丽

壮剧是壮族戏曲剧种的统称，因方言、音乐唱腔、表演风格和流行地区不同而"兵分多路"，有壮族师公戏（又称壮师剧）、南路壮剧和北路壮剧等。百年来，壮族人之所以迷壮剧，因为其剧情不但是壮族人熟悉的，且唱词、道白也是壮族的方言土语，让人听来备感亲切。那慢板、中板、快板、散板等，无不来自壮族人所熟悉的民歌曲调。多年来，广西壮剧创作、改编和演出的《红铜鼓》《夜明珠》《玫瑰花》《百鸟衣》《一幅壮锦》等，都博得观众的好评。

Zhuang Opera is a blanket term for several kinds of arts performed by the Zhuang people, which differ in dialects, melodies, performance styles and regional factors, including the Zhuang master operas, the Nanlu Zhuang opera, and the Beilu Zhuang opera. Over the course of more than a hundred years the Zhuang opera has been the favorite of Zhuang people because the story, lyrics and dialogues are very familiar to them. Slow, medium, fast and free-form styles are all encompassed in these songs. Over the years, many notable original Zhuang productions have been adapted and performed, such as Red Copper Drum, Luminous Pearl, Rose Blossom, Hundred-Bird Dress, A Bolt of Zhuang Brocade and others, all of which have gained very high praise from audiences.

天籁之琴的神韵

Sounds of Nature

文：翟香丽

眼前，壮族的天琴少女蹁跹而至，她们身着黑衣壮的传统民族服饰，手拿天琴，足悬脚铃，坐在老房子前弹奏了一曲又一曲的壮族声韵……天琴，是壮族使用的一种弹拨类弦鸣乐器，壮语称“鼎叮”，由乐器发声的谐音而得名。天琴音色圆润明亮，常用于独奏或为歌舞伴奏。在学者们看来，天琴是壮族最古老的三大乐器之一，也是骆越文化的主要曲艺形式之一，至今已有上千年历史。

Zhuang dancers flits about before the eyes, clad in traditional black clothing with a stringed instrument called Tianqin, or Heavenly Zither. Bells ring out at the feet as they play one Zhuang song after another. This traditional instrument is called the “ding ding” in the Zhuang language, a reference to the sound it makes. It has a sound that’s clear and pleasing, and is employed in solos as well as dances. Scholars say that it is one of the original three major instruments of the Zhuang people and a musical form of the Luoyue Culture that has persisted for more than a thousand years into the present day.

邕剧票友中的传说

Yong Opera

文：覃兰

邕剧是南宁独有的地方剧种，因南宁古称邕州而得名。邕剧早在清朝道光年间，就已在南宁及周边一带流传开来，不过那时人们只亲切地称它“老戏”“大戏”“本地班”。一个流传于邕剧票友中的传说：一位青年艺人随戏班去越南演出，邂逅了一位越南女子，两人迅速坠入爱河。当戏班结束在越南的演出时，两人只得惜别。谁料几十年后，一位越南海军舰长带着一张照片到南宁寻找自己的亲生父亲，照片中的那位男子就是当年戏班的那位青年艺人。

邕剧剪影　摄影：张小宁

Nanning Opera, the city’s unique art form, is also known as “Yong Opera” due to the old name of the city, Yongzhou. It began in the Daoguang era of the Qing dynasty and became popular in and around the city, where it was called intimately “old opera”, “big opera” or “local opera”. There is a legend among the fans, a troop of young performers went to Vietnam, where one of the members met a young Vietnamese woman, and they quickly fell in love. When their tour was finished, they could only part. Decades later, a Vietnamese navy captain went to Nanning with a picture in hand to search for his birth father; the man in the picture was the opera performer from all those years ago.

行走的“故事会”——客家竹板歌

Story Club

文：覃兰

只见那人手持竹板，左手三块，右手一块，或敲或击或锯，“沙沙乐、沙沙乐、沙乐沙乐沙沙乐”。他走街串巷，随编随唱，张口就来，“见人说话，见鬼打卦”，总能博得听众的欢心。这是流行在贺州市的一种客家民间曲艺——竹板歌。旧时艺人夜晚还会为劳苦大众免费表演。《梁山伯与祝英台》《孟姜女哭长城》《赵玉林》《胡中庆》《高文举》等故事在客家地区可谓家喻户晓，这主要归功于行走的“故事会”——客家竹板歌了。

One sees a man with bamboo clappers in hand; three in the left and one in the right, tapping, striking, or cascading them to make that running “click-clack-clack-clack” sound. He walks the streets and the alleyways, singing his songs impromptu. He’s always well-received by audiences. This is a traditional art form popular in Hezhou – bamboo clapper songs. In olden times, performers would put on shows for free for the tired laborers at the end of the day. Classics such as Butterfly Lovers, Lady Meng Crying at the Great Wall, Zhao Yulin, Hu Zhongqing, and Gao Wenju are familiar to everyone here. The bamboo clapper performances are like a kind of walking story club.

零零落，长板落

Ling Ling Lo

文：覃兰

桂林有个别具地方特色的曲艺——零零落。零零落源于宋、元时代贫苦人歌唱的乞食词莲花落。相传清乾隆年间，桂林设有 4 所专门收容流民和流浪艺人的养济院，由于官府所发钱米不足维持最低生活，院中收容的一些女盲人便仿效莲花落的曲调，沿街卖唱。其音乐后来与桂林官话结合，受当地民歌小调的影响，逐渐演变成零零落。

There’s a special kind of song in Guilin, Ling Ling Lo, which originated in the Song and Yuan dynasties as a form of performance art among beggars. It’s said that during the Qianlong era of the Qing dynasty there were four shelters for the homeless and itinerant performers. The grain allowances they were given weren’t enough to sustain their basic needs, and thus some blind women wrote some beautiful songs which they performed on the street. These musical pieces were later merged with the tradition of Guilin Mandarin, and influenced by local folk ditties to gradually become “Ling Ling Lo”.

桂剧剪影　摄影：张小宁

桂剧的魅力

The beauty of Gui Opera

文：彭匈

开演之前要打一通很长的锣鼓，叫做“打开台”，起“预备铃”作用。开台锣鼓由多牌子组成，名称有点怪，但很好听：三炮擂、四门进、乱插花、滴溜子、摇摇令、狗咬羊、十八槌……锣鼓声中隐伏着一种令人难耐的急促和焦虑……用桂林方言演唱的桂剧，就是桂林人另一种说话方式，细腻而富有岭南地区的生活气息。

At the start of a performance, the stage is “opened” by striking percussion instruments, as a “ready” signal. There are all kinds of arrangements of drums and gongs, some names of which are a bit odd but sound good: “three beats”, “flowers abound”, “eighteen hammers”, “dog bites lamb” and the like. The sounds of the instruments contain a kind of energy that makes people feel driven and anxious. Gui opera, performed in Guilin dialect, is another way of speaking for Guilin people, smooth and full of the character of life in the Lingnan Area.

开开合合，开开合合

Bamboo Pole Dance

文：朱燕

每当收割时节的晚上，壮族人民就会愉悦地跳起竹竿舞，庆祝丰收。“开开合合，开开合合……”人们随着竹竿的节奏，跳跃、狂欢、释放，多么机灵，多么轻快，多么准确；节奏逐步加快，多么紧张，多么痛快，多么奔放，人心沉醉，欢乐弥漫……

Each year at night during harvest time, the Zhuang people come together to happily dance the bamboo pole dance and celebrate the bumper year. “Come together, come apart, come together, come apart…” People dance, celebrate and cut loose to the rhythm. It’s sharp and quick; the pace picks up and so does the heartbeat, people get worked up and let it all out, taken in with the exhilarating dance…

桂林市最珍贵的特产

Most Precious Product

文：覃兰

一方水土养一方音乐。北京有国粹京剧，东北有二人转，江淮一带有黄梅戏，在山奇水秀的广西则有文场，又称“文玩子”“小曲”等，是流行于桂北官话地区的传统说唱艺术。著名音乐家贺绿汀先生访问桂林时，对文场很是感兴趣。考虑到时间有限，他原计划只听一小时，可一听就停不下来了，竟足足听了一整天，还意犹未尽，于是欣然题词：“广西文场是桂林市最珍贵的特产”“国际旅游者要买当地特产，如能得到它的录音或激光唱片（CD），比任何纪念物都好”。

Where people live so, where will music grow. Beijing has Peking Opera, the Northeast has “duo performances”, Jiangsu and Anhui have Huangmei Opera, and Guangxi has its own art forms called Wenchang, Wenwanzi or Xiaoqu, which are popular in the northern, Mandarin-speaking portion of Guangxi. Famous composer He Lüting visited Guangxi and became very interested in these performances. His time was limited, and he originally planned on listening for one hour, but ended up listening for an entire day. He was moved, and wrote, “These performances of string and wind instruments are the most precious local product that Guangxi has.” “If tourists from abroad want to pick up a local specialty, they should buy a CD here; it’s better than any other souvenir.”

渔鼓声声道桂林

Fishing Drum

文：覃兰

“我想去桂林呀我想去桂林，可是有时间的时候我却没有钱……”这首曾风靡一时的流行歌曲，道出了众人对桂林的神往。这朗朗上口的曲调，是由最具桂林地方特色的桂林渔鼓素材谱曲而成。渔鼓，是扎根桂林本土的传统说唱艺术。宋代曾在桂林任通判的周去非在《岭外代答·平南乐》中记载：“广西诸郡人多能合乐，城廓村落，祭祀婚嫁、丧葬，无一不用乐，虽耕田亦必口乐相之，盖日闻鼓笛声也。”描写的仿佛就是桂林人唱渔鼓的情景。

“I want to go to Guilin, I do want to go, but when I have time I haven’t money”. This song was popular for a while, and lead to a surge of interest in Guilin. Did you know, however, that the basis for the song is the simple traditional songs of Guilin itself? The “fishing drum” is a kind of traditional local performance with roots in Guilin. During his term as an administrator of lawsuits in Guilin, Zhou Qufei of the Song dynasty wrote, “The people of Guangxi excel at music all over; at rituals, weddings, funerals, even in the fields, one will always hear the sounds of drums and flutes.” It seems that he was describing scenes of the “fishing drum” music.

童年晒场上的演唱会

Songs upon the Threshing Ground

文：翟香丽 覃兰

“小时候，最是期待夜晚在田间晒场上的牛歌戏了。牛歌戏帮都是村子里的人自发组成的，在农闲时为大家表演，不收门票，但总有热情的乡亲自发送上稻米充当戏金……”据载，最早的牛歌戏剧目是《阿赖卖猪》，取材于民间故事，诙谐幽默，生动活泼，一出现就受到群众的热烈欢迎，并很快流传开来。

“When I was young, I always looked forward most to the 'cow opera' performances upon the threshing ground in the fields. The performing troupe consists of people from the village. It was a performance during the slack season. Nobody had to pay for tickets, but the villagers would always contribute rice…” Records show that the earliest “cow opera” was Ar-Lai Sells His Pig. The plots come from folk stories, and the performances are humorous, active and full of life. They became quite popular and spread far and wide after they first appeared.

唱神必跳神，跳神必戴相

Dance with Mask

文：朱燕

师公戏 摄影：陈炜平

区别于其他祭祀舞蹈，广西壮族师公戏主要标志是“唱神必跳神，跳神必戴相”。“相”即为面具。只见师公穿着长而鲜艳的宽袖大袍，戴上刻有“作神”形象的木制面具，在台上作揖致礼后开始唱……先表演一段独舞或双人舞，示意神灵已降临人间，接着坐下演唱该神的身世业绩，歌颂他的力量与功德。后来，随着剧目增多及人神形象比例的变化，师公的面具逐渐为化妆所代替，师公戏遂演变成一个新剧种——壮师剧。

Different from other sacrificial dances, the standard of the Zhuang master operas is that “one must sing, one must dance, and one must wear a mask”. Traditionally, the master danced in a brightly-colored wide-sleeved robe while wearing a wooden mask. On the stage, after bowing and saluting, a solo or duo dance was performed to signify the arrival of the spirits. The performer then sat and detailed the virtues of the spirit, and praised its power and character. Over time as the repertoire of these performances expanded and styles shifted, the masks were gradually replaced with makeup, and the grandmaster dance became a style of performance all of its own, an essential part of Zhuang opera.

壮乡哭嫁歌

Wedding Lament

文：朱燕

男方的彩礼已送到门外，就等着新娘拜别父母。新娘子走出闺房，与父母兄弟道别，唱起哭嫁歌。“爷呀娘！”刚一开唱，那泪珠便顺着腮帮滚落。顿时，宴席上众人安静下来。一开始，只有新娘与她的好姐妹的附和帮唱，后来，来参加宴席的妇女也被感染，加入到合唱的人群中。那曲调时而激昂悲壮，时而缠绵悱恻，撼动全场，催人泪下。

The groom waits for his bride to part with her parents after he delivers the wedding gifts. As she leaves the home in which she grew up, and her parents and siblings, she will sing the “Wedding Lament”. Tears flow down her cheeks as she says farewell to the family. Suddenly, the banquet becomes quiet. At the start, only the bride’s friends sing the accompaniment; later the older women are also taken up in the sentiment and join in. The song swells to a chorus powerful and poignant, and sometimes pained, always moving – it brings tears to the eyes.

唱山歌的瘾头

Mountain Songs

文：彭匈

柳州人的生活，有一个外地人难以望其项背的节目——唱山歌。“讲起唱歌心就开，半夜三更我就来。衣服没穿披起走，鞋子没扣踏起来！”柳州人唱山歌的瘾头很大。柳州市中心的鱼峰山，传说当年刘三姐就是在这里骑着鲤鱼成仙的。山下常有对歌，时见精妙之作。周边县份的人劲头更大。他们以歌代言，以歌传情。到这些地方去做客，必须能够对上几首，否则一切免谈。

Life for the people of Liuzhou contains a performance that’s hard to top: singing mountain songs. “One’s heart opens up when talking about singing songs; I wakc up in the middle of the night; I have neither time to get fully dressed or do up my shoes!” Singing the songs is quite a rush. It’s said that Yufeng (“fish peak”) Hill in the center of the city is where Liu Sanjie rode the fish to become a fairy. The base of the hill is a place where one frequently hears songs and sees exquisite works. The people who live in counties nearby are even more into it. They express themselves and their feelings through songs. When you come here, you really should make sure you know enough to join in for a bit of singing.

评论

千人打榔舞
Pole Dance

文：朱燕

在“打榔舞之乡”天等举行的榔舞比赛，有1000多人参加，少长咸集。比赛分自编舞蹈（舂榔调）和统一舞蹈（千人打榔舞）两部分。伴随着音乐，天椒广场上响起阵阵有力的击打声，“咚咚咚”的节奏让人振奋。所有参赛队伍都穿着壮族特色服饰，以稻作工具为道具，用木杵有节奏地击打榔壁、榔底、榔边。从原生态打榔到具有各乡镇特色的现代风格的打榔……精彩纷呈、气势磅礴，当然是一场视觉盛宴。

There is a kind of dance competition in Tiandeng that involves the use of a long wooden pole – more than 1,000 people participate, both young and old. There are two sections – original dances, and the coordinated “thousand-dancer” section. Along with music, in Tianjiao Plaza, the “donk-donk-donk” sounds of the tapping of the poles ring out with energy. Each team wears unique Zhuang clothing, using these rice-farming poles as props, tapping on the sides, edges and base of a kind of wooden box rhythmically, from the original rhythms of times past to more modern styles that with the characteristics of individual villages. It’s an exciting scene, one full of robust feelings and impressive sights.

有画的石山
Painted Mountain

文：朱燕

泛舟崇左境内左江、明江河段，岸边悬崖峭壁，红影绰绰，骆越先人穿越2000年的时光，驻留石上。那是世间最传奇的红色，如生命不息，永不褪色；那是壮乡最盛大古老的生活群像，如江畔木棉，花开似锦。古朴、粗犷、壮观，整体规模宏大，单体气势雄伟，个体强壮硕大，花山于山河沉静与刚劲之处，震撼人心。2016年，花山壁画列为“世界文化遗产”，为广西第一处。

Boating upon the Zuojiang and Mingjiang Rivers in Chongzuo, one sees cliffs and red shadows all about. The traces of the Luoyue Culture from more than 2,000 years ago are still here upon these rock faces. This legendary red has persisted all this time without fading, a testament to the strength of lives – it stands there like the kapok trees that line the banks. Old, simple, strong and solid, the feeling is grandeur and bravery. Observing these sights is a moving experience. In 2016, these rock paintings upon Mount Huashan (“flower mountain”) were listed as a world cultural heritage – the first in Guangxi.

评论

花山岩画　摄影：张小宁

马山壮族三声部

Trio

文：朱燕

说起马山壮族三声部的传承与发展，不得不提及广西著名民歌专家范西姆。1980 年，范西姆陪上海电影制片厂的编辑到古零镇采风，遇到了被当地称为“三顿欢”的壮族民歌。范西姆经过细致考察，确定这就是三声部民歌。该民歌由 3 个人唱 3 种声调，甚至是轮换担任高、中、低音部，歌声和谐，乐律淳朴。而在此之前，世界音乐史上一直有“中国没有多声部民歌”的说法。

When talking about the traditions and development of the trio songs of the Mashan (“horse mountain”) Zhuang people, one must mention famous Guangxi songwriter Fan Ximu. In 1980, he was working with the Shanghai Film Studio and visited Guling Town to gather some shots; where he encountered these Zhuang folk songs. Through careful exploration, he confirmed that they are a kind of trio folk songs. They are sung by three people in three parts, each performer changing between high, middle and low parts. They’re harmonious, full of musicality, and pure. They proved wrong the previous misconception abroad that “China has no polyphonic music”.

阿妹的嫁衣歌声

Zhuang Brocade

文：潘惠娟

“壮锦是阿妹的嫁衣歌声；壮锦是阿哥的木叶酒盅；壮锦是山坡上吃草的成群牛羊；壮锦是田坝里生长的五谷丰登……”壮锦是广西民族文化瑰宝，与云锦、蜀锦、宋锦并称中国四大名锦，据传起源于宋代。《柳州府志》载：“壮锦各州县出，壮人爱彩，凡衣裙巾被之属，莫不取五色绒，杂以织布为花鸟状，远观颇工巧炫丽，近视而粗，壮人贵之。”

“Zhuang brocade is the wedding dress of the girl, Zhuang brocade is the wooden leaf wine cup of the young man. Zhuang brocade is the sustenance of the sheep and cattle upon the mountain slopes, Zhuang brocade is the plentiful grains growing in the fields.” Zhuang brocade is a cultural treasure of Guangxi, one of the four famous styles of brocade historically in China. It’s said to have originated in the Song dynasty. In Local Chronicles of Liuzhou, it is written, “Zhuang brocade comes from all cities and counties, and is much loved by the people. Garments and scarves come in various colors, bearing patterns of birds and fish; even when viewed from afar it looks elegant; viewed up close it can look a little rough. It is quite valued by the Zhuang.”

评论

壮乡铜鼓

Zhuang Drums

文：覃明君

若谈壮族文化，一定离不开铜鼓。我国共有 8 种不同类型的铜鼓，而广西就有 7 种之多；在全国收藏的 1400 多面铜鼓中，广西馆藏就有 900 多面。铜鼓腹中空，曲腰鼓胸，且无底。在鼓身上有许多的纹饰：太阳纹、云雷纹、翔鹭纹、羽人舞蹈纹、十二生肖纹、几何纹，还有青蛙的立体雕像。这些纹饰既是一种装饰，更是一种信仰与崇拜。时至今日，我们仍不能完全参透其中的奥秘。

The copper drums are a topic that must be mentioned when talking about Zhuang culture. There are eight types of copper drum in China, seven of which are in Guangxi; of the more than 1,400 collected copper drums in the entire country, 900 are in Guangxi. The shell of the drum is hollow, the waist thick, and there is no base. There are all kinds of patterns upon each drum, such as sun, cloud, soaring egret and feathered dancers, as well as astrological signs, geometric shapes, and frog decorations. These are not only decorations but also have ritual significance as signs of respect. Even today, we still can't wholly unravel their secrets.

壮族铜鼓舞

Copper Drum Dance

文：朱燕

每逢春节，村里赛铜鼓时，铜鼓队便把四面铜鼓吊挂在村头的那棵大榕树上，由四个青年持竹片敲击。还有一面大皮鼓放置场地中心，鼓舞者双手持鼓槌，或正击、反击，或转身、翻身，不停变换动作边击边舞，舞姿矫健洒脱。青年配合舞者的表演击铜鼓，时轻时重，时缓时急。围观助兴的群众，听见“咚咚”的铜鼓响，脚也开始渐渐发痒起来，一个个情不自禁地汇聚到大皮鼓周围跳起舞来，或就在原地踩着铜鼓的节奏起舞。

Every year at the Spring Festival, there is a copper drum competition in the village. Teams of drummers hang four drums upon the big banyan tree, and four youths beat the drums with bamboo in hand. A large leather drum is placed in the center. The drummers hold mallets with two hands hitting on the front or back side, or spinning and flipping as they continuously drum and dance with smooth movements. The youths provide accompaniment with their copper drums to the dancers, sometimes heavily, sometimes lightly. The audience gets an urge to dance as they watch all of this, letting loose as they start to move their legs and feet all about, or just stand in place going along with the beat.

评论

得之我幸，不得我命

Lucky Me

文：潘惠娟

坭兴陶雕刻大师刘明洲在坯体上刻纹　摄影：谢勇云

钦州坭兴陶，中国四大名陶之一，坯泥取自钦江，泥质软硬谦和，以为坭兴陶筋骨。将花鸟山水于坯体上刻纹，刻痕中嵌套不同泥料，打磨，窑制，至涅槃。而神奇的窑变，是坭兴陶借天工之手谋得的斑斓色彩和绚丽纹理，颇有“得之我幸，不得我命”的宿命。烧制好的坭兴陶，色泽光润、耐酸耐碱，茶叶置于坭兴陶罐可数年无霉变。风雅天然，成无定格，品珍独一。坭兴陶谓为：天成之美意，巧手偶得之。

The Nixing pottery of Qinzhou is one of the four most famous in China. The ceramic paste is taken from the Qinjiang River and has a good character that is neither too hard nor too soft; it forms the physique of Nixing pottery. Birds, flowers, or landscapes are carved into the work, and different pastes are filled into the crevices. Then the work is sanded down and fired. Incredible changes happen in the kiln, which is one of the hallmarks of this art form. When luck is good, beautiful patterns and variations will emerge during the process. Fired Nixing pottery has a brilliant luster, withstands both acid and alkali, and can preserve tea while preventing mold for years. It's an elegant and valuable craft, a fusion of natural beauty and human skill.

评论

一贝藏天地，一刀刻乾坤

Carved Shells

文：潘惠娟

“天上有多少星星，海里就有多少贝类……”广西北海地处北部湾畔，滨海的地理位置让北海得到了来自海洋的馈赠——贝雕。北海贝雕利用贝壳的天然色泽、纹理、形状等，依势取形。无论山水人物还是花鸟虫鱼，都自然逼真、意蕴丰富，大有“一贝藏天地，一刀刻乾坤”之大气。1989 年，北海贝雕作品《程阳桥》被悬挂在人民大会堂广西厅。

“The kinds of shells in the sea is as many as the stars in the sky.” In Beihai City and along the shores of the Beibu Gulf, there are treasures that come from the sea – carved shells. These are beautiful works of art with luster, patterns and forms that reflect the natural state of the unworked source material. Landscapes, human figures, birds, flowers, insects and fish… all the designs are realistic and full of vibrancy. It’s said that they are carved in harmony with Great Nature. In 1989, the carved shell Chengyang Bridge was hung in the Guangxi Chamber of the Grand Hall of the People.

壮家姑娘心灵巧

Zhuang Skills

文：刘源祥

咱们壮家姑娘心灵手巧，从小就得为自己准备出嫁的盛装。因此，在很小的时候，我们练就了一手针线活。织布、染色、裁剪、绣花、装饰，样样都精通。在奶奶的细心教导下，我还学会了织壮锦，这是我的最爱。一丝一线，凝聚着壮家人的勤劳和智慧，也织出了我们幸福、甜蜜、祥和的美好新生活。

We Zhuang girls are good at crafts. From the time we are young we prepare to make our wedding outfits. For this reason, when we’re very little, we already have learned how to use a needle and thread. Weaving cloth, dying, cutting and stitching, embroidering, decorating, are all things we learn. Under the careful guidance of my grandmother, I learned how to make Zhuang brocade which I love most. Each thread, each string is a concentration of the wisdom and hard-working nature of the Zhuang people, as well as evidence of the prosperous, sweet and lucky lives we live.

评论

南丹县中堡乡苗族妇女在竹篓上织锦绣花腰带　摄影：张小宁

服饰·遗风
Clothing and Customs

黑衣壮服饰　摄影：张小宁

黑色的衣，银色的鱼

Black Clothing, Silver Fish

文：覃兰

黑衣、黑裤、黑头巾、黑布鞋，没有哪个民族比黑衣壮更“黑”了。黑衣壮妇女还会搭配各种银饰，银簪、银链、银项圈等，其中银项圈尤为特别。项圈两端制成鱼的形状，有如双鱼对吻。这双鱼对吻银项圈是黑衣壮婚嫁时的必需品之一，是黑衣壮独特的鱼图腾崇拜，因为黑衣壮的祖先们相信，人死后灵魂化而为鱼，再入轮回转世。

Black shirt, black trousers, black headscarf, black cloth shoes – no ethnic group has blacker clothing than the black Zhuang. The women dressed in black will wear all kinds of silver accessories, such as hairpins, chains, and necklaces. The necklaces are quite special – the two ends are in the form of fish as if they were kissing each other. These “kissing fish silver necklaces” are an essential item for black Zhuang women when they marry; the black Zhuang revere the fish as their totem animal. As their ancestors believed that after people die their souls turn into fish as they are reincarnated.

“混搭风”的“三层楼”

Mixed Style

文：翟香丽

一眼望去，隆林壮族女子服饰分上、中、下三层：上衣较短，仅及腰间，衣身下摆两侧开叉；上衣下配一条黑色或者蓝色百褶片裙，长及膝盖，以浅色布做裙头、系带；裙子内着黑土布长裤，长及脚踝。这样耀眼的“混搭风”，就是当地壮族女子服饰的“三层楼”。

Looking at the Zhuang women of Longlin, you see that their outfit is in three pieces. They wear a short garment at the top that only extends to the wait, with two openings at the bottom. Under that is a black or blue skirt that extends to the knee, with many pleats and a light-colored waistband and rims. Under the skirt are long black cloth trousers that extend to the ankles. This kind three-part of “mixed style” is the norm for local Zhuang women.

隆林壮族女子服饰　摄影：玉时阶

戴“高帽”

“High Hats”

文：翟香丽

很难想象，头顶上带着十来斤甚至更重的帽子是什么感受。贺州尖头瑶因为头顶高高尖尖的帽饰而著称。或许只有他们才能理解，靛青棉布上那一格格、一排排、一列列密密匝匝的针线间，瑶胞的生命情感和历史密码；而作为他者，我们看到的只是那些白色、红色饰边的青色布帕，一层层富丽堂皇地重叠成尖头竹笋的形状。

贺州尖头瑶服饰　摄影：张小宁

It’s hard to imagine what it feels like to wear a hat that weighs five or more kilograms. The “pointy-headed Yao” of Hezhou get their name from this piece of attire. Maybe only they can understand the history and feelings behind these indigo cloth hats with rows of tight stitching all upon them. As outsiders, we see these white- or red-brimmed indigo hats as grandiose accessories.

一半春风在里湖

Living Cultural Fossil

文：翟香丽

在南丹里湖，身处在浓厚的白裤瑶气息中是件很幸福的事。白色裤子上的五指印、“两片衣”上的盘王印、悠悠晃动的百褶裙流动在过往的男的女的老的少的白裤瑶人身上，地为T台，天为观众，柴米油盐酱醋茶为道具，像一场盛大的生活走秀，艺术含量却极高，绝不愧对联合国教科文组织认定的“人类文明的活化石”这一称号。

At Lake Lihu in Nandan, it's nice to be in the environment of the “white-trousers Yao”. Upon their trousers they have handprints; upon their vests, they have the mark of King Panwang. They wear many-pleated skirts, male and female, young and old. The ground is the stage, the sky is the audience, and everyday items are the props, as if a large show of everyday life is being put on. It has a very artistic field, and is worthy of UNESCO's designation of a “living cultural fossil”.

天地间，点点红

Red Dots

文：翟香丽

一串串冰挂点缀在龙胜的深山里，一夜间世界银装素裹。红瑶女子是雪中红雀，叽叽喳喳地来闹冬。数码相机、智能手机，拍不尽家乡的雪景，拍不完生活的幸福。殊不知，“你站在桥上看风景，看风景的人在楼上看你”。在别人的镜头里，白雪红衣才最美。

Icicles hang off the trees in the forest of Longsheng, and white is all around. The women of the “red Yao” are like cardinals in the snow, chirping as they move about. Digital cameras and smartphones can capture the scenes, but not the joy of life. It's like the poem “you look at the scenery from the bridge, but you're a part of the scenery for the person in the building watching you”. In other people's lenses, white snow and red clothing are the most beautiful.

龙胜红瑶女子服饰 摄影：张小宁

白裤瑶女子服饰　摄影：张小宁

盛装的竞技

Dolled Up

文：覃兰

蜡染在隆林苗乡世代传承，苗家的姑娘们更是自幼便学习蜡染技艺。时至今日，身在隆林苗乡的女子每逢民族节庆、走亲访友等场合，都会身着自制的蜡染裙，拎着蜡染包。尽管一套九层的盛装会让她们行动不便，但姑娘们可不会放过这么一个显示自己聪明才智的机会。于是，盛装也成了一场竞技，一场悦己悦人的美丽竞技。

Batik is a tradition in the Miao villages of Longlin. Girls in Miao families learn the craft of wax-dying from a young age, and even today whenever times for festivals or visits come around, Miao girls wear batik skirts and carry batik bags they have made themselves. Although a nine-layered outfit might make walking a bit inconvenient, the girls won't miss out on this opportunity to show off their talent and intelligence. Thus, this clothing becomes a kind of competition, one of joy and beauty.

三江侗族服饰　摄影：玉时阶

低调的奢华

Low-key Luxury

文：翟香丽

在三江侗族地区，人们的衣服布料泛光，色彩斑斓，银饰繁多，银光闪闪，甚是“奢华”。但是穿在淳朴的侗族朋友身上，艳而不俗，洋溢出的是自信与幸福。白色、蓝色、暗红色，银项圈、银盘、银手镯、银头饰，摇曳多姿；时尚的男子还会在内里穿上白衬衣，打上红领带，更是颜值满满的了。

The clothing worn by the Dong people of the Sanjiang area is full of color and vibrancy, adorned all over with silver, but when worn by the Dong doesn't appear flashy or loud – instead, it's bright and full of self-confidence and joy. White, blue, deep red, silver necklaces, silver plates, silver bracelets, and hair ornaments are in all forms here. Fashionable young men wear white shirts with red ties for a sharp effect.

隆林花苗服饰　摄影：王时阶

仫佬服色尚青

Mulao Clothing

文：翟香丽

在罗城仫佬族自治县，用蓝靛染成的土布被视为珍贵的布料，用之做成鞋子送给老人，是对长辈最大的尊敬。蓝靛土布，色青，承载了仫佬族先祖躬耕社会里自种、自纺、自织、自染、自缝的岁月积淀。多少姑娘曾用它做成“送嫁衣”和“同年鞋”，又有多少老年人用它做成了“防老衣”，它见证了仫佬族人最重要的人生礼俗。

In the Luocheng Mulao Autonomous County, the indigo cloth is the most precious material. A pair of shoes made of this kind of cloth for an elder is a huge sign of respect. The deep color is a testament to the age-old customs of planning, spinning, weaving, dying and sewing their clothing. Many girls use the material for wedding costumes or love gifts. Many old people make “anti-aging” clothing with it, a testament to the customs of the Mulao people.

头戴顶卡花

Bamboo Hat

文：翟香丽

对一个非服装专业的人来说，不用去费劲地分右襟、对襟、琵琶襟、滚边……在环江，只要看到头上戴着顶卡花（花竹帽）的，那就一定是毛南族女子了。随着社会的变迁，顶卡花如今不仅仅是遮阳挡雨的用具，更是珍贵的装饰品，是流淌在毛南族人生活里的代代相传，是区别于其他民族最明显的特征。

For someone who’s not an expert in clothing, one needn’t differentiate diagonal, front and side lapels... In Huanjiang, one need only see the bamboo hats to recognize a girl of the Maonan people. As society has changed over time, these hats aren’t just used to block sun and rain; they are valued accessories, a part of the customs of the Maonan people, and an explicit identifier that distinguishes them from other groups.

评论

伏波将军的“时尚秀”

General Fu Bo's "Fashion Show"

文：翟香丽

碧海蓝天，一顶顶圆锥形京笠，白里透黄，随着或黄或红的曼妙身段穿梭移动。在防城港京族地区的沙滩渔船边，一眼就能认出身着单色绸衣的京族女子，海风过处，衣袂飘飘。传统的京族女子服饰胸前有一块菱形“胸掩”。据说当年伏波将军来到交趾，见妇女们同男人一样袒胸，觉得不文雅，便亲自设计了一块“胸掩”相赠。自此，“胸掩”便流传开了。

A deep blue sea and azure clouds, conical hats, yellow within white, and yellow or red clothing… In Fangchenggang City, one can see the Jing women in their single-colored outfits by the fishing boats on the beach, clothes fluttering as the sea breeze blows. The traditional women have a rhomboid patch upon their chests – it's said that when General Fubo went to northern Vietnam, he found that both the women and men here went topless. Thus he designed a "chest cover" for the women to make them look more cultured. Since then, the chest patch was widely accepted.

京族女子服饰　摄影：玉时阶

再现彝族历史

Yi History

文：翟香丽

相传远古时期彝族的妇女勇敢善战，本领高强，打仗时佩戴的腰环刀枪不入，女神白佐所赐与的胸裙因可以发出闪耀的光芒而击退了征杀彝族人的天敌。至今，那坡白彝女子腰间还会围一块黑色的榆树皮腰环，其胸裙两端顶角或者腰环的锦带上贴有锡片或银片，那是作战的护身符演变而来，而锦带的尾饰也是为了抵挡敌人的弓箭。

The women of the Yi people in ancient times were brave warriors, skilled and strong. They wore almost impenetrable waist guards in battle; it was said that the legendary chest guards they wore could emit a light that would strike down those who sought to kill them. The Yi women of Napo still wear a black elm bark waist guard, and upon it and the chest guard there are pieces of tin or silver which evolved from protective talismans in battle. The brocade they wear upon their backsides arose from a shield to protect against arrows.

评论

奢华的“马尾”

Horse Tail

文：翟香丽

在南丹六寨镇南部一些多民族杂居的村寨中，偶尔会看到身着一身青衣，肩挂花丝点珠、盘龙团凤银饰，胸戴马尾绣胸牌的水族女子。水族与马有着天然的联系。相传，水族的先民曾骑着马四处征战，马是水族人农业劳作的重要工具，而且他们在水族传统节日“端节”中赛马。被称为“刺绣中的精品”的马尾绣也在水族女子的巧手中应运而生。

In some villages of multiple ethnic groups in Liuzai Town, Nandan, you'll occasionally see Shui girls with blue coats, upon which floral beads and silver dragons or phoenixes are decorated, and traditional chest pads are added. The Shui people have a natural relationship with horses. Legend has it that the ancestors of the Shui rode horses into war all over; the horse is also an important agricultural tool, and horses are raced on the traditional Duanwu Festival. The excellent traditional embroidery style of the Shui people is known as "horse-tail stitch".

水族女子服饰　摄影：玉时阶

偏爱筒裙

Tube Skirts

文：翟香丽

相对于百褶裙的灵动，隆林仡佬族妇女更爱无褶筒裙的婀娜。初见身着传统服装的仡佬族妇女，会惊讶于她们用色的大胆。彩色绸缎和花边，各种树木花草和房屋人像等图案鲜艳夺目。筒裙的上半节系吊着数条 2 到 5 寸长的彩色丝绒，虚盖着各色飘带，斑斓而厚重。

In contrast with the smart many-pleated skirts, the Gelao women of Longlin enjoy wearing un-pleated tube skirts. When you first see them, you'll be surprised by the bold colors. Silks with fancy borders, all kinds of patterns of trees, grasses, flowers, people and buildings will catch your eye. The top of the skirt has a band of velvet a few inches long covered in all manner of colors, which appears bright and graceful.

图书在版编目(CIP)数据

微观广西:汉英对照/彭匈主编. 一北京:
商务印书馆,2019
(微观中国)
ISBN 978-7-100-16827-4

Ⅰ. ①微… Ⅱ. ①彭… Ⅲ. ①广西—概况—
汉、英 Ⅳ. ①K926.7

中国版本图书馆CIP数据核字(2018)第259022号

微观广西
(汉英版)
彭 匈 主编

商 务 印 书 馆 出 版
(北京王府井大街36号 邮政编码100710)
商 务 印 书 馆 发 行
北京中科印刷有限公司印刷
ISBN 978-7-100-16827-4

2019年9月第1版 开本787×1092 1/16
2019年9月北京第1次印刷 印张14
定价:68.00元